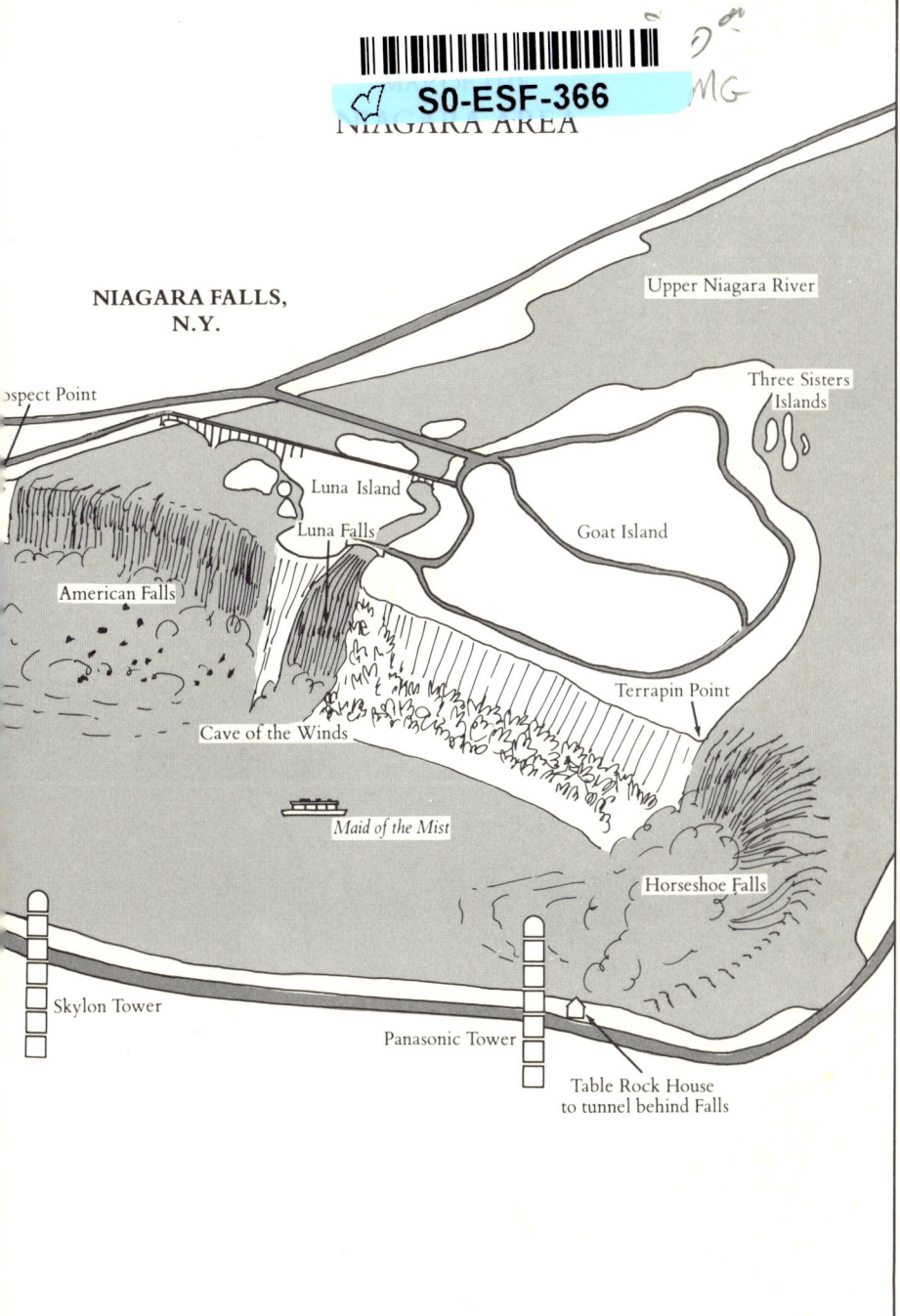

Also by Gordon Donaldson

FIFTEEN MEN

BATTLE FOR A CONTINENT

Niagara!

NIAGARA!
The Eternal Circus

GORDON DONALDSON

Doubleday Canada Limited, Toronto, Canada
Doubleday & Company, Inc., Garden City, New York

1979

Library of Congress Cataloging in Publication Data

Donaldson, Gordon, 1926–
  Niagara!: The eternal circus.
  Bibliography
  Includes index.
  1. Niagara River region, N.Y. and Ont.–History. I. Title.
F127.N6D66 1979   974.7′99
ISBN: 0-385-12309-4
Library of Congress Catalog Card Number 79-7328

COPYRIGHT © 1979 BY GORDON DONALDSON
ALL RIGHTS RESERVED
PRINTED IN THE UNITED STATES OF AMERICA
FIRST EDITION

For Isobel and Rosalie

ACKNOWLEDGMENTS

A story told by Corky McKenzie, CBC news cameraman and former Niagara River Rat, gave me the idea for this book. While filming the movie *Niagara*, Marilyn Monroe appeared on the main street of Chippawa, the village where Corky was born and grew up. She recognized him as a photographer who had tried to sneak pictures of her elsewhere. As the village watched in awe, the world's reigning sex symbol yelled, "Hi, Corky!" and beckoned the hometown boy over to join her. It reminded me that almost everybody who is, or was, anybody visited Niagara at some point and contributed to its tumultuous history. God created the falls, but man has done some strange things with them and around them.

So, I'm grateful to Mr. McKenzie, and also to the following: Donald E. Loker, city historian of Niagara Falls at the Earl Brydges Library, New York; Clyde Helfter of the Buffalo and Erie County Historical Society; Mario J. Pirastru and John Seager of the Niagara Frontier State Parks Region; Ron Devereux of the Niagara Parks Commission; Jim Moir of the Niagara Falls (Ontario) Resort and Tourist Association; Dick McLeod of the Niagara Falls (New York) Convention and Visitors Bureau; Alex Rigby of Ripley International; Robert Crichton and Linda M. Goodwin of Ontario Hydro; Dorothy Dalton of the Ontario Ministry of Industry and Tourism; Colonel John Gondek of Old Fort Niagara; Isabelle Hickman, Librarian, and

Fletcher Clarke, Managing Editor, of the Niagara Falls (New York) *Gazette*; John Brunton of Insight Productions, Toronto; the staffs of the Ontario Archives, the Metro Toronto Reference Library, and the Library of the Ontario Legislature. And to the many others who helped, thank you.

Gordon Donaldson
Toronto, Canada
February 6, 1979

Contents

	ACKNOWLEDGMENTS	ix
1	*The Dam Breaks*	1
2	*Hinu's Lair*	7
3	*Rum Versus Brandy*	31
4	*The Devil's Hole*	59
5	*Mrs. Hustler Invents the Cocktail*	71
6	*Came the Apocalypse*	91
7	*The Colonel Invents the Tourist Trap*	117
8	*A Boy with a Kite*	141
9	*Blondin the Great*	161
10	*The Awful Eye*	181
11	*Power and Glory*	209
12	*In Fifi's Footsteps*	227
	BIBLIOGRAPHY	261
	INDEX	265

Niagara!

1
The Dam Breaks

Even the beginning was spectacular. First came a trickle, then a torrent, then a stupendous onslaught of water as an inland sea burst its banks and the cataract thundered into life. No one witnessed its birth. There were men on earth, but not at Niagara. For a million years much of North America had been clamped in the Great Ice Age. Life was stilled. Bones of dinosaurs and fossils of tropical plants lay entombed by glaciers three miles thick, with mile-high snowdrifts piled on top. The continent had been scraped, gouged, and flayed by the creeping ice-fronts. It lay dead and deserted, mourned by howling winds.

Niagara Falls was no place for tourists.

Then, mysteriously, the world warmed up again. The glaciers retreated northward, leaving great seas of meltwater in the basins they had dug. The greatest, ancient Lake Algonquin, spread over a thousand miles, out and beyond the area of the present Upper Great Lakes Erie,

Huron, Michigan, and Superior. It was one grim sea of churning, grinding ice floes and it rose as they melted, building up behind the rock dam that held it back from Lake Iroquois, ancestor of Lake Ontario, and the St. Lawrence escape route to the Atlantic.

That dam was the Niagara Escarpment, a ridge heaved out of a Palaeozoic sea of trilobites. Its cap is hard Lockport dolomite rock but below that lies softer Rochester shale. The pent-up waters probed for a weak spot—and found it at the Niagara frontier. After centuries of freezing and thawing, sapping and buffeting, the shale crumbled. The hard cap came loose and the dam broke. Lake Algonquin leapt down upon Lake Iroquois, 250 feet below. It was a sensational opening to the ever-theatrical display of Niagara Falls.

In the seventeenth century, Niagara became the first giant waterfall to be discovered by Europeans. It puzzled geologists, who wondered why such a violent upheaval of nature had taken place in an otherwise flat and placid landscape. It intrigued theologians, who assumed that the secret of the Creation must lie somewhere in this most awesome of God's marvels. So for nearly two hundred years, scientists, preachers, and scholars argued over the age of the falls. When did the dam break?

Father Louis Hennepin, a Récollet priest who traveled with the explorer La Salle to the Niagara River, viewed the falls in 1678 and wrote the first published description of them. Hennepin was a bit of a liar—the first of a long line of liars to visit Niagara—but he raised an important question: Why was there "such a big river with no mountains?"

The geologists pondered for nearly a century, then produced the answer: the river was no ordinary river. It had

The Dam Breaks

carved a deep gorge for itself through erosion and the power of its mighty falls. Niagara Falls had been born not where Hennepin found them, but nearly seven miles downstream at a break in the cliffs overlooking Lake Ontario. They had then dug their way backward toward Lake Erie. They were still moving back.

Here geology and theology collided. In a footnote to the 1611 King James Bible James Ussher, Archbishop of Armagh, Ireland, had stated definitively that the world was created at 9:00 A.M. on October 23, 4004 B.C. The archbishop had spent long, dedicated years working this out from biblical references and it was widely accepted by Christians.

But if God created heaven and earth and Niagara Falls at the same time, the gorge must have been dug at incredible speed. The case against Ussher's Creation date was put by Robert McCauslin, an American thinker who had lived by the falls and observed them for nine years. In 1789 he told the American Philosophical Society: "If we adopt the opinion of the falls having retired six miles and if we suppose the world to be 5,700 years old, this would give about sixty-six and a half inches for a year [erosion rate] or sixteen yards and two-thirds for nine years, which I venture to say has not been the case since 1774."

Ussher's disciples agreed that the falls could not be moving at a rate of five and a half feet a year, so they challenged the whole theory of erosion. The gorge, they said, must have been formed suddenly and completely by an underwater earthquake.

The geologists struck back by stretching the age of the earth. In 1790 one expert estimated the earth and the falls had been created simultaneously 55,440 years earlier. Another maintained that the falls had existed "since the first rain fell upon earth" 36,960 years before.

The religious argument was finally quashed by the British geologist Sir Charles Lyell, who visited Niagara in 1841. He took rock samples that proved the gorge had been eroded by the river, and estimated this had taken 35,000 years. But, he said, the rock of the escarpment was much older than that, so the earth had been created long before the falls. At this, the theologians abandoned them as a time clock, but scientists continued to probe into their history.

Accurate surveys of the brink began in 1842 and soon demonstrated that the falls were moving upstream faster than anyone had believed possible. Between 1875 and 1905, the Canadian falls were eroding by between 66 inches and 78 inches a year—the speed McCauslin couldn't credit. (Erosion slowed down when water was diverted to hydroelectric power generators. The American falls is now nearly stationary, and the Canadian moves at one foot a year or less.)

Recent carbon 14 dating of fossils found on the shoreline of ancient Lake Iroquois indicates that the lake existed until about 12,000 to 13,000 years ago. This would mean that the dam broke around 10,000–11,000 B.C.—a few seconds ago on the geological clock, a blink in time compared to the world's history of two and a half billion years—so Niagara and its violent gorge is one of the newest of natural wonders.

It is the third-greatest waterfall in the world in terms of power and volume of water. The greatest, Sete Quedas, on the border of Brazil and Paraguay, drops 470,000 cubic feet a second from a height of 130 feet. Stanley Falls, on the Congo River, carries an even greater volume, but is only 10

The Dam Breaks

feet high. The heights of Niagara are usually reckoned at 167 feet for the American falls and 158 for the Canadian—although these figures can vary by 30 feet either way as the water level in the gorge drops in summer and the ice piles up in winter. There are a hundred falls of greater height, but without Niagara's power. Niagara's average volume is 212,000 cubic feet a second. In one hour it could flood a roadside ditch stretching from coast to coast.

But statistics cannot measure the magic of Niagara. Since the white man discovered it, and probably long before that, it has lured men and women and charmed them into performing feats of bravery and brilliance and idiotic antics that could not have occurred anywhere else. Explorers, soldiers, stunters, inventors, poets, and charlatans have been challenged by it. There is a genial madness about the place that brings out the best and the worst in people. Nature ran amok there, and man seems determined to follow suit. Niagara is a circus, the New World's oldest continuous show, refreshed by new acts every season. There is nothing quite like it.

2
Hinu's Lair

The first visitor to Niagara Falls probably arrived between 9,000 and 7,000 B.C.—a wandering hunter whose remote ancestors had crossed the frozen Bering Strait from Mongolia in search of better weather. At the time, the river would have excavated about three miles of gorge and been nearing the site of the present Whirlpool Rapids, ready to make a right-angle turn and create that deadly vortex.

The visitor would have gasped at the sight of a single plume of water, 250 feet tall, perhaps marveled for a time, then moved on. For although stone tools tentatively dated 7,000 B.C. have been found in the area, there is no evidence of permanent settlement and agriculture until the Christian Era. The Mound Builders, a primitive tribe from the Ohio Valley who buried their dead in peculiar hillocks, left traces of a fort near Lewiston, New York, just below the birthplace of the falls. Human skeletons found there had been cremated and buried about 160 A.D. The Mound

Builders may have been massacred or driven out, for there are no further traces of them in the area.

By 1000 A.D. various Indian tribes had established semi-permanent villages at the falls and along the river. They sowed fields of corn, beans, and pumpkins, and planted orchards of fruit trees. Every twenty years or so, when the fields no longer bore crops and the supply of firewood ran out, they would move their villages; but they were no longer nomads. As historian Samuel Eliot Morison points out, Europeans delighted in classing all Indians as nomads in order to grab their land. But in the case of the Niagara Indians, that excuse was invalid long before the Europeans arrived.

The area was settled, unsettled, and resettled as tribes fought over it. It was ideal fishing and hunting country. Salmon and huge sturgeon swarmed in the gorge, and the heights above were alive with wildfowl, including fat, waddling turkeys, which were easy to catch and provided food and ornamental feathers. Along the east bank was the Niagara portage—a rugged nine-mile trail from Lewiston that bypassed the falls and led to the upper river above the first set of rapids. Although part of it was so steep the Indians called it the Crawl-on-All-Fours, it was the most convenient route between the Upper and Lower lakes. Much of the canoe traffic of the continent passed over the portage, and it became an important Indian trading center. It was also a strategic site, for whoever controlled the portage commanded the vital water route. And there was flint for arrowheads to be found in the rock strata.

So the lords of Niagara had food, trade, power, and weapons. When written Indian history began, these were the Neutrals—so called because they tried to stay out of the wars between the larger Huron and Iroquois nations. In

Hinu's Lair

the end, their neutrality did not pay; they were all wiped out by the Iroquois.

The Jesuit priest Jean de Brébeuf visited them in 1641 and reported:

> They embroider their robes with much care and industry and try to ornament them in divers fashions. They also make figures upon their bodies from head to foot with charcoal pricked into their flesh . . . so that we see their faces and breasts figured like the helmets and cuirasses of soldiers in France.

He noted that the Neutrals seemed to have great affection for their dead:

> A corpse often passes the whole winter in the wigwam and when they place it at last outside upon a scaffold to decay they draw out the bones as soon as possible and exhibit them to sight arranged on one side or the other of their wigwams until the feast of the dead. These objects being constantly before their eyes renew the sense of their loss and make them cry and lament with lugubrious songs, but this is only done by the women.

Father Brébeuf tried to convert the Neutrals to Christianity, but failed. They clung to their natural gods—the spirits of the wind, the rain, the sun, the dark forest—and the thunder god Hinu, who lived in the great falls. Sometimes his rumble was drowned by the other thunder god in the sky, but there was no voice of such constant authority as his. And he sent up a tower of mist, shimmered by rainbows. His lair was a sacred place.

Hinu lives on, long after his worshipers were massacred, in the dubious legend of the Maid of the Mist. The story first appeared in Burke's *Descriptive Guide to the Falls*, published in 1851, and has been a gold mine to tourist guides ever since.

According to Burke, the thunder god had to be propitiated by the annual sacrifice of a canoe sent over the falls with a cargo of fruit and game. At some unspecified period, the Indians concluded that this was no longer enough. They were dying of a strange disease, their graves were being desecrated, and the bodies eaten by a monster. Obviously Hinu was upset.

So the tribe tried human sacrifice. The most beautiful maiden of the year was added to the cargo of gifts. This didn't work either. The sickness and desecration continued. As a last resort, Lelawalo, daughter of Chief Eagle Eye, was chosen to join the previous "maids of the mist." As her canoe was set adrift in the rapids, her father jumped into his own canoe to follow her. Both vessels slid over the brink. However, the maiden was caught by Hinu's sons, who leaped out of a cave behind the falls and through the curtain of falling water. They told her the sickness and grave robbery were the work of a great water snake that lived on the river bottom.

The maid returned in spirit form to tell her people that the snake was poisoning their water. They must avoid their wells, drink only from springs, and prepare to kill the snake when it appeared.

When the snake crawled out of the upper river, the Indians attacked it with arrows, spears, and tomahawks. Mortally wounded, it wriggled back into the water and was swept to the brink. There the gods arranged for its head to be wedged in the rocks on one side and its tail on the other. As it died, it writhed into the form of a horseshoe, thus molding the Canadian falls.

Burke doesn't say what happened to the girl's father.

The question today is not whether anyone believes this yarn, but whether anyone ever *did* believe it. Some historians have written it off as the concoction of a mid-Victorian hack.

Whoever created it, it now has an honored place in the legends of Niagara. It could even be based on a small portion of truth. From time immemorial, people have gone over the falls, accidentally or deliberately, in canoes, boats, barrels, and rubber balls. Maybe there *was* an original Maid of the Mist who returned in spirit form. The Burke version doesn't say she came back alive. And his story is probably tame by comparison with the tales told by long-dead Indian storytellers as they awed and entertained their audiences in the long evenings, eyes watering in the kippering smoke of the longhouse, while the great voice of the thunder god shouted nearby.

Samuel de Champlain, founder of New France, heard Indian tales of the great falling waters soon after 1603, when he built his first tiny settlement under the Rock of Quebec. They interested him, for he had been royal geographer of France, and he inked in their supposed position on a map he drew in 1612. At that time no Frenchman had been farther up the St. Lawrence than Montreal, and Champlain's drawing of Lake Ontario, which led to the falls, was based largely on the information that it took fifteen days' paddling to get from one end to the other.

No doubt Champlain would have liked to view them for himself, but he was too busy with the affairs of his poor, often-starving colony and his war with the Five Nations Iroquois. So the first white man to see the falls was probably Étienne Brûlé, who has been aptly described as an immortal scoundrel. He was one of the first of a new breed of

North American, the French-Canadian *coureurs-de-bois* (wood runners) who rollicked and rampaged through the savage land, running wild with the Indians, drinking, debauching, and horrifying the priests and the few sober settlers. They did more to open up the continent than the pious and mercenary English and Dutch, but they were constantly hounded by their own countrymen. They were outlawed at the behest of the priests because they fed the Indians brandy in exchange for furs while the missionaries were trying to feed them Christianity. Brandy proved more palatable, and the bishops mourned that every fur gained meant a heathen soul lost to the Church. From time to time *coureurs* were hanged or sent as slaves to row the king's galleys, but they were never tamed. By the mid-eighteenth century, there were as many *coureurs* as settlers in New France.

Brûlé came to Quebec from France in 1608 as a sixteen-year-old servant in Champlain's household but soon took to the woods, lived with the Hurons, and learned their language. Although the stern Champlain disapproved of the wild young man, he would use him as an interpreter and link with the Hurons, who were to be his allies against the Iroquois.

By picking a fight with the wrong Indians, Champlain made a fatal mistake. The Iroquois, who proudly and justifiably called themselves the "Men of Men" were the toughest, cruelest, most implacable of enemies, and they haunted Champlain and his successors until New France was no more. The Five Nations confederacy, consisting of the Mohawks, Cayugas, Oneidas, Onondagas, and Senecas, had been formed in 1570, and these Iroquois tribes held sway over most of New York State and the eastern seaboard. They subscribed to the Great Immutable Law that all members were free and equal and pursued the quest for a Great Peace, which would be achieved by conquering any outside tribe that offended them.

(The Great Immutable Law was to be quoted as a model for the Constitution of the United States, and the Great Peace theory has been used by every aggressive military alliance in history.)

As Champlain's Indian agent, Brûlé was free to roam and roister as a *coureur* without becoming an outlaw. A powerful, reckless adventurer, he explored more for fun than for profit in furs or for the glory of France. He was happiest with a paddle in his hand and a squaw by his side, skimming ahead to the farthest tip of an unknown lake and on to the portage beyond.

Brûlé traveled the lands of the Neutrals in 1615 and brought back accounts of these Indians that encouraged Father Brébeuf to try to convert them. It was on this journey that he probably saw the falls. Unlike Father Hennepin, who arrived fifty-three years later and described perhaps more than he actually saw, he leaves no written description because he couldn't write. Six years later, he may have revisited Niagara on his way to discover Lakes Erie and Superior.

Brûlé's 1615 trip began on the shores of Lake Simcoe in the heart of the Huron country. He was there with Champlain, planning an attack on the Five Nations' homelands on the New York side of Lake Ontario. Champlain sent him, with twelve Huron warriors, on a mission to allies of the Hurons who lived on the upper Susquehanna River. He was to rouse them and inspire or bribe them to join the assault on the Iroquois.

Brûlé made his way by river and portage down to Lake Ontario, arriving at the mouth of the Humber River, the site of present-day Toronto. Brûlé is hailed as the "discoverer" of Toronto, although at the time there was nothing to discover but one tiny Huron village.

It's unlikely that Brûlé headed straight across Lake Ontario, for that would have taken him straight into Iroquois territory. He could have taken several routes to the Susquehanna, but the most direct was over the Niagara portage, controlled by the relatively friendly Neutrals. Undoubtedly his Huron companions knew that route. It was as familiar to canoe travelers as the New York Thruway is to today's motorists.

We know that Brûlé did reach the Susquehanna tribesmen, but by the time he had persuaded them to go on the warpath, the battle was over. Champlain's Hurons had made their assault and been beaten back. Brûlé was taken prisoner by the Iroquois and tortured—mildly, by Iroquois standards, for he lived to travel the woods and paddle his canoe once again. He seems to have convinced his captors that he had the unholy power to cause a thunderstorm—one of the few things in heaven or on earth that could frighten an Iroquois—so they let him go free.

Brûlé's discoveries were either ignored or claimed by others because, although Champlain used him, he never trusted him. To the merchants and clergy of New France, he was an outcast. Even his one respectable French friend, Father Gabriel Sagard, allowed sadly that Étienne was "much addicted" to Indian women.

Spurned and castigated, Brûlé turned traitor. In 1629 he piloted the British privateer brothers Kirke up the St. Lawrence to Quebec. Their three ships pointed their guns at Champlain's little fort, and the governor was forced to surrender himself and his entire colony. As he was being shipped to England—a prisoner, since England and France were supposedly at war—Champlain was allowed ashore at Tadoussac on the St. Lawrence. There he met Brûlé. A laundered version of what the choleric prisoner told his former servant appeared in the Jesuit *Relations*. Even with the expletives deleted, it was powerful stuff. The contemporary French historian De Creux wrote:

> It is clear that Brûlé was a bad man and guilty of every vice and crime . . . Champlain taunted Brûlé with this perfidy and pointed out how disgraceful it was for a Frenchman to betray King and country and for an orthodox Catholic to ally himself with heretics, share their foul intoxication and eat meat on days when, as he knew, Catholics were forbidden to do so. The impious man answered that he knew all that, but since a comfortable life was not before him in France the die was cast and he would live with the English.

But there was to be no life for him with the English. When the Kirkes reached London, they learned that their capture of Quebec was illegal. England and France had made peace while they were sailing up the St. Lawrence although, of course, they weren't in a position to know this. Four years later, France got her colony back and Champlain returned to Quebec.

Brûlé had now given up all trappings of civilization. Abandoned by the English and the French, he was living as a half-naked Indian on Penetanguishene Bay. But when his Indian brothers learned the French were coming back, they, too, turned on him. He was killed, boiled, and eaten.

De Creux had no sympathy:

> He died by treachery; perhaps for this very reason, that he might perish in his sins. Deprived of those benefits by which the children of this Church are prepared for a

happy issue from this mortal life, Brûlé was hurried to the
Judgment seat to answer for all his other crimes and espe-
cially for that depravity which was a perpetual stumbling
block to the Hurons, among whom he should have been a
lamp in a dark place, a light to lead that heathen nation to
the Faith.

Father Brébeuf, a larger man both physically and spiritu-
ally, had a kinder thought for the renegade. He visited
Penetanguishene Bay and wrote: "I saw the spot where
poor Étienne Brûlé was barbarously and brutally murdered,
which made me think some day they might treat me in the
same manner . . ."

They did. In 1648 he was slowly tortured to death and
eaten by the Iroquois.

In pursuit of the Great Peace, the Five Nations defeated
the Hurons and totally obliterated the Neutrals. The Seneca Iroquois took over the great gorge and the lair of the
thunder god. They had a name for it: *Onguiaahra*. The
fierce and beautiful word "Niagara" comes from a French
attempt to write it down.

The Iroquois were prodigious orators, but the majesty of
the falls seems to have defeated their vocabulary. *Onguiaahra* simply means "throat."

The falls were a ripple in the river compared to the immense scheme of the next great explorer to stand beside
them. René-Robert Cavelier, Sieur de la Salle, planned to
seize the entire West, beginning at Niagara and extending
as far as the imagination could reach. He would build a
line of fortified trading posts out to the Upper Lakes and
down the Ohio Valley to the Father of All Rivers, the Mississippi, which, he believed, led to the Gulf of Mexico. This
would pen the English, Dutch, and Spanish colonists into

little enclaves along the eastern seaboard and leave the vast interior to France—and to La Salle, for Louis XIV had granted him limited rights to trade in the new territory he opened up.

He was thirty-five, arrogant, impatient, and totally dedicated to his dream of empire. The arrogance came with his noble birth; the dedication from his years of study as a Jesuit. The impatience was fueled by an urgent need to make money. He had signed away his inheritance to his brothers when he entered the Jesuit novitiate and they refused to hand it back when he left the order.

La Salle was a hard man to get along with. His only real friend was the swashbuckling Italian sailor Enrico de Tonti, the Man with the Iron Hand. Enrico was the son of Lorenzo, the Neapolitan banker who devised the tontine—an elaborate gamble in which subscribers put up money, drew only the interest, and left their shares to the survivors. The last survivor took the pot.

It sounds foolproof, but the first Royal Tontine of France ended in a royal row among the promoters, and Lorenzo went to the Bastille, leaving Enrico fatherless for most of his youth. He joined the French Navy, lost his right hand in battle, and had it replaced with a heavy metal one, enclosed in a leather glove. He became an excellent left-handed swordsman. Since he could also crush heads with his iron fist, he was a formidable fighter.

He and La Salle made an imposing pair—both tall and thin with large, overbearing noses and deep, burning eyes. When they set off to conquer the West, they took with them another adventurer, La Motte de Lussière and the bustling, talkative Dutch priest, Father Louis Hennepin.

La Motte and Hennepin were sent up Lake Ontario, ahead of the main expedition, to set up a base at the mouth of the Niagara River. Their small ship reached there on December 6, 1678, and Hennepin took his famous first look at the falls:

> On the sixth, St. Nicholas Day, we entered the beautiful river Niagara which no bark had yet entered. . . . Four leagues from Lake Frontenac Lake Ontario there is an incredible Cataract or Waterfall, which has no equal. The Niagara River near this place is only an eighth of a mile wide but it is very deep in places, and so rapid above the great Fall that it hurries down all animals which try to cross it, without a single one being able to withstand its current. They plunge down a height of more than five hundred feet and its fall is composed of two sheets of water and a cascade, with an island sloping down. In the middle these waters foam and boil in a fearful manner. They thunder continually and when the wind blows in a southernly direction the noise they make is heard for more than fifteen leagues. . . .

This version was first published in Paris in 1683, soon after the priest returned from the New World. He had more than tripled the height of the falls, generally reckoned at about 160 feet, and magnified the Great Voice beyond the red man's wildest fantasy. The keenest hunter's ear never heard it fifteen leagues (forty-five miles) away. But Hennepin was only warming up.

Fourteen years later he rewrote his story, adding another hundred feet to the height of the falls:

> We pass'd by the great Fall of Niagara and spent half a Day in considering the Wonders of that prodigious Cascade. I could not conceive how it came to pass that four great lakes, the least of which is 400 leagues in compass, should empty themselves into one another and discharge themselves at the Great Fall, and yet not drown a good

Hinu's Lair

part of America. . . . Our surprise was still greater when we observ'd there were no mountains within a good two leagues of the Cascade; and yet the vast quantity of water discharg'd by these four fresh seas stops or centres here and so falls about six hundred foot down into a Gulph which one cannot look upon without Horror. . . .

This account, translated and published in London in 1698, gave the English-speaking world its first impression of Niagara. It was accompanied by a highly imaginative engraving by an unknown artist which would be retouched and copied for more than a century. It remained the standard view of the falls until the early 1800s, when artists arrived to paint the scene at first hand.

It would be charitable to presume that Father Hennepin's memory was slipping when he wrote his second book or that he magnified the cataract for the greater glory of the Lord, but the rest of the book suggests he did it for the greater glory of Hennepin. He took the drama of La Salle's exploration of the Mississippi and recast it with himself as hero. In the introduction he promised to solve "the mystery of this discovery which I have hitherto concealed that I might not offend Sieur de la Salle, who wished to keep all the glory and knowledge of it to himself."

The nineteenth-century historian Francis Parkman calls Hennepin "the most impudent of liars." He points out that La Salle was still alive when the friar published his first book, so he had to be careful. The explorer was dead when he wrote the second and he could really let himself go.

In 1703 another traveler went one better. The Baron de Lahontan wrote, in *New Voyages to North America:* "As for the waterfall of Niagara, 'tis seven or eight hundred foot high and half a league broad."

The falls had gained 300 feet in twenty years, but were about to be shrunk to size. The Jesuit Pierre de Charlevoix looked at them in 1721 and wondered if Lahontan had ever been there. He put the height at 140–150 feet. And the Swedish botanist Peter Kalm, who surveyed the natural history of New France between 1748 and 1751, made it exactly 137 feet. He was not deafened by the thundering waters; he held conversations just beside them without raising his voice. Hennepin, he wrote, "has gained little credit in Canada; the name of honor they give him there is *un grand menteur* or the great liar; he writes of what he saw in a place he never was. 'Tis true he saw this fall. But as it is the way of some travellers to magnify every thing; so he has done with regard to the fall of Niagara . . ."

Still, Hennepin had the story first. His tall tales grabbed and held his European audience. While the pious accounts of massacres in the Jesuit *Relations* lured black-robed zealots ripe for martyrdom, Hennepin, who belonged to the gentler gray-robed Récollets, brought visitors. He is rightly revered as the founder and patron saint of the Niagara tourist trade.

La Salle, however, considered him a nuisance. When he arrived at the river mouth on January 3, 1679, he found his advance party idly fishing while Hennepin prayed in the bark-and-pole cabin he was using as a chapel. No base had been established and no stockade erected; they hadn't even unloaded their ship. La Salle had no time for sightseeing. He barely mentions the falls. While Hennepin prayed and wrote his journal, the men of action built Fort Condé on the east bank of the river.

Named after Louis de Bourbon, Prince de Condé, La

Salle's principal patron in France, the fort was built by permission of the Iroquois, who at the time were more or less at peace with the French. In wearying weeks of flowery speeches, feasts, and drinking sessions with the sachems of the Five Nations at their stronghold, Boughton Hill (near Rochester, New York), La Salle had persuaded them to allow him to set up a trading post on their territory. He fortified it, naturally, because he didn't trust them; and he chose a commanding position at the river's mouth. In the wars that followed, that position would be taken and retaken by French, British, and American troops. Old Fort Niagara stands there today.

La Salle's forty men finished the fort's blockhouse and stockade in a week, hacking down hardwood trees, dragging them to the site, adzing them square, and doweling them together. Meanwhile the explorer, accompanied by Tonti, scrambled and crawled up and over the old Indian portage to the upper river, looking for a place to build a ship. He found it at the mouth of Cayuga Creek, an inlet five miles above the falls on the American side. There was a gentle slope of firm ground, suitable for a shipyard, and beyond it an anchorage of calm water sheltered by a small island.

La Salle's great scheme required a ship. Since he couldn't spirit one up the falls or drag it over the Crawl-on-All-Fours, he had to make one—the *Griffon*, first vessel other than a canoe to sail the Upper Lakes.

Construction got off to a bad start. The barque that brought the cordage, sailcloth, blacksmith's forge, anchors, and two brass cannon for the new ship was wrecked in a storm at the mouth of the Niagara River. The pilot, a seven-foot Danish giant named Luc, had moored it carelessly, and it lurched onto a rock and sank. Its cargo had to be salvaged from the freezing river before being hauled over the portage to the new shipyard.

"The Anchors and Cables were saved," Hennepin wrote, "but several Canows of Barks of Trees with Goods and Commodities were lost. These Disappointments were such as would have dissuaded from any further Enterprise all other Persons but such who had formed the generous design of making a New Discovery in the Country."

On January 26 the trunk of a white oak had been stripped, squared, and slotted at Cayuga Creek. The keel of the *Griffon* was ready, and the master carpenter Moyse Hillaret placed the first iron pin to attach the knee of the sternpost. Hennepin claims that La Salle invited him to hammer it home but he declined the honor because of his cloth, so the explorer did it himself. He then laid down his hammer, promised Hillaret ten gold louis if the ship was completed promptly, and left on snowshoes for Fort Frontenac (Kingston, Ontario) to face the creditors who were threatening to seize his property. (La Salle was constantly in debt and surrounded by enemies. There had been two attempts to poison him in Montreal. At one dinner party he was offered a salad dressed with hemlock, and at another there was so much arsenic in the wine that it turned cloudy. He avoided such dubious feasts.)

Tonti, who knew ships but had never built one, was left in charge of construction. He had a handful of men, few tools, and was surrounded by suspicious Indians, but he managed it in three months by raging, threatening, and waving his iron fist.

Hillaret selected crooked trees, which his axemen felled, then squared and scarfed together to form the natural curves of the ribs. These were slotted into the keel with its rearing stem and sternposts while the sawyers sweated in their snow-lined sawpits, ripping out two-inch planks for the sides. The blacksmith, known only as La Forge, molded and hammered the sizzling iron bolts.

The Senecas watched uneasily as the monster canoe grew. *Griffon* had a capacity of 45 or 60 tons, depending upon which of Hennepin's accounts we believe, and was probably about 60 feet long. A floating fortress with its own cannon. A threat to the Men of Men. They waited for a chance to burn the beast before it defiled their waters.

Hennepin's engraver pictures a brave attacking the muscular La Forge, who drives him off with a red-hot iron bar. The ship's keel is careened on one side as Tonti's men ram caulking into her starboard quarter and there is a griffin (*griffon*) carved on her transom. For despite the rush to launch her and the primitive conditions, Hillaret found time to carve the decorations that were supposed to boost a ship's pride, drive off devils, and bring her luck. La Salle named her after the mythical half-bird half-beast on the arms of Count Frontenac, the governor of New France on whom he depended for support.

But there would be no luck for the *Griffon*.

She was levered and pushed down a log slipway and into the creek in the spring of 1679 while La Salle was still away trying to sort out his finances. Hennepin records:

> Fir'd three guns and sang Te Deum, which was attended with loud Acclamations of Joy; of which those of the Iroquois who were accidentally present at the Ceremony were also Partakers; for we gave them some Brandy to drink as well as our men, who immediately quitted their Cabins of the Rinds [barks] of Trees and hang'd their hammocks on the deck of the Ship, there to lie with more security than as-shoar. We did the like, insomuch that the

very same day we were all on board and thereby out of reach of the insults of the Savages.

She rode easily at the anchors salvaged from the river below. Her two masts were stepped and rigged. According to one of La Salle's letters, her mainsail had a spread of 21 feet and the lateen sail on the mizzen, 16 feet. She also carried two small "bonnets" as topsails.

Griffon made a pleasant refuge from the increasingly hostile Indians, but the first attempts to sail her were discouraging. Once out of the creek, she was grabbed by the current and twice nearly sucked downstream and over the falls.

"The Best Designs," Hennepin mused, "are often crossed by some unexpected Accidents which God permits to try Men's Constancy." He had fallen out with Tonti, who objected to his hanging around taking notes and had tried to burn his diary. Hennepin took "Precautions to secure my observations." Presumably he hid the diary.

La Salle returned in August and the *Griffon* set off on her first and last voyage. Twelve men with two ropes towed her along the riverbank until she was safely out of reach of the deadly current and found a favorable west-southwest breeze. The men scrambled aboard, and she surged forward into Lake Erie. La Salle urged the pilot Luc to make all possible speed. He needed to have the *Griffon* back at Niagara with a cargo of pelts within two months. These would go over the portage to Fort Condé, reach Montreal before the freeze-up, and restore the explorer's credit. His backers had seized and auctioned off all the furs he had acquired on previous voyages but he was still in debt. According to his agreement with France and his understanding with the Iroquois, he was permitted to trade only in buffalo hides, not the more valuable beaver, but La Salle was desperate for money and determined to take the best furs available. Money would buy off the French officials, and the Indians could be soothed by brandy. His great scheme depended on the fur trade, and bribery was a tool of that trade.

Griffon reached the Detroit River within a week, and Hennepin waxed enthusiastic over the "panorama of plenty" spread before him. The countryside was rich in fruit trees and abounded in turkey cocks, wild goats, and bears which, he noted, were not as fierce as European bears and tasted better than the ship's salt pork.

In Lake Huron, La Salle had a violent row with Luc and took over the navigation of the ship. Then a storm blew up; the crew hauled down the main yards and topmast and let the *Griffon* drive at the mercy of the wind.

Hennepin wrote:

> Although he was a courageous man, M. La Salle began to fear and told us we were undone. We all fell upon our knees to pray and prepare for death—except our Pilot, whom we could never oblige to pray. And he did nothing this while except curse and swear against M. La Salle. He raged that M. La Salle had brought him here to perish in the nasty lake and lose the glory he had acquired through long and happy navigations on the ocean. However, the wind abated somewhat and we made about two leagues headway.

On August 27 *Griffon* reached the end of the "nasty lake" and anchored off a Huron village in the calm Strait of Mackinac. A round was fired from one of the brass cannon and La Salle went ashore, dressed in his best wig and scarlet cloak trimmed with gold lace. Here he got the first news of a fifteen-man fur-trading party he had sent ahead by canoe months before. They had passed through the straits, but several had deserted and headed north toward Sault Ste. Marie. La Salle flew into another of his rages and sent Tonti off by canoe to find the deserters and bring them back in chains.

His rage and impatience were to wreck the expedition. By depriving himself of his one loyal friend, the explorer left himself alone with his disaffected crew. He waited six days for Tonti to come back, then sailed on to Green Bay, Wisconsin, where he found the rest of his fur-trading party camped beside an impressive pile of beaver and buffalo skins. At least part of the grand plan was working. Tools and rigging for the construction of a second ship were unloaded, and the furs weighed, sewn into bags, and stowed in the hold. All the *Griffon* needed now was a skipper to take her back to Niagara while La Salle headed south to destiny. There was still no sign of Tonti, so reluctantly he ordered Luc to take command, with a skeleton crew of five.

The pilot protested that five men were not enough. La Salle roared at him and the ship sailed, with sullen, mutinous men on deck. As she slipped away she fired one gun in derisive salute to the angry aristocrat in the scarlet cloak. He watched her fade into the autumn mist. A storm was moving in from the West.

Here the *Griffon* vanishes and a mystery begins.

Nearly three centuries later, a slotted keel of ancient white oak, the remains of thirteen ribs, and a collection of iron pins were salvaged from a shallow lagoon on Russell's Island, off the tip of the Bruce Peninsula in Georgian Bay. Orrie Vail, a fisherman from nearby Tobermory, first saw the remains as a boy in the early 1900s. His family had known of it for three generations before that.

Hinu's Lair

In 1955 John MacLean, a reporter for the Toronto *Telegram*, heard Vail's story and connected the wreck with the *Griffon*. He and Vail ferried the parts over to the mainland for scientific examination.

No conclusive evidence such as carved griffins or dated cannon was available, but none was to be expected. In the years it had lain in shallow water Indians or early white settlers would have stripped away anything of value. But the size of the keel corresponded to the probable dimensions of the *Griffon*, and the iron pins and an iron bolt secured by a wedge rather than a threaded nut fit the period of La Forge and his anvil.

Marine architect Rowley Murphy and Great Lakes historian C. H. J. Snider examined the wreckage and declared that it most probably was the *Griffon*. The curvature of the stem matched the engraving that followed Hennepin's description and existing models of seventeenth-century French ships.

Murphy wrote: "As the *Griffon* was the only vessel built on the Lakes by the French above Niagara Falls and as no other Upper Laker of my acquaintance of any date shows such a stem, I think it reasonable to feel that this keel and stem are from the *Griffon*."

If so—if the timbers now lying among the fishing tackle in Orrie Vail's shack are all that's left of La Salle's ship and cargo—then it was treachery, not a storm, that robbed him of his treasure and set back his great scheme.

At the time Hennepin concluded that the pilot Luc, who couldn't navigate and refused to pray, simply lost the ship through a combination of incompetence and impiety. But La Salle suspected Luc, whom he had never trusted. Francis Parkman reports ancient rumors that (a) Luc and his five men stole the furs and scuttled the ship or (b) Ottawa Indians boarded her, murdered the crew, and burned her.

John MacLean claimed that the position of the Russell Island remains, assuming they *are* the *Griffon*, proves the ship didn't get there by accident. They lay in a well-hidden and protected inner cove:

> The *Griffon* was carefully steered into the narrow channel entrance to the first cove. Then she was angled four degrees to starboard and probably towed through the next and narrower channel by men on shore. Once inside the inner cove she was turned completely around and fitted carefully into the "C" [of a C-shaped rock berth] like a billiard cue into a rack. Her bow faced 70 degrees, pointing back out into the lake.

MacLean argues that only Indians would know of such a secret hiding place, but no Indian could handle such a ship, and most Indians feared the "floating fortress" too much to try. He believes that Luc hid the ship with Indian help. After that, either the Indians killed the crew and took the cargo, or they provided the white men with canoes in return for a share of the spoils, and Luc and company vanished eastward toward Montreal.

No explorer faced such a series of disasters as La Salle did in 1680. In January he finally accepted the fact that the *Griffon* was gone for good. He was then on the Illinois River, at Peoria, building another fort and shipyard. He named it Fort Crèvecoeur—Fort Broken Heart.

By Easter he was back at Niagara, discovering that Fort Condé, his stronghold at the river mouth, lay in ashes. It had burned down, through either the carelessness or the treachery of the sergeant left in command. (Treachery is

Hinu's Lair

more likely, since Sergeant La Fleur subsequently turned up in the service of the British.) Soon La Salle received word that Fort Crèvecoeur, too, was no more. The shipwright Moyse Hillaret had led a mutiny against Tonti and burned it. On top of that, a ship from France bringing him 22,000 *livres'* worth of supplies had been wrecked in the St. Lawrence.

The plan was a shambles. Tonti was missing, probably dead. La Salle's creditors were meaner than ever. Yet it never occurred to him to give up. Two years later, on April 9, 1682, he would stand on the shore of the Gulf of Mexico, plant a column and a wooden cross, and claim for France "Possession of this country of Louisiana" from the Ohio down the Mississippi to the southern sea.

Beside him stood the iron-fisted Tonti, rescued from the wreckage of Fort Crèvecoeur, and a thin line of Frenchmen and Indians who had made the first voyage down the "Father of Rivers." They fired a musket volley, shouted "*Vive le Roi,*" and sang the hymn of the V*exilla Regis*:

> *The banners of Heaven's King advance*
> *The mystery of the Cross shines forth . . .*

The great explorer was no colonizer. When he returned in 1687 to settle the empire he had discovered, his men mutinied once more and murdered him. He was left to the buzzards in a Texas swamp while his colonists died of malaria or were killed off by Indians.

According to an Indian tale, La Salle had been forewarned of his doom back at Niagara. The Iroquois chief Gironkouthie took him into the Devil's Hole cave in the gorge to hear the voice of the river god. As interpreted by Gironkouthie, the boom of the waters, echoing in the cave, told La Salle that his southern odyssey could end only in his death.

La Salle was impressed, but ignored the warning. Neither the might of Niagara nor the wisdom of its gods could deter him from his quest.

3
Rum Versus Brandy

The House of Peace at Old Fort Niagara is a masterpiece of deception. It looks like an eighteenth-century French manor house, a graceful setting for wine-bibbing nobles and their crinolined ladies. But its granite walls are four feet thick, and its harmless-looking attic windows conceal gunports for heavy cannon. It is a fortress in disguise. When it was built in 1725, it was a powerful stronghold and a symbol of France's determination to control the Niagara trading route. Behind its six-inch oaken door lived a hundred "trading personnel" who were, in fact, French soldiers.

However, the Iroquois, who still occupied the surrounding area, and the British, who were attempting to divert the fur trade from New France to New York, were told that the big stone *Maison de la Paix* was a simple trading post, a boon and a blessing to red men and white.

The deception was planned by Louis Joncaire, a will-o'-

the-wispish figure who led a double life so mysterious that he appeared to be in several places at once and was believed by some to be in command at Niagara twenty years after his death. Joncaire was a "white Indian": a Frenchman who not only understood Indians but at times thought like one. He and his sons after him wielded an almost magical influence over the Five Nations Iroquois and almost, but not quite, won them over to the side of France. They lost in the end to another "white Indian" on the British side: William Johnson.

Louis Thomas de Joncaire, Sieur de Chabert, first appears in 1687 as a seventeen-year-old junior officer on a punitive expedition against the Five Nations led by the newly appointed governor of New France, the Marquis de Denonville.

Denonville, under orders to subdue the Iroquois and stop their treacherous fur-trading with the British, believed that "resolution" was all he needed for success—the resolution of the steady lines of troops he had commanded on the battlefields of Europe. After a few months in the tangled, bug-ridden forests of the new land, he abandoned resolution and turned to the local weapon: treachery. He invited several Iroquois chiefs to a peace conference at Fort Frontenac, seized them, and shipped them in irons to France, where they were exhibited as freaks at the royal court and then sold into slavery.

That done, he advanced upon the leaderless Indians at the Five Nations' principal village, Boughton Hill. He had 2,000 Frenchmen and 600 Indian allies but they were ambushed and nearly routed by a mere 500 Senecas.

Baron de Lahontan, the man who raised the purported height of the falls by 200 feet, was there as a company commander. He wrote to Denonville:

Had you but seen, sir, what disorder our troops and militia were in amidst the thick trees you would have joined me in thinking that several thousand Europeans are no more than a sufficient number to make head[way] against 500 barbarians. Our battalions were divided into straggling parties who fell into the right and left without knowing where they went. Instead of firing upon the Iroquois we fired upon one another. 'Twas to no purpose to call in the soldiers of such-and-such a battalion for we could not see 30 paces off. We were so disordered that the enemy were going to close in on us with their clubs in their hands when the savages on our side, having rallied, repulsed the enemy and pursued them to their villages with such fury that they brought off the heads of eighty and wounded a great many. In this action we lost ten savages and a hundred French.

Most of the hundred French were killed but thirteen, including young Joncaire, were taken prisoner by Senecas. These were the unfortunates.

The Iroquois torture ritual was partly a religious ceremony, part entertainment, and part education. A brave was hardened by inflicting torment and, by watching the victim, he might learn how to withstand it, should it happen to him.

The prisoner was hoisted on to a platform so that everyone, including squaws and infants, could watch. He was stripped and chained to a stake, scorched by flaming torches, then scalded with boiling water from camp kettles. His fingernails were torn out and fingers and toes crushed between stones. Sometimes a collar with several red-hot tomahawks attached was placed around his neck, so that every move he made brought a searing bite from a hatchet. His torn body would be encased in bark smeared with pitch and set afire. As he roasted, his tormentors would carve slices from his arms and legs, eating them as he died. If he lasted a long time without showing fear, the braves would fight for the privilege of eating his heart.

The ritual was well known to the French. Jesuits and *coureurs* like Étienne Brûlé had described it. La Salle and Tonti had been invited to watch prisoners being burned during their negotiations with the Senecas.

So Joncaire knew just what was happening as he lay trussed by ropes in a longhouse at Boughton Hill and heard the hellish screams from the reeking platform outside.

His twelve companions died on that platform. Before his turn came he managed to free himself, batter his guard in the face, and make a run for it. He was caught, but his courage had impressed the sachems. They offered him his life if he could run the tribal gantlet without showing fear. He ran—was kicked, clubbed, whipped, and lashed by chains, but survived—and was adopted into the tribe as an Iroquois warrior.

At this point, Joncaire melts into the forests and vanishes for ten years. We know that he married a Seneca woman and had a large half-breed family. He learned several Iroquois dialects and apparently excelled as a fighter, hunter, and probably torturer, for he was elected a sachem of the tribe. Nowadays, every semiprominent politician can become an honorary Indian chief. They're as common as Kentucky colonels. But Joncaire was a real one.

Joncaire re-emerges around 1700 as a French agent, conducting diplomatic and trade negotiations with his Seneca brothers and handing them gifts and silver medals from "your great father across the sea." He also explained the Senecas' problems to the authorities in Quebec and Montreal. If France wanted to win back that portion of the fur trade which had been allowed to slip away to the British, she should offer them better prices and provide bigger and fancier presents for the sachems. Joncaire was trusted by both sides because he was loyal to both. As he saw it, neither the French nor the Indians had anything to gain from further wars.

The French were beginning to agree with him. Denonville's 1687 attempt to crush the Iroquois by force and treachery had failed dismally and so had his efforts to re-establish a fort on the Niagara.

While Joncaire was awaiting the torture platform in 1687 the governor set 1600 soldiers to work building a log blockhouse on the site of La Salle's burned-out Fort Condé. It took them three days. Then, as Seneca scouts watched from the surrounding woods, Denonville ordered most of his battalions into their canoes and flat-bottomed *bateaux* and departed. He left 120 men to winter at the fort. They had no boats—not even a canoe—and when they opened the barrels of food the governor had left them, they found the flour wet and the biscuits crawling with weevils.

The Senecas did not attack the fort. They didn't need to. When the snow came, the garrison was starving. Hunting parties went out to look for game and were scalped by the Indians. The remainder crouched behind the log walls, hearing the howl of wolves and the shrieks of the warriors. They died of hunger, scurvy, and fright. An officer wrote: "The woodchoppers one day, facing a storm, fell in the drifts just outside the gate; none durst go out to them. The second day the wolves found them—and we saw it all . . ."

When the first ship arrived in the spring of 1688 only twelve men were alive. A Jesuit buried the dead under an 18-foot oak cross. The fort was abandoned that summer, and the Senecas burned it. Only the charred cross was left standing as a memorial to Denonville's war policy.

Meanwhile, the British were courting the Iroquois in the style they appreciated. In Albany, sachems were received splendidly by Governor Thomas Dongan of New York and presented with dazzling raiment, iron pots, and rum. Denonville protested to Dongan about the rum: "Think you, sir, that Religion will make any progress while your merchants will supply, as they will, *eau-de-vie* in abundance which, as you ought to know, converts the savages into demons and their cabins into counterparts and theatres of hell?"

Dongan stoutly replied: "Our Rum does as little hurt as your Brandy and in the opinion of Christians is much more wholesome."

Besides rum, Albany offered bargains. The Indians could buy a musket for two beaver skins and a blanket for one. The prices in Montreal were five skins and two, respectively. And Albany was closer and more convenient than Montreal.

To offset its attractions, the French needed a new trading post in Iroquois territory, preferably at the Niagara portage. This time, they realized, it had to be built with the permission of the Iroquois and Joncaire, the Seneca sachem, was the man to negotiate this. It took him nearly twenty years. When he finally received the go-ahead from his fellow chiefs, they stipulated that he—Joncaire—maintain personal control over the post "forever."

This was the start of the "Jean Coeur" myth that would persist long after he was dead. In 1706 Joncaire married a Montreal woman, Magdelene le Guay, and set up house there. He spent the next fifteen years commuting by canoe between his busy Seneca home in New York State with its numerous brood of half-Indian children and his Montreal home, where he rapidly acquired another ten children by Magdelene. Two of his Montreal sons, Philippe and Daniel, followed him into his Indian life as soon as they were big enough to paddle canoes and wield little hatchets of their own.

Their exploits in the hectic years that followed became so jumbled together in frontier tales that the three Joncaires blended into one legendary figure known to the British as "Jean Coeur," a white-Indian Scarlet Pimpernel who refused to die.

The senior Joncaire erected his first store in 1721 near Lewiston, at the base of the Crawl-on-All-Fours part of the portage. Indian women and children still humped bundles of goods up and down that cliff, but by this time ponies were being used to carry them along the edge of the gorge to the boat landing at Cayuga Creek. The Seneca porters lived in a village at Lewiston and were available for hire to any expedition—Indian, French, or, occasionally, British— that used the portage. In 1702 they had carried the luggage of the first white women to visit Niagara—Madame de la Motte-Cadillac, wife of the founder of Detroit, who was on her way to join her husband there, and her companion Madame Alphonse de Tonti, sister-in-law of the Man with the Iron Hand. The ladies managed the Crawl-on-All-Fours with the help of the buckskinned *coureurs* who guarded them, and ponies took them safely over the Niagara rattlesnakes that infested the pathway above.

The lieutenant-governor of Montreal, Baron de Longueuil, opened Joncaire's trading post grandly, naming it the *Magazin Royal.* Joncaire had coached the baron in tact, so he explained carefully to the Senecas that the shop was not a fort. As it was made of bark and poles, it could easily be destroyed by a few fire arrows. The company of soldiers were not going to remain at Niagara; they were on their way to Cadillac's post at Detroit. The Senecas were welcome to see them on their way to the Upper Lakes. Baron Longueuil saluted the lilies of France as the flag fluttered over the modest royal store, then went to Lake Onondaga to meet the rest of the Iroquois leaders and assure them of France's peaceful intentions.

Governor William Burnet of New York received detailed reports from his Indian spies a few days later and didn't like what he heard. He hinted that the new store could be burned with a couple of fire arrows; maybe someone should try it. The Five Nations had signed a treaty with him, placing themselves under the protection of "His Greate Majesty, George II," and Burnet understood that this gave His Majesty a monopoly over their furs. But since the mysterious "Jean Coeur" had somehow suborned the Seneca nation, the governor had to mount a new diplomatic offensive. He sent messengers into Iroquois territory, inviting every chief of consequence to attend a "council of friendship" at Albany. The council began with the presentation of unusually lavish gifts, including red cloth, linen shirts, mirrors, scissors, muskets, ammunition, twelve dozen Jew's harps, six and a half barrels of good tobacco, and a hogshead of rum. Proceedings were delayed, as was the custom, by a week-long drunk. This time the usual uproar of shrieking, whooping, and fighting was accompanied by the twanging of Jew's harps.

When Governor Burnet expressed his disapproval of the new French store, the chiefs promptly threw down their wampum belts—the sign of a solemn promise—and swore that they would have no more truck or trade with the

French. Then they spent the rest of the night dancing and drinking the king's ale.

Burnet knew his allies well enough not to believe them implicitly. They would be back at the *Magazin Royal* as soon as they recovered from the king's hospitality. What he did *not* know was that one of the blanket-swathed natives who had thrown down a belt, pledged allegiance to the great Hanoverian, drunk his share of the rum and the ale, and played his Jew's harp was the manager of the *Magazin Royal:* Joncaire.

Although Burnet set up a trading post of his own first, unsuccessfully at Irondequoit bay near Rochester and later, with success at Oswego, Joncaire's store prospered. By 1725 it was time to expand. Baron Longueuil, coached again by Joncaire, met the sachems of the Senecas, Cayugas, and Onondagas at Boughton Hill to tell them that the bark store was now falling apart. The roof was leaking, rotting the fine trade goods within. There was also a fire hazard—as the baron had said before when explaining how harmless the place was. A stone house would be better for everyone. And the French begged permission to build larger ships to bring better presents; they'd like to build the house at the river mouth—where forts Condé and Denonville had stood. But, of course, this would not be a fort. Just a House of Peace.

The baron's speech, translated by Joncaire, was interminably long, embellished by the flourishes and flattery the Iroquois loved, complete with boring passages they could snooze through, and altogether satisfying. It convinced the chiefs that a stone house would be harmless and profitable. At the last moment the Mohawk and Oneida sachems, friends of the British, came to object. But the House of

Peace was approved by a majority vote, and construction began in the summer of 1726.

The new, larger ships—probably schooners of about 60 tons—brought granite blocks quarried near Fort Frontenac; the architect Gaspard Chaussegros de Léry wanted stronger material than the erodable rock of the Niagara gorge. He built innocent-looking attic windows that overhung the courtyard with holes in the overhang through which soldiers could fire on anyone below. The massive front door, strong enough to withstand a battering ram, had a peephole just too high for the average man to reach. A visitor had to pull himself up with both hands to show his face before being admitted. This meant he had to drop his weapon. But apart from these defensive features, the building looked peaceful enough. Its secret was in the attic, where batteries of cannon stood, supported by heavy oak beams.

The cannon were shipped up Lake Ontario after the building was finished, and smuggled ashore after dark, thickly wrapped in canvas. As the Indians would certainly notice a rope and pulley hanging from the roof, they had to be manhandled through the front door, then up two flights of stairs. This was done between midnight and dawn.

Despite this secrecy, word reached the governor of New York that the House of Peace was not what it appeared to be. He called the Five Nations chiefs to an emergency council meeting and bluntly accused them of allowing the French to build a fortress on their land. He demanded—and got—their agreement to hand over a strip of land 60 miles long on the south shore of Lake Ontario and the east bank of the Niagara.

Since the 1724 Treaty of Utrecht between France and Britain, the Five Nations had been recognized by both

Rum Versus Brandy

sides as wards of Great Britain, but this had not stopped their trade with the French or ended the Senecas' affection for Joncaire. The Iroquois never took the white man's treaties very seriously. Pieces of paper did not impress them.

They ceded their Niagara land to the British on paper but remained in possession of it. Business continued as usual at the House of Peace, which would soon become a house of war and a focal point in the struggle between Britain and France for the continent of North America.

William Johnson was a huge, lusty Irishman, fierce and reckless as an Iroquois, but with a canny eye for property values. He was brought up on the 200 acres his parents farmed for the Earl of Fingel in County Meath, but they soon recognized that 200 acres—or even the whole of Ireland—was too small to contain him. His mother described him as "a great lout, too wild in his ways for the likes of here."

So when she received a letter from her brother in America offering to take the lout as overseer of his huge estate, she jumped at the chance. William, then twenty-three, was encouraged to round up ten local families who wished to emigrate with him and get on the next boat. There was no suggestion that he ever come back. Nor did he.

William and the families were each promised 200 acres of the 14,000 acres of "good" wilderness in the Mohawk Valley, owned by his uncle, Captain Peter Warren of the Royal Navy. Warren had bought it for 25 cents an acre thanks to the political connections of his wife's *patroon* family. The immigrants would get their lots for the same 25 cents—once they had hacked down every tree, hauled out every stump, planted crops, and repaid their passage money. Life was hard for the humble Irish who didn't marry money, but they had no intention of remaining humble. Johnson was never humble to begin with; soon he would outshine and outrank his uncle, and eventually he would conquer Niagara for Britain.

A coarse, rough-hewn man, Johnson didn't try to emulate the gold-braided Warren's success in the drawing rooms of Albany and Manhattan. Power, as he learned, lay with the Indians, not with the powdered fops who regarded him as a ferocious peasant. The threat of the torture platform convinced Joncaire to become a white Indian. Johnson never had to face that threat; he chose the path for himself. He reached the Niagara hinterlands in 1738, a year before Joncaire died, and spent the next twenty-one years struggling with the Joncaire sons and the "Jean Coeur" legend for control of the Iroquois. In the end, he won.

From the start Johnson distrusted the old New York aristocracy. On the advice of Captain Warren he had bought six horses from an Albany gentleman with the revered name of van Rensselaer. Five of them promptly died on him. After that, Johnson found his own kind of people—the German refugees from the Palatinate who had settled along the Mohawk because earlier immigrants wouldn't have them in the older parts of the colony, and the Mohawks themselves, fierce, devious, but too primitively honest to sell a man spavined horses.

He began by opening a frontier store and tavern on Warren's land—Warrensburg—for the Germans. He provided a free lunch of smoked herring with old cheddar mixed with rum and sprinkled with caraway seeds. He bought every third round of drinks himself, so business flourished. An innkeeper has to hear the drunken meanderings, the sorrows, and the spilled secrets of his customers; so the wild colonial lad learned to listen.

He hired a German girl, Catherine Weisenberg, as clerk and barmaid. She soon became his mistress and produced three children. There is doubt whether they ever married but they lived together until she died in 1759. When Johnson became a baronet, the editors of Debrett decided to give Catherine the benefit of the doubt and list her as the first Lady Johnson. She deserved the honor, for William was not an easy man to live with. While Joncaire maintained two families, the Irishman sired entire tribes.

Although Johnson occasionally lived as an Iroquois and followed their customs, he overlooked their ban on sex before battle. Apparently they forgave him for this and were awed by the giant's sexual prowess. According to longhouse legend, he acquired 700 half-breed children during his prodigious career as a womanizer. There are records of only three—his children by his second wife, the Mohawk Molly Brant, whose brother Joseph became principal chief of the Iroquois nations.

Johnson was introduced to the Mohawks by their chief Tiyonaga, whom the British called King Hendrick. He was a hatchet-scarred veteran who had been presented to Queen Anne in London, spoke elegant French and English, but liked to play the role of ignorant savage. The "king" took the ferocious-looking newcomer under his wing and taught him the subtleties of the Mohawk tongue and the intricacies of tribal ceremonies.

After four years' instruction Johnson could outhunt, outfight, and outdance most braves. In 1742 he was formally adopted as a Mohawk blood-brother and given the name Warraghiyagey, "the man who undertakes great things." He was never the complete Iroquois brave like

Joncaire in his Indian periods but he, too, led a double life and was equally at home in the smoky longhouse or with Catherine among the whiskey fumes, the smoked herring, and the German settlers.

By 1746, when his role in the history of Niagara begins, the unruly lout had become a rich and important, if still unruly, squire. The Mohawks had presented him with a tract of land 12 miles square in Herkimer County, New York, and he had built an enormous house, Johnson Hall, "to shelter my whores and bastards," as he put it. There he staged Indian feasts and Irish jollifications, sometimes together, with few distinctions made as to the race or the rank of the guests.

Uncle Peter was furious. His uncouth nephew had overtaken him in wealth and power, and he had done it without marrying money or cultivating the Albany snobs.

In 1744 the European War of the Austrian Succession spread to America, where it was called King George's War. Nobody in America cared who took the throne of Austria. The important point was that the shaky truce between New France and the British colonies was over and both sides were free to fight for trading rights instead of haggling, bribing, stealing, and threatening.

In a straightforward fight between the 60,000 whites of New France and the 1,000,000 in the British colonies, the outcome would have been easy to predict. But the wars of the New World were never straightforward. Both sides relied on "their" Indians to do much of their fighting. The Iroquois were the best fighters, so victory or defeat depended on which side could hold their loyalty. King George's War became a struggle between William Johnson and the Joncaires for control of these key Indian nations.

Louis Joncaire died at Niagara in 1739, leaving his sons

Philippe and Daniel to carry on his work in his name. They did this so successfully that seven years later even Johnson, with all his Indian contacts, did not know the father was dead. He launched a hunt for "Jean Coeur," believed to be a French priest living among the Senecas. In return, Daniel Joncaire offered a bounty of £1,000 to any Indian who would bring him Johnson's scalp. None did. The Irishman was as feared and respected by his Mohawk brothers as the Joncaires were among the Senecas.

The Joncaires began their war by rousing the Senecas, Cayugas, and Onondagas to attack British supply routes to their trading post—the rival to the House of Peace—at Oswego, on Lake Ontario. Four hundred French and two hundred Indians plundered and burned settlements along the Hudson Valley toward Albany and hijacked cargoes of rum and trade goods on their way to Oswego.

Governor George Clinton of New York called on Johnson to settle the score. The white Indian shaved his shaggy black mane, leaving only a sharp ridge and scalp lock on top, daubed war paint on his bare chest and arms, and led his Mohawks, leaping and shrieking, to a conference at Albany. Governor Clinton promised that the Great Father in England would send many soldiers to drive out the French. Meanwhile, the Mohawks must attack them at Niagara. After much haggling, a price was arranged: £10 for each male French scalp, nothing for female scalps, £20 for every adult male captured alive.

(While European officers professed horror at the North American practice of carving up the dead and near-dead and tried to stop it from time to time, everyone was guilty. The French and British-American militiamen fought alongside the Indians and took scalps as a matter of course. When regular troops arrived from Europe in the 1750s, many of them were soon carrying scalps dangling from their belts. Major-General James Wolfe, the hero who took Quebec, strictly forbade his troops to scalp Europeans, but allowed them to slice the heads of Indians and Europeans disguised as Indians. By the rules of the period, it would have been acceptable to scalp either Johnson or the Joncaires, for those were the savage rules they lived by.)

Johnson was now a British official. Clinton had appointed him "Colonel of the Six Nations." The Six were actually only five and a half. The sixth, the Tuscaroras, had been driven out of Georgia in 1722 and were under the protection of the Oneidas, but they did not have a vote in the councils of the Iroquois Confederacy. However, Clinton needed the support of as many nations as he could muster, so, in the 1740s the Five Nations became the Six.

The new colonel led some small raids into New France, but his assault on Niagara was postponed for many years because the "many soldiers" from England took a long time to arrive. Only the Mohawks and a few Oneidas were betting on the British to win. The majority of the sachems, who had dealt with both sides, favored the French. They were impressed not by numbers, but by the spirit of a man and his strength of purpose. They didn't think much of the sober New Englanders or the quarrelsome Southerners and didn't believe the colonies could stop arguing over their local problems long enough to agree on any kind of concerted action. At the time they were right.

Johnson, always a showman, pranced through the streets of Manhattan with a band of painted Mohawks waving the scalps he had taken on his raids, but failed to stir up much enthusiasm for the distant war, which was at a standstill. From Niagara the Senecas sent a warm expression of their great love for King George, but they continued to trade at

Rum Versus Brandy

the House of Peace. The war ended officially in 1748 with the peace treaty of Aix-la-Chapelle, but there was neither peace nor war at Niagara; only a mounting hostility that sooner or later must lead to battle.

In 1751 Daniel Joncaire was appointed Master of the Niagara Portage—a job that would lead him to a cell in the Bastille along with the great thieves and swindlers of New France. For Niagara was a link in the golden chain of corruption strung by François Bigot, the *intendant* (business manager) of New France. Bigot was not only the greatest crook of his time; he has yet to be equaled in North America. Today's crime bosses are petty pilferers compared to the man who looted an empire. Through his syndicate, *La Grande Compagnie*, he stole from all levels of society— from the king of France to the peasant farmer who had to buy his own grain back from the officials who commandeered it to feed nonexistent soldiers.

"Profit by your place," Bigot advised a pupil, "clip and cut—you are free to do as you please." His company collected kickbacks on every cargo that moved in New France —by ship, boat, canoe, or pack train. It took all the supplies the king shipped over to the colony and resold them—often back to the king. Fraud touched everyone in New France, including the Master of the Niagara Portage, although his share of the graft was small because Bigot installed his own agent at Niagara, Major Jean Péan.

The frontier post had seen wild men, bad men, traitors, and murderers but Péan was the first smooth, elegant swindler to ply his trade there. Others would follow.

He arrived in suitably discreditable circumstances. Bigot, fat, fiftyish, and pimply, was nonetheless a charming rogue with an eye for a fine woman. That eye fell upon Péan's wife, Angélique. The ungallant major agreed to hand her over to the *intendant* in exchange for a commission to buy and sell grain at an assured commission of 400 per cent. (If a farmer haggled over the price, troops confiscated his harvest.)

Angélique was installed as Bigot's mistress and became the Madame Pompadour of New France, while her husband moved discreetly from Quebec to Niagara, where crime paid equally well. Niagara was the base for a new military and commercial push down the Ohio—*La Belle Rivière*, as the French called it. Strongpoints were re-established there, British poachers cleared out, and the dream of La Salle revived for the profit of the Bigot gang. Daniel Joncaire built a new fort, "Little Niagara," near La Salle's old shipyard on Cayuga Creek, while Péan organized the burgeoning portage traffic over the Crawl-on-All-Fours. In the summer of 1753 he earned his graft. Twelve thousand bundles, each weighing 80 pounds, were heaved across on the backs of every man, woman, and child the major could lay his hands on. Among them were four Mohawks spying for Johnson.

"Everything goes ahead, day and night," Péan reported to Quebec. "One shift works while the other sleeps and eats; there is no interruption. Some bring the *bateaux* to shore; others carry them up; one part makes the portage, another fills the sacks, still others sew them."

More than two thousand militiamen crossed the portage, followed by a few wives and several hundred "joy girls." The House of Peace became a house of revelry. "I have made thirty seamstresses as nimble as our girls of Montreal," Péan writes ambiguously. "I begin to have hope . . . Gaiety reigns."

But there was a sour note amid the gaiety. Péan, the 400 per cent swindler, was aghast to find that thefts were taking place. His human beasts of burden were looting their 80-pound bundles on the portage. So were officers and clerks at the House of Peace.

"I have endless anxieties. At Niagara, they have found barrels filled with stones instead of pork. . . . The casks of wine and brandy have nearly all been opened. They are but half full."

You can't trust anybody, he told Bigot—who had never trusted a soul in his life.

Corruption rotted the colony and prepared it for eventual defeat. ("What a country," wrote the Marquis de Montcalm, "where rogues get rich and honest men are ruined.") But defeat was slow in coming. Although outnumbered twenty to one, the French with their Indian allies ruled the frontier lands, outwitting and terrorizing the British.

The Seven Years' War, which was to decide the ownership of North America, did not start officially until 1757, but actually began three years earlier, when twenty-one-year-old Major George Washington and his straggle of Virginia militiamen fired on a French patrol near Pittsburgh, Pennsylvania. That volley killed ten men, including the French commander, and brought a counterattack by a much larger force that led to Washington's surrender at Great Meadows.

After this, Britain and France each sent a general with a small army of regulars to end this ill-disciplined skirmishing in the woods and win proper parade-ground battles in the European manner. Both men failed.

Britain's Major-General Edward Braddock was a no-nonsense Guards officer of the old school. When William Johnson urged him to attack Niagara and "sever the throat of New France," he turned his back. He had not come all this way to be lectured on strategy by a scruffy Irish colonial who dressed up as an Indian. So he marched his shining redcoats along Washington's ill-starred route to Pittsburgh and straight into an ambush on the Monongahela. Braddock kept them lined up ramrod-straight and beat them with the flat of his sword when they tried to take cover. *Coureurs* and Indian snipers gleefully slaughtered them from behind trees. Four horses were killed under the general. He was on his fifth, still shouting for discipline, when a bullet brought him down. He died murmuring, "We shall better know how to deal with them another time."

France's general, the German baron Ludwig August von Dieskau, was equally courageous and pigheaded. He had no time for Indians, including those attached to his army, and only contempt for British colonials who, he was told, were the worst troops on earth. "The more there are," he declared, "the more we shall kill." *Boldness Wins* was the baron's family motto. In his case, it didn't. Dieskau was tramping south to meet Braddock when, at Lake George, he ran into a large force of the despised colonials and their Indians commanded by Johnson. To his surprise, he found that "they fought like good boys in the morning, like men at noon and like devils in the afternoon."

The baron was shot in the leg but refused to be carried to the rear. He sat under a tree, confident that his white-coated regulars would crush the colonials. Instead they were routed. He was captured and taken to Johnson's tent.

The giant received him courteously and they chatted about military matters while their wounds were dressed. Johnson found the baron, like Braddock, so unaware of the realities of life in the wilderness that he might have arrived from another planet. When a group of Mohawks burst

Rum Versus Brandy

into the tent, shrieked at Johnson, then left in a fury, Dieskau mildly inquired what they wanted.

"What do they want?" echoed the white Indian. "To burn you, by God, eat you and smoke you in their pipes!" Their great chief and his mentor King Hendrick had been bayoneted to death in the battle.

Dieskau was escorted to New York and put on a ship for Europe, still puzzled by the wild ways of the New World.

His victory at Lake George made Johnson a hero and gained him his baronetcy and a reward of £5,000 from Parliament in London. But it was inconclusive. Most of the French regulars escaped and, rather than pursuing them, his colonial officers held a council of war and voted to go home for Thanksgiving. The new Sir William Johnson went home to Johnson Hall, leaving France in possession of the Ohio forts and the key to the interior, the Niagara frontier.

Another British expedition, aimed at Niagara, had reached as far as Oswego, built two 40-foot warships and 233 flatboats, then given up on hearing rumors of reinforcements at Niagara and approaching storms on Lake Ontario.

"O tell it not in Quebeck!" parodied an editorial in the Boston *Gazette*. "Nor publish it in the streets of Montreal! Let the daughters of the Popish Nunneries rejoice, and the British name be had in derision by the slaves of the haughty Louis!"

The Joncaire brothers were back at Niagara with canoeloads of British scalps and boots and uniforms taken from Braddock's dead. They had fought with their blood brothers at the Monongahela, and the blood brothers, having seen how easily the redcoats fell, were now ardent for the cause of France. Daniel agreed to accompany a delegation of Cayugas and Oneidas to Quebec, where they would present symbols of loyalty to the governor, while Philippe accepted an invitation to a friendly powwow with the Iroquois chiefs at Onondaga Hill.

(Meanwhile the Onondagas were assuring the governor of New York that they had driven out "Joncuer, [sic], a Frenchman who has resided among the Senecas several years past.")

Only the Mohawks remained true to Britain because of their beloved Johnson, and they had been badly shaken by the loss of "King Hendrick." The Joncaires were winning; they had convinced most of the Six Nations that New France reigned supreme, and they had convinced the British that the House of Peace was impregnable.

In fact, New France was rotting, and so was the House of Peace. The governor at Quebec reported to Paris:

> In regard to Niagara, it is certain that, should the English attack it, it is theirs. I am informed that the fort is so dilapidated that it is impossible to put a peg into it without causing it to crumble. Stanchions have been obliged to be set up against it to support it. Its garrison consists of thirty men without any muskets.

February 1757 was a hard month at Niagara. Ice silenced the falls and choked the gorge. The portage path shone glassy and empty. On campfires at the river mouth, soldiers were burning logs intended for a new palisade. Food was scarce because, back in Quebec, Intendant Bigot was using army grain to fatten fowl for his table. Hungry Indians hovered around the fort, scrounging and scavenging, selling wild turkeys to the French for a penny each, and stewing Niagara rattlesnakes for themselves. They could get a pint of brandy for a deer, but deer were hard to find, and the

French were watering the brandy. Times were hard, but hard times make for good theater. So, in that dismal February, the first theatrical performance was staged at the House of Peace.

Le Vieillard Dupé (*The Old Man Duped*), written and produced by some unknown soldier, was performed on the main floor of the fort by members of the garrison in homemade costumes. Good or bad, it attracted attention as far away as Quebec, where Montcalm, the new commanding general, mentioned it in his diary. Historically, it ranks as the first frontier stage play. There were a few wives and many joy girls in the audience, as well as English and German women who had been captured by Indians along the Ohio and sold to the garrison for a blanket or two, to become cooks or washerwomen. About a hundred British prisoners heard the show from their cells.

The House of Peace, now known as Fort Niagara, was being refurbished and extended. Its commander, the engineer Captain François Pouchot had shored up the sagging walls and refaced them with fresh stone shipped from Kingston. New earthworks had been erected to take cannon captured from Braddock, and a new barracks was added. When spring came, the garrison troops and the prisoners dug a new moat.

The fort seemed secure, but the Senecas were unhappy. Although their chiefs presented Daniel Joncaire with a sack containing thirty-eight scalps as proof of their diligence in attacking the British, the porters at Niagara were restless. Despite Joncaire's promise of permanent employment, they were being replaced on the portage by horses and carts. And they complained bitterly about the watered brandy. This was no small matter, since the frontier functioned largely on brandy or rum. The fabulous canoe journeys of the *voyageurs* were seldom made without *eau-de-vie* before breakfast, the militia wouldn't fight without their daily ration, and the loyalty of the Indians, whether in trade or in war, was best assured by keeping them in a state of stupor.

In August 1758 the British took Fort Frontenac (Kingston) and with it all the supplies destined for Niagara and the Ohio forts. The brandy barrels dried up, and the Indians sniffed the winds of change. The British were coming, bearing rum and promises. The long-awaited assault on Niagara was near.

It came the following year. Sir William Johnson summoned the sachems of the Six Nations to a grand council at Canajoharie. A deputation of sixty Senecas accepted the invitation and brought along some Shawnees from the Ohio. Johnson roasted oxen and broached kegs of rum. Parleying droned on for a day and a night. Gifts were exchanged. At the appropriate moment, the baronet stripped off his shirt and breeches, striped himself with paint, and leapt into his war dance. The chiefs whooped approval as he writhed, shrieked, and sweated, the paint running down his square Irish features. Suddenly he silenced the drummers, screamed, and hurled a war belt to the ground. A chief snatched it up and shouted for French scalps. Others followed. War fever ran high. When the council ended, eight hundred Iroquois, including the Seneca delegation, joined the Niagara expedition.

The expedition was part of a three-pronged attack on New France. Major-General James Wolfe would sail up the St. Lawrence to make a frontal assault on Quebec while his superior, General Jeffrey Amherst, advanced from Albany along Lakes George and Champlain to Montreal. Brigadier General John Prideaux's 2,000 redcoats and

American militia, with Johnson's Indians, would seize the Niagara throatway and choke off the French left in the West. This impressive force assembled at Fort Oswego. Thirteen hundred men were left to guard that fort while the rest sailed for Niagara in an armada of whaleboats.

At sunrise on July 7, 1759, Captain Pouchot looked out from the House of Peace to see the river mouth black with boats and the woods to the east swarming with hostile Indians.

Prideaux, a cool professional, took his time. His men rowed twelve boatloads of heavy artillery over to the west bank of the river mouth, facing the fort. It took them a week to dig out gun positions and lever the big guns onto platforms. When they had been trained with plumb bob and wedge, the general observed the traditional nicety of gentlemanly warfare: He sent a junior to Pouchot, under a white flag, to suggest that the captain surrender. Pouchot poured him a glass of wine and wrote a polite note: "Before I make any terms, I wish an opportunity to gain your esteem."

Pouchot had only 429 men of his own, plus about seventy whom the Joncaires had brought from Little Niagara, which was abandoned and burned when the siege began, but his fort was strong—"stronger than we expected," a British officer wrote—and there was hope of relief by a French force from the Ohio. The Joncaires still believed they could win over Johnson's Iroquois, and a truce was arranged while they sent an elderly Seneca to talk with them. While that parley continued, Prideaux dug trenches on the east side of the river, extending them almost to the outer palisade of the fort. The Joncaire persuasions failed, and another hundred Iroquois arrived to join Johnson.

An artillery duel began. Prideaux's siege guns coughed

hollow incendiary shells across the river, setting fire to the log barracks and the roof of the fort. The House of Peace boomed cannon balls at the trenches.

On July 20 General Prideaux was watching a crew fire a new mortar for the first time when it blew up and killed him. Sir William Johnson took command of the siege.

The French relief force arrived, but instead of crossing to the west bank of the river and silencing the siege guns, as Pouchot had advised the commander by messenger, it attacked Johnson's troops on the portage and was cut to pieces.

Johnson wrote: "I divided up among the several [Indian] nations the prisoners and scalps amounting to 246 . . . The officers I released from them by ransom and good works."

At this, Pouchot surrendered. The House of Peace was surrounded, torn by shellfire, and partly burned. The cannon dragged up to the attic thirty-five years before had been knocked out, and Pouchot's men had fewer than a hundred muskets still in working order. Gallant to the end, he invited Johnson and his staff officers to dine with him in what was left of the main hall. Wine was poured and civilities exchanged. The Irishman met the Joncaires for the first and last time. Unfortunately, we don't know what was said; only that Johnson had Philippe and Daniel locked in a dungeon for their own protection against "his" Iroquois, then sent them to France where they would face trial for the sins of the Bigot conspiracy.

After the polite dinner party, the victorious officers helped themselves to all the fort's china, silverware, and what valuables they could find, then opened the main gate and allowed the Indians in to drink, plunder, and wreck what was left. In one wild drunken night they did as much

Rum Versus Brandy

damage as the siege guns. It took weeks to clean up the fort —let alone repair it.

Thus France lost Niagara and, a year later, the rest of her North American possessions. One French ghost remained behind at the House of Peace. According to nineteenth-century stories, a headless man in a white officer's tunic haunted the ground floor of the fort, looking for his head, which had been sliced off in a duel and plopped into a well. He had been buried without it. But there was no well, so the ghost seemed to be looking in the wrong place. However, in 1927, the American custodians of Fort Niagara received from Paris a copy of de Léry's original plans, showing the location of a well. Workmen broke through the stone floor and there it was. Johnson's men had sealed it while repairing the fort, suspecting that Captain Pouchot had poisoned the water as he awaited his conquering dinner guests.

No skull was found down there, so the Headless Frenchman may still be around, looking.

4
The Devil's Hole

About a mile below the Whirlpool Rapids, the Niagara River veers to the left, slashing at the rock walls on the American side and tearing out a cave. This is Devil's Hole, the turbulent grave of ninety men.

On a drowsy September day in 1763, John Stedman, new master of the portage, led a convoy of covered wagons along the cliff-top path above the Hole. The wagons were his idea—they carried more goods more efficiently than the carts the French had used or the Seneca porters who were now used only on the Crawl-on-All-Fours. The path had been widened and smoothed to take iron-bound wheels and teams of horses. British ingenuity was conquering the perils of the portage and Stedman was pleased with himself. His patron, General Jeffrey Amherst, governor general of all British America, had granted him a handsome tract of land, along with the contract to manage the Niagara traffic, and he had moved into a new log house near the falls as one of the first three permanent settlers.

The Indians' friend, Sir William Johnson, had protested to Amherst, reminding him that the Iroquois had been promised that no whites would settle—or even hunt—along the Niagara. The area would remain a military strongpoint and trading center. Nothing more.

Amherst paid no attention. He detested Indians even more than he detested Johnson, the white Indian. When the war with the French ended, he cut down the supply of bribes to the chiefs and weapons to the braves and ignored their resentment over Stedman's improvements at Niagara. He didn't think the Indians had any fight left in them. He was wrong.

In the fall of 1762 Pontiac, paramount chief of the western Ottawas, called for a holy war on the white man. His medicine man had communed with the Master of Life, who told him the time had come to give up rum and guns and drive out the intruders with arrows and hatchets. In fact, the time had already passed. If the quarreling tribes had received that message several generations earlier, they might well have driven all the Europeans back to the sea. Instead, they allowed themselves to be divided and debauched by the bottle and the gun and sent raging after scalps in the name of one White Father or another. Even the Six Nations, best organized of all the Indian tribes, never managed to unite completely against a common enemy.

A delegation of Ottawas paddled from Lake Michigan to Niagara, carrying war belts and tomahawks painted blood red and bearing Pontiac's war message to the Seneca sachems. The Seneca chiefs were unimpressed. They rejected the war belts, but some of their warriors went back

The Devil's Hole

with the Ottawas to join Pontiac. Others planned a rebellion of their own.

The Pontiac rising of 1763 caused more British casualties than the 1759 battles against the French. About 500 soldiers and 2,000 settlers died; many of them were tortured and eaten. Small undermanned forts on the Upper Lakes were overwhelmed and their garrisons wiped out. Pontiac laid siege to Detroit for four months.

Still, Niagara seemed to be at peace on that September day as Stedman's wagons creaked along above the gorge. Then, from behind the trees, came the bloodcurdling scream of a Seneca war cry. Flaming arrows streaked at the canvas wagon tops, and tomahawks sliced into the drivers. Stedman hugged his horse's neck and galloped toward the falls, leaving his twenty-four men to be butchered. The only other survivor was a small drummer boy who managed to hide in a bush after being thrown from a wagon as its terrified horses overturned it. The Seneca raiders pushed the wagons and horses over the brink and down into the gorge.

The shrieks of massacre and the crash of falling vehicles was heard downstream at the outposts of Fort Niagara. Two companies of the 80th Regiment scrambled to the rescue and ran into a second ambush. Most of the soldiers were slaughtered on the spot or hurled alive over the precipice.

Two days later, a British regiment cautiously approached the scene. They found eighty bodies, all scalped, lying on the portage trail and the horrid remains of more men, horses, and wagons wedged on the rocks below.

It is still unclear whether the massacre was ordered by Pontiac to block the portage and stop delivery of supplies to besieged Detroit, or an act of terrorism by the local Senecas thrown out of work by Stedman's wagons. In either event, it failed. The wagons were replaced, and Detroit was supplied by the schooner H.M.S. *Michigan*. Pontiac abandoned his siege in mid-October and moved south, where his followers began to desert him and his rebellion collapsed. The chief reached for the rum bottles he had preached against, and sank into oblivion.

A year later the Senecas were made to pay for their day's scalping. Johnson called a great conclave on the banks of the river that had swallowed Stedman's wagon train and demanded that the Indians surrender, once and for all, all claims to the Niagara portage, including strips of land four miles wide on both sides of the river. In return, he promised in the king's name that white settlement of America would stop at the watershed of the Alleghenies, and would leave all the western lands to the Indians.

Two thousand of Pontiac's allies gathered around Fort Niagara for the conference. Their chiefs were sobered by the threat of a British punitive expedition into their territory, then cheered by the prophecy of a Chippewa seer: "Sir William will fill your canoes with presents; with blankets, kettles, gun powder and shot, and large barrels of rum such as the stoutest will not be able to lift." They made their crosses on a treaty, handing over the Niagara strip to King George and his heirs. They received barely two canoe-loads of gifts. Pontiac was not among them, but two years later he showed up, drunk and disillusioned, to sign the treaty and bury his hatchet at Johnson's feet. Soon after, he was stabbed to death in a brawl. The great chief's name now adorns a General Motors car.

Over the chanting, speechifying, and foot-stamping of the Niagara conclave hung the air of insincerity that marked such gatherings. No arrangement between Indians and whites would last forever. Johnson was the Indians'

The Devil's Hole

friend and brother—he had his Mohawk squaw Molly Brant there to prove it—but he knew as well as his listeners that the treaty was a ploy to calm them down and slow, rather than stop, white colonization of the West. Settlers would be encouraged to fill the empty spaces in eastern Canada, Nova Scotia, and the Floridas instead. But western expansion was inevitable, for the colonies had spawned a race of land speculators. As Johnson handed out silver gorgets, wampum belts, and assurances to the chiefs, he was probably thinking of his own scheme to colonize "Charlotania," which involved grabbing most of Illinois and Wisconsin. Thus the only lasting effect of the treaty was that the Senecas lost Niagara.

Captain John Montresor, a British army engineer, was sent to Niagara in the aftermath of the Pontiac Rebellion with instructions to strengthen the fortifications. But his inventive mind ranged beyond blockhouses, palisades, and gun positions. He wandered the river banks and climbed down into the gorge, sketching and measuring. He selected sites and drew plans for eleven new two-story log blockhouses along the portage trail. While a battalion of troops erected them, he devised a new means of hauling goods up the Crawl-on-All-Fours—North America's first elevator.

Montresor built it during June 1764, about the time the first experimental "plateway" was used to haul coal in English mines. He left no complete description but it seems to have consisted of two wooden tramways leading from a dock on the river to the top of the cliff. Two sleighs or cradles were linked by a rope over a pulley at the top so that when one moved down one tramway with its load, the other moved up. Montresor records in his journal: "The lower cradle broke this day by which 14 barrels of provi-

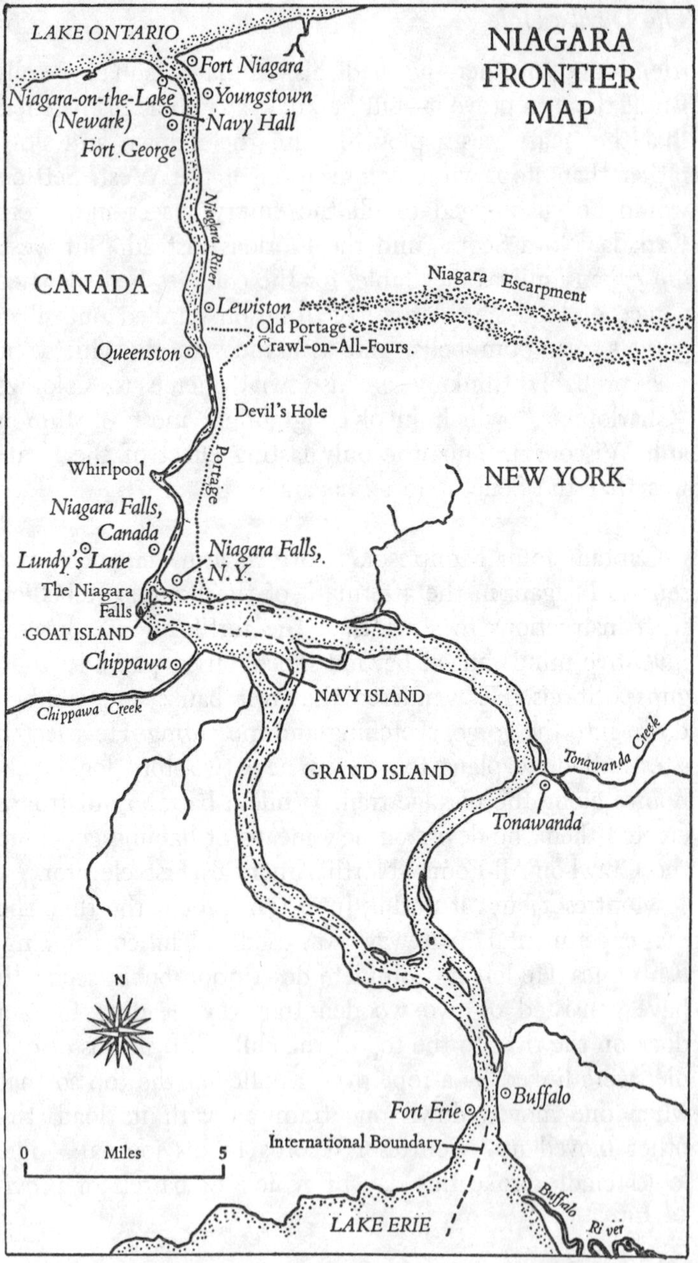
NIAGARA FRONTIER MAP
LAKE ONTARIO
Fort Niagara
Youngstown
Niagara-on-the-Lake (Newark)
Navy Hall
Fort George
Niagara River
CANADA
Niagara Escarpment
Lewiston
Old Portage
Crawl-on-All-Fours
Queenston
Devil's Hole
Portage
Whirlpool
NEW YORK
Niagara Falls, Canada
Lundy's Lane
Niagara Falls, N.Y.
The Niagara Falls
GOAT ISLAND
Chippawa
NAVY ISLAND
Chippawa Creek
GRAND ISLAND
Tonawanda Creek
Tonawanda
N
Buffalo
Fort Erie
International Boundary
0 Miles 5
LAKE ERIE
Buffalo River

The Devil's Hole

sions were lost in the river." He doesn't say that the lower cradle carried the entire fourteen barrels. Presumably, if the lower one dumped its load, the upper one, relieved of its gravity counterweight, would come crashing down.

Whether the cradles carried seven or fourteen barrels per load, the invention revolutionized transportation at Niagara. It was still working forty-six years later when surveyors came to prepare for the next step forward—the building of the Erie Canal, which would bypass the portage altogether.

Montresor spent only four months in the area but did an incredible amount of work. In addition to the tramways and the line of blockhouses, he built the original Fort Erie at the headwaters of the river on the Canadian side and designed two massive stone redoubts beside de Léry's House of Peace at Fort Niagara. His work made the frontier secure against Indian raids, and for ten years there was peace. The next upheaval would be a fratricidal struggle between whites—the American War of Independence—during which Niagara served as a base for Loyalist raiders.

Sir William Johnson did not live to see it. He died in 1774, sick at the prospect of Englishmen fighting Englishmen and the thought of having to lead his Indians against his colonial friends. His funeral at Johnstown was attended by 2,000 people. Among the chief mourners were the Mohawk chiefs, wearing black blankets and gloves and black crepe on their headbands. He was, they declared, "as a tree with roots sunk deep in our affection."

The tree had many branches. Johnson's family was as large and confusing as Louis Joncaire's. As with the Joncaires, the next generation took over the founder's work. Sir John Johnson, his son by his union with Catherine Weisenberg, inherited the title when that union was legitimized by Debretts, but the post of chief superintendent of Indian affairs went to Guy Johnson, another immigrant from County Meath who may or may not have been Sir William's nephew but was certainly his son-in-law, since he had married one of Catherine's daughters. Another son-in-law, Daniel Claus, became one of Guy Johnson's deputies. The other deputy was Sir William's friend and neighbor, John Butler. Joseph Brant, who is remembered as a brother of Sir William's Indian wife Molly but may have been one of his many bastards, became paramount chief of the Six Nations. Peter Brant Johnson, first known son of Sir William and Molly, would command a Mohawk army. These Johnson kin, with Butler, were key figures in the next phase of Niagara's history. They persuaded the Iroquois nations to fight for King George or at least stay neutral in the Revolutionary War. And they led the frontier raids that revived the horrors of the French-Indian wars.

In 1777 the British general "Gentleman Johnny" Burgoyne surrendered to Washington's army in the Hudson Valley. The main British force under Sir William Howe retreated from Philadelphia, leaving the "loyal" colonists who had welcomed them at the mercy of raging "patriot" mobs. Loyalists were stripped of their property, tarred and feathered, put in pillories, and—occasionally—hanged. Streams of Loyalist refugees headed north and west to the relative safety of the Niagara frontier and the forts Montresor built.

There, according to a Niagara tourist guide published in the United States in 1839:

> were congregated the leaders and chiefs of those bands of miscreants that carried death and destruction into the remote American settlements. There, civilized Europe revelled with savage America; and ladies of education and refinement mingled in the society of those whose only distinction was to wield the bloody tomahawk and scalping

The Devil's Hole

knife. There the squaws of the forest were raised to eminence and the most unholy unions between them and officers of the highest ranks smiled upon and countenanced; there they planned their forays and there they returned to feast until the hour of action came again.

This obviously biased description is probably not too far from the truth. Johnson Hall, where wild Sir William had reveled among his "whores and bastards," had been wrecked by the revolutionaries, and Sir John and most of his clan were now at Niagara, raising irregular regiments and planning revenge. Regular officers like Colonel Allan MacLean of the Royal Highland Emigrants detested "all of that Johnson tribe," but His Majesty's forces needed their special skills more than ever.

From the able-bodied Loyalist refugees, Sir John raised his regiment of Royal Greens, and John Butler his more famous (or infamous) Butler's Rangers. Colonel Butler, a chubby, peppery man in his fifties, lacked the Johnson wildness but shared the clan's ability to deal with the Iroquois. His estate, Butlerbury, had been plundered and his wife taken hostage, so he was bitter and vengeful.

On orders from General Sir Frederick Haldimand, he enlisted eight Ranger companies, each fifty strong. Two companies were to be formed of "people speaking the Indian language and acquainted with their customs and manner of making war" and the others of "people well acquainted with the woods." They were highly paid at up to four shillings a day—eight times as much as a regular private—and outfitted with bucket-shaped leather hats and green jackets trimmed with yellow. Their job was to raise havoc and spread terror, and this they did. Their raids were heroic, according to British accounts; wanton and despicable to the Americans, who called Butler and his men fiends and devils. They fought alongside Joseph Brant's Mohawks and a band of Cayugas led by the hatchet-wielding warrior queen Esther Montour, so there was always the danger of Indian massacre.

Massacres did take place. About 300 colonists were scalped or burned at Forty Fort (Wilkes Barre, Pennsylvania) in the Wyoming Valley and 35 at Cherry Valley, New York. The Rangers committed atrocities of their own, using the raids to settle old frontier scores with their former neighbors. Guerrilla bands on the American side did the same.

Butler's rangers, with Sir John Johnson's Royal Greens and other irregulars, burned crops, barns, and gristmills to deprive Washington's Continental Army of food. Their aim was to divert the Continentals away from the main British army under Sir William Howe, and they succeeded. In the summer of 1779 Washington ordered one third of his forces to march on Niagara and stop the raids.

General John Sullivan led 6,000 men against the hotbed of Loyalism but did not get beyond the Genessee Valley. Harassed by Rangers and Iroquois skirmishers, he turned back, but not before carrying out Washington's orders to "lay waste all settlements around, so that the country may not only be overrun but destroyed."

Sullivan's men leveled forty Iroquois villages, burned their cornfields, and killed their livestock. Five thousand homeless Indians fled to Fort Niagara but found no help there. An American blockade at the mouth of the St. Lawrence had choked off supplies from England. The fort could neither feed nor house another soul, and the soldiers were living off the bodies of geese, ducks, and swans killed going over the falls. In the hard winter that followed, hun-

The Devil's Hole

dreds of Iroquois starved or froze to death in brush huts and dugouts around the fort.

The war continued but the Niagara raids petered out. Sullivan had broken the spirit of the Six Nations. After the "Starvation Winter" of 1779, vegetables and fruit trees were planted on both sides of the Niagara River, and the first Loyalist families rowed across to settle on the empty west bank where Prideaux's siege guns had stood, and to begin the colonization of Upper Canada.

5
Mrs. Hustler Invents the Cocktail

Colonel John Graves Simcoe, first lieutenant-governor of Upper Canada, sailed into the mouth of the Niagara on July 26, 1792, to establish a capital for the new British province in the tiny village of Newark, now Niagara-on-the-Lake, Ontario. The merchants of Kingston, where he stopped off on his way up Lake Ontario, had warned him not to go. They told him there were few houses there, fewer provisions, and that he would certainly catch the ague. They were right about the accommodations. The governor and his wife Elizabeth stepped ashore from the topsail schooner *Onondaga*, took one disapproving look at their official residence, Navy Hall, and pitched large tents they had brought with them.

The Hall consisted of four broken-down frame barracks used as billets for schooner captains. They were being repaired and redone as a very modest governor's mansion, but were still open to wind and weather.

Elizabeth was not upset. She had survived the horrors of an Atlantic crossing in a small frigate and a dubious lake voyage—"the men who navigate the ships on this lake have very little nautical knowledge," she observed—and was happy to be ashore. At twenty-six, she was a bright, birdlike little woman, five feet tall and tough. Her mother had died giving birth to her, hence her middle name Posthuma, and her father died soon after. She was raised by an aunt, living the sheltered life of a wealthy orphan in the west of England. Her journey to Canada with her grim soldier husband was her first great adventure, and she recorded it in rich detail in her diary and in sketches and watercolors.

While so much of the early history of Niagara is taken up with scalpings, torture, and musketry, Mrs. Simcoe's diary adds the trivia we need to remind us that the frontiersmen didn't spend all their time killing one another. Nowhere else do we learn that cotton from the wild asparagus made excellent pillows and featherbeds. One could stuff a muff with it. And that pounded crayfish was the cure for the bite of the now-extinct Niagara rattlesnake.

Instead of complaining about the ramshackle state of Navy Hall, she writes: "Our marquees command a beautiful view of the river and the garrison on the opposite side . . . and the poorness of the building is not remarked at this distance, from which a fine picture might be made."

That garrison, Fort Niagara, was still held by the British, as were the other strongpoints along the river, although peace had been signed between King George and the New United States of America nine years earlier. Britain held on to the frontier in the hope of prying $45 million out of the Americans in compensation for the property they had seized from the 40,000 fleeing Loyalists. The new republic

Mrs. Hustler Invents the Cocktail

didn't have that kind of money and the Americans' attitude toward the Loyalists had hardened since they beat the British. Peace or no peace, they were still regarded as traitors and would not be allowed to return home. In return, the British refused to permit Americans to travel or settle along the Niagara. Until 1796, when the dispute was settled and Britain withdrew, there was practically no settlement along the east bank. The New York State census for 1790 lists 25 residents west of the Genessee Valley.

Meanwhile, the Canadian side flourished. In 1780 General Haldimand, an amateur gardener, had proposed "The Niagara Plan for Edible Annex to Fortresses," and ordered wheat and vegetable seeds from Montreal. He had examined the soil and believed the area would bloom and bear richly once men could be found to clear it. He found the men among Butler's Rangers who, of all the Loyalists, were most likely to be hanged if they went home. Butler led them across the river, where they built barracks. When the Rangers were disbanded, the colonel and 260 of his men were given grants of Crown land. They and their families founded a village and called it Newark. Their chaplain told them it was an Anglo-Saxon word meaning "new work."

They hacked down the tangled white pine and cedars, stripped the bark from ancient elms to make their cabin roofs, and burned what was left to clear their patches. These former ravagers and destroyers were good farmers. Soon wheat waved peacefully along the river bank—the beginnings of the "Edible Annex" that would exceed Haldimand's greatest expectations and become the richest food belt in Canada.

Elizabeth Simcoe noted the fine turf that led to the woods above Newark and the "good" road that took her calèche over the new eastern portage all the way to the falls. The drive was delightful, and the hills reminded her of her home in Herefordshire:

> I descended an exceedingly steep hill to get to the Table Rock, from which the view is tremendously fine. . . . The prodigious spray which arises from the foam at the bottom of the fall adds grandeur to the scene, which is wonderfully fine, and after the eye becomes more familiar with the objects I think the pleasure will be greater in dwelling upon them. After taking refreshment on Table Rock we went three miles to Chippawa Fort, admiring the rapids all the way. . . . People cross from Chippawa to Fort Schlosser [on the American side] but great caution is necessary, the current is extremely strong and if they did not make exactly the mouth of the Chippawa the force of the water below it would inevitably carry them down the Falls without redress.
>
> Eight soldiers, who were intoxicated, met with this accident in crossing the river some years since. Their bodies were taken up entire some distance below the Falls. An Indian was asleep in his canoe near Fort Schlosser. The canoe was tied to a tree; some person cut the rope; he did not wake until the canoe had got into the strong current. He found all his efforts to paddle ineffectual and was seen to lay himself down, resigning himself to his fate, and was soon carried down the Fall.

Mrs. Simcoe returned to her marquee at Navy Hall and was disgusted to find the ground around covered with winged grasshoppers—"hard, scaly and ugly as rhinoceros and the color of dead leaves." But next day she was admiring some tame raccoons and noting that black squirrel tasted as good as young rabbit.

A month after they arrived, the Simcoes entertained Niagara's first royal visitor, Prince Edward, the king's

Mrs. Hustler Invents the Cocktail

twenty-four-year-old son. To make way for him, they had to move out of the relative comfort of their marquee and into Navy Hall. Elizabeth writes: "So here we came in a cold, blowing, dismal night. I sat by myself in a dismal, unfinished, damp room, looking on the lake where it blew quite a gale, the *Bear*, a gunboat, tossing about terribly and not a cheerful thought passing through my mind."

Prince Edward could be trying—which was why his father sent him off to Canada to command the garrison there. He was tall, handsome, charming to the ladies, and enamored of life in Quebec, where he kept his long-time mistress, Madame St. Laurent. The chatelaines of Newark's log huts swooned over him. But when he saw soldiers on parade, his eyes glazed with memories of his German military training, and he went slightly mad. Military floggings and hangings delighted him, and his harshness had brought on a mutiny at Quebec. Elizabeth's rubicund, square-jawed husband had similar ideas of discipline. Fortunately for the Niagara garrison, the two officers had little chance to discuss their ideas for, at Edward's ceremonial welcome at Fort Niagara, Simcoe stood too near to a saluting cannon, and the noise affected his head, sending him to bed for two weeks.

Three weeks later, Elizabeth writes, rather mysteriously: "He is now recovered, and has a pain in his foot, which perhaps would more effectually relieve his head if it were more violent."

Prince Edward left Niagara and moved on, through years of military sadism and bliss with Madame St. Laurent, to the one act that assured his place in history: he married a proper princess and fathered Queen Victoria.

Governor Simcoe was left nursing his head and foot while Elizabeth collected the seeds of the white-petaled may apple, admired the black and yellow meadowlark, a swamp blackbird with red-tipped wings, and a new scarlet creature called the kingbird. She feasted off the Niagara whitefish and sturgeon, netted from the then-clear river:

> The [whitefish] are so rich that sauce is seldom eaten with them, but it is a richness that never tires, it is of so delicate a kind. They are usually boiled or set before the fire in a pan with a few spoonfuls of water and an anchovy, which is a very good way of dressing them. The sturgeon are about six feet long. Those that are caught here are infinitely better than those which go to sea: cooks who know how to dress parts of them, cutting away all that is oily and strong, make excellent dishes from sturgeon, such as mock turtle soup, veal cutlets etc.; and it is very good roasted with bread crumbs. The 5th Regt. have caught 100 sturgeon and 600 whitefish in a day in nets.

She also tried Indian cooking, a cake made of dried hurtleberries "which was like Irwin's patent black currant lozenges but tastes of smoke."

The first winter was mild and pleasant; so was the society "within a certain circle." Mrs. Simcoe pointed out in her letters home that Niagara, though small, had fortnightly balls in a candlelit hall, with seldom fewer than eighteen couples and "as many feathers, flowers and gauze dresses" as back in Herefordshire. She spent most evenings playing whist and drawing maps of Canada—her hound Trojan ate her best effort—and entertaining dinner guests with such delicacies as turtle, chopped up and served like oysters in scallop shells.

Her main problem was the lack of decent servants: "The worst people do you a favor if they only wash dishes for twenty shillings a month."

As Elizabeth recorded her gently snobbish little

Mrs. Hustler Invents the Cocktail

thoughts, soldiers were being flogged by cat-o'-nine-tails within earshot of her marquee. Deserters were hunted down by Indians and dragged back to barracks to be shot. One private was made to kneel on his own coffin on the parade ground of Fort Niagara while a firing squad riddled him with bullets. She mentions none of this in her diary. She does write: "I lately dreamed of being fired at by small shot in passing through a wood and have since had quite a horror of the sound of a musquet or anything military."

One wonders what she and her husband discussed during their evenings in the tent, for Simcoe was preoccupied with things military although his principal task was to set up a civil government for the fledgling province. He had commanded a Loyalist regiment during the Revolutionary War and had seen some of his men hanged after the surrender at Yorktown. This left him with a lasting hatred of all republicans, and he was constantly thinking ahead to the next war with the United States. The French philanthropist the Duc de la Rochefoucauld, who visited the Simcoes, noted that the governor was distinctly anti-American and relished the memory of Butler's raids.

(Mrs. Simcoe, usually so genteel in her writing, described the duke and his party as "perfectly democratic and dirty" and added, "I dislike them all.")

Dirty or not, the duke was the first Niagara visitor to foresee that trade and settlement could do even more than war to ruin the beauty spot. In an account of his travels, written in 1779, he proposed that government take over and preserve the falls and the land around them. A century later, his suggestion would be acted upon when New York State and the province of Ontario set up their Niagara parks commissions.

The duke also foresaw the need for vantage points from

which to view the falls. He had to struggle through thickets and swamps and over rocks to get near the river. He wrote:

> It is much to be regretted that the government of a people which surpass all other nations in fondness for travel and curiosity should not have provided convenient places for observing this phenomenon at all possible points of view. It is pleaded in excuse that the number of travellers whom curiosity leads to this spot is inconsiderable, that even they who travel this way on account of business and stop here to view the falls are few in number, that only hunting Indians and idle children form the idea of creeping down to the falls, and that consequently nobody would be benefitted by the money expended in providing an easy access. Yet all these pleas cannot justify a saving of thirty dollars, for which expense the greatest curiosity in the known world would be rendered accessible.

Mrs. Simcoe was more impressed by visiting Indian chiefs, whom she found to be "much civilized." Joseph Brant, who dined at Navy Hall, had "a countenance expressive of art or cunning. He wore an English coat, with a handsome crimson silk blanket, lined with black and trimmed with gold fringe, and wore a fur cap; round his neck he had a string of plaited sweet hay. It is a kind of grass which never loses its sweet scent."

The governor and the Iroquois leader never trusted each other. As a reward for their services in the war and in compensation for the loss of their homes in the Mohawk Valley, Brant's warriors had been given 800,000 acres of land along the Grand River northwest of Niagara. It had taken the chief years of diplomatic negotiation to achieve this. He made two trips to England where he was lionized and patronized, like King Hendrick before him, as a splendid savage who could use a knife and fork. Playing that role, he

Mrs. Hustler Invents the Cocktail

proudly refused to kiss the king's hand but said he'd be delighted to kiss the queen's.

Now he was comfortably settled in Upper Canada with his own property and even his own church. The first Protestant church in the province was a wooden structure with steeple and bell built near Brantford for Mohawk Anglicans like Brant. He was gradually reorganizing the Six Nations federation, which had been broken during the war. But within the civilized churchgoer stirred the old dreams of Pontiac. Brant wanted to unite the Six Nations with the Ohio tribes into one Indian people who would stop further white expansion and save the western hunting grounds for their original owners. He would play the role of peacemaker one day, warmonger the next.

In 1791, the Shawnees, Potawatomis, and Miamis took to the warpath and slaughtered an American force along the Wabash. This convinced the United States government that it needed Brant's co-operation. The Secretary of State invited the villain of the Wyoming Valley massacre to come to Philadelphia and meet the President. Brant rode into the American capital with the same aloof dignity he had displayed at the royal court. Nobody patronized him this time. He was offered 1,000 guineas, plus twice the half-pay and pension the British were giving him, to pacify the Ohio warriors. He refused the money but said he would try.

Brant actually did urge their chiefs to deal with a delegation of American commissioners, but they refused. In 1794 their uprising was crushed by an overwhelming American force at Fallen Timbers, near Toledo, Ohio, and Brant's ambitions faded. Two young chiefs who escaped from Fallen Timbers would carry on where Brant left off—Tecumseh and his mystic brother, The Prophet.

The first legislature of Upper Canada assembled at Newark under the stern eye of Governor Simcoe. It was not an impressive assembly. Simcoe had not come to set up another United States Congress or any kind of freewheeling democracy. He wanted a tight elite group—a transplanted English aristocracy that would form a buffer state between the republican rabble to the south and the remnants of French feudalism in Quebec (which became Lower Canada). The legislature had sixteen elected representatives, supervised by a seven-man council appointed by the governor from the Anglican clergy and what nobility he could find. This was to be the kernel of a new "New England" that would replace the one that had gone sour and revolted.

Grants of 3,500 acres each were handed out to council members and leading citizens in the hope that they would become the new landed aristocracy of British North America. This never happened because Simcoe's instant aristocrats preferred to speculate in land rather than work it, but the conservative clique of clergy and snobs that he created, later known as the Family Compact, ruled Upper Canada until its downfall fifty years later.

The first election to Newark's mini-Parliament was held in the summer of 1792. It was restricted to voters possessing acreage worth at least two pounds a year and candidates owning a house and five pounds a year in land, but apparently it was conducted in style. Candidate D. W. Smith wrote from Niagara to his agent in Kent County:

> The French people can easily walk to the hustings, but my gentry will require some conveyance: if boats are necessary you can hire them, and they must not want for beef or rum—let them have plenty—and in case of success I leave it to you which you think it will be best to give my

Mrs. Hustler Invents the Cocktail

> friends, a public dinner and the ladies a dance, either now or when I go up; if you think the moment the best time you will throw open Forsyth's Tavern and call for the best he can supply . . . push the bottle. The more broken heads and bloody noses there be, the more election-like.
>
> Have proper booths erected . . . Employ Forsyth to make large plum cakes with plenty of fruit &c. Be sure to let the wine be good and plenty. Let the peasants have a fiddle, some beverage and beef . . . Forgive me, I worry you out. I have quite an election fever.

Despite this fever, only seven of the sixteen winners bothered to attend the opening session of the legislature that fall, so they were vastly outnumbered by the governor's military escort and the citizens in their Sunday best and Indians in blankets, feathers, and scalp belts who came to watch. According to varying accounts, they met either in Navy Hall, Butler's barracks, in a tent, or under an old tree called Parliament Oak.

In its four years at Niagara, the legislature passed the basic laws that distinguished the new province from its French and American neighbors. The old judicial system of Quebec was abolished and the English system substituted. Jails and courthouses were built and property registered. "Irregular" marriages (arranged without the benefit of clergy) were legalized, but the right to perform future marriages was given exclusively to Church of England ministers, although only a tenth of Upper Canadians were Anglicans. There was a great deal of bitterness over this, and some settlers crossed into the States to be married. Even more controversial was Simcoe's Slave Bill, which stopped further importing of slaves into the province and called for the gradual abolition of slavery. It was one of the world's first abolitionist measures, and it irked upper-class Loyalists who had brought their slaves with them.

When, in 1796, Britain finally handed over the forts on the American side of the river and settled the partition of the continent, Simcoe decided the Canadian bank was indefensible against the American attack he still believed was coming, so he moved his capital across Lake Ontario to York, now Toronto, and the legislators found new quarters there. When the British flag was hauled down at Forts Niagara and Schlosser, the troops crossed to the new Fort George at Newark, and most of the civilian population went with them. A new wave of immigrants from the States moved into Upper Canada. The old Loyalists sneered at them, calling them "late Loyalists," but Simcoe welcomed them, for the land cried out for people. Despite his prejudice against Americans, he recognized that they made good settlers.

Behind the settlers came a new generation of visitors to give the outside world a more accurate view of the Niagara frontier and its fabulous falls.

Engravings of the falls had sold briskly in Europe throughout the first half of the eighteenth century. All were done by artists who had never been within a thousand miles of the place and all followed the Hennepin version of the scene, showing two cascades of approximately the same size and shape, separated by a prowlike parapet of rock. Indians, soldiers, and gentry were added for decoration. An illustration for Herman Moll's 1715 map of North America shows the area populated by giant beavers chewing trees and some smallish bears.

The first on-the-spot artist came in 1762. Thomas Davies was a British officer trained as a watercolor painter at the

The Maid of the Mist of Indian legend. (Painting by James Francis Brown, 1891. Buffalo and Erie County Historical Society)

The falls, an engraving from the 1770s. (Ontario Archives)

Old Fort Niagara, dominated by the original French "House of Peace." (Earl Brydges Library, Niagara Falls, N.Y.)

*The Governor's Lady,
Mrs. Elizabeth Simcoe.
(Ontario Archives)*

*Below, Colonel John Butler
of Butler's Rangers.
(Ontario Archives)*

*General Sir Isaac Brock.
(Ontario Archives)*

*Below, Tecumseh.
(Public Archives of Canada: C 7042)*

*The Battle of Lundy's Lane.
(Buffalo and Erie County
Historical Society)*

*Right, the Canadian heroine
Laura Secord.
(Ontario Archives)*

The Pirate, MICHIGAN,

WITH A CARGO OF FEROCIOUS ANIMALS, WILL PASS THE GREAT RAPIDS AND THE FALLS OF

NIAGARA,

8TH SEPTEMBER, 1827, AT 3 O'CLOCK.

THE first passage of a vessel of the largest class which sails on Erie and the Upper Lakes, through the Great Rapids, and over the stupendous precipice at Niagara Falls, it is proposed to effect, on the 8th of September next.

The *Michigan* has long braved the billows of Erie, with success, as a merchant vessel; but having been *condemned* by her owners as unfit to sail longer proudly "*above;*" her present proprietors, together with several publick spirited friends, have appointed her to convey a cargo of Living Animals of the Forests, which surround the Upper Lakes, through the white tossing, and and the deep rolling rapids of the Niagara, and down its grand precipice, into the basin "*below.*"

The greatest exertions are making to procure Animals of the most ferocious kind, such as Panthers, Wild Cats, Bears, and Wolves; but in lieu of some of these, which it may be impossible to obtain, a few vicious or worthless Dogs, such as may possess considerable strength and activity, and perhaps a few of the toughest of the Lesser Animals, will be added to, and compose, the cargo.

Capt. *James Rough*, of Black Rock, the oldest navigator of the Upper Lakes, has generously volunteered his services to manage this enterprise, in which he will be seconded by Mr. *Levi Allen*, mate of the Steamboat *Niagara*—the publick may rest assured that they will select none but capable assistants. The manager will proceed seasonably with experiments, to ascertain the most practicable and eligible point, from which to detach the Michigan for the Rapids.

It is intended to have the *Michigan* fitted up in the style in which she is to make her splendid but perilous descent, at *Black Rock*, where she now lies. She will be dressed as a *Pirate*; besides her *Menagerie* of Wild Animals, and probably some tame ones, it is proposed to place *a Crew* (in effigy) at proper stations on board. The Animals will be caged or otherwise secured and placed on board the "*condemned Vessel*," on the morning of the 7th, at the Ferry, where the curious can examine her with her '*cargo*,' during the day, at a trifling expense. On the morning of the 8th, the Michigan will be towed from her position at *Black Rock*, to the foot of Navy Island, by the Steamboat *Chippewa*, from whence she will be conducted by the Manager to her last moorings. Passage can be obtained in the Michigan from *Black Rock* to *Navy Island*, at *half a Dollar* each.

Should the Vessel take her course through the *deepest of the Rapids*, it is confidently believed, that she will reach the *Horse Shoe*, unbroken; if so, she will perform her voyage, *to the water in the Gulf beneath*, which is of great depth and buoyancy, entire; *but what her fate may be, the trial will decide*. Should the Animals be young and hardy, and *possessed of great muscular powers*, and *joining their fate* with that of the Vessel, remain on board until she reaches the waters below, there is great probability that many of them, will *have performed the terrible jaunt, unhurt!*

Such as may survive, and be retaken, will be sent to *the Museums* at New York and Montreal, and some perhaps to London.

It may be proper to observe, that several Steamboats are expected to be in readiness at *Buffalo*, together with numerous Coaches, for the conveyance of Passengers down, on the morning of the 8th. Coaches will leave *Buffalo*, at 2 o'clock, on the afternoon of the 7th, for the Falls on both sides of the River, for the convenience of those who may be desirous of securing accommodations at the Falls on the 8th. Ample means for the conveyance of Visitors, will be prov... *awania*, at *Lockport*, at *Lewiston*, a... and at *Fort George*, to either side...

As no probable estimate can now be made, of... the proposed exhibition may bring together, great... regarding the extent of our accommodations, may... pated by some; in respect to which, we beg leave... pective friends and the publick in general, that, in a... which are large, (and will on the occasion be furnish... limits,) there are other Publick Houses, besides... which comfortable entertainment can be had, for... the Falls on the present occasion—an occasion w... velty and the remarkable spectacle it will present,... the annals of *internal* navigation.

August 2, 1827.

P. WHITNEY, Keeper of Eagle Hotel, United States Falls.

WM. FORSYTH, } Keepers of the On...
JOHN BROWN, } Pavilion, C...

The first great stunt: a shipload of wild animals over the falls, 1827. (Buffalo and Erie County Historical Society)

The Little Rebel
of 1837:
William Lyon Mackenzie.
(Ontario Archives)

Below, Mackenzie's steamer
Caroline, *set ablaze and cut
adrift by Canadian forces.*
(Ontario Archives)

The first tourist attraction, the Terrapin Tower, seen in an 1837 engraving by William Henry Bartlett. (Earl Brydges Library, Niagara Falls, N.Y.)

A ferryboat landing on the American side, 1838. A Bartlett print. (Earl Brydges Library, Niagara Falls, N.Y.)

Royal Military Academy, Woolwich. (In the days before photography, armies used artists to sketch the lie of the land and enemy positions with photographic detail. They were still being sent into the field in Vietnam.)

Davies painted a sparkling, idyllic falls, broader, lower, and less frightening than the Hennepin concept. With its careful detail of eddies, rock formations, and vegetation, it is probably the most accurate representation of the period.

The first American to paint the scene was John Vanderlyn, last of the American neoclassic school, who did several studies in 1801–2. His view from Table Rock—the jutting ledge that dominated the Canadian end of the Horseshoe Falls until it collapsed into the chasm in 1850—gives a fierce impression of the might of the waters and the height of the spray plume.

The first detailed description of the area comes from Isaac Weld, an Irish traveler, who rode up the western portage road from Newark in September 1796 and stabled his horse at a hamlet of a few straggling houses which was the beginnings of Niagara Falls, Ontario. Weld, a trained draftsman, decided that there was more to the scene than met the eye:

> It is impossible for the eye to embrace the whole of it at once; it must gradually make itself acquainted in the first place with the component parts of the scene; each one of which is in itself an object of wonder, and such a length of time does this operation require that many of those who have had an opportunity of contemplating the scene at their leisure, for years together, have thought that each time they have beheld it each part has appeared more wonderful and sublime, and that it has only been at the time of their last visit that they have been able to discover all the grandeur of the cataract.

Weld found a guide to take him down into the gorge—an indication that Niagara was preparing for tourists even then. He looked at the "Indian ladders," which the Senecas had used to descend the cliffs—slender, shaky pine trunks notched every couple of feet to provide footholds. Weld found them old and unsafe but still in use. He decided not to try them; instead he moved downstream to descend "Mrs. Simcoe's ladder"—a series of stoutly built wooden-runged ladders erected for the use of the governor's lady. These were safe enough, he says; "to descend over the rugged rocks, however, the whole way down to the bottom of the cliff is no trifling undertaking and few ladies, I believe, could be found of sufficient strength of body to encounter the fatigue of such an operation."

Down below, he found

> great numbers of the bodies of fishes, squirrels, foxes and various other animals that, unable to stem the current above the falls, have been carried down them and consequently killed. . . . A dreadful stench arises from the quantity of putrid matter lying on the shore and numberless birds of prey, attracted by it, are always seen hovering above the place.
>
> As you approach the Horse-shoe Fall, the way becomes more and more rugged . . . without a guide, a stranger would never find his way to the opposite end; for to get there it is necessary to mount nearly to the top, then crawl on your hands and knees through long, dark holes where passages are left open between the torn-up rocks and trees. After passing these mounds you have to climb from rock to rock close under the cliff and those rocks are so slippery, owing to the continual moisture from the spray, which descends very heavily, that without the utmost precaution it is scarcely possible to escape a fall.
>
> There is nothing whatever to prevent you from passing

Mrs. Hustler Invents the Cocktail 85

    to the very foot of the Great Fall; and you might even proceed behind the prodigious sheet of water that comes pouring down from the top of the precipice . . . caves of very considerable size have been hollowed out of the rocks at the bottom of the precipice, owing to the violent ebullition of the water, which extend some way underneath the bed of the upper part of the river.
    I advanced within about six yards of the edge of the vast sheet of water, just far enough to peep into the caverns behind it; but here my breath was nearly taken away by the violent whirlwind that always rages at the bottom of the cataract, occasioned by the concussion of such a vast body of water against the rocks. I confess I had no inclination at the time to go farther; nor, indeed, did any of us [he had two companions] afterwards attempt to explore the dreary confines of these caverns where death seems to wait him that should be daring enough to enter their threatening jaws.

Although Weld and his party didn't venture into the thunder god's haven behind the falls, he makes it clear that others did, so one of today's most popular tours had been discovered. So had the white calcite rock found in the gorge which the locals called "petrified spray." Weld got a chunk for nothing; future visitors would have to pay for it. Niagara "petrified spray" is still sold, but since the local supply has run out, the calcite is imported from England. Another trip Weld did not take was a boat ride down the upper river to Goat Island, which perches on the cliff top, dividing the two main cataracts. The boats had to be kept exactly on course in the middle of the river. Any deviation to right or left and they'd miss the island and go over the falls where, he noted "destruction must inevitably follow." Weld marveled that people actually made this voyage just to say they'd done it. The Niagara madness was beginning.

Weld spent three years touring North America and his book, *Travels Through the States of North America and the Provinces of Upper and Lower Canada*, published in 1799, became the most popular of its kind and period. Despite his enthusiastic prose, Weld decided at the end that he never wanted to see North America again. He liked Canada a little better than the States, but not well enough to stay there.

Not everyone was bowled over by the view of the falls. The Englishman John Maude tells of a New York lawyer who arrived in 1800, took one look, said, "Is that all?" and journeyed on without even bothering to get off his horse.

On the other hand there was Thomas Moore, the first poet visitor, who was so enchanted that he found the English language inadequate to describe the falls. But he did his best with it. He wrote to his mother:

> I have seen the Falls and am all rapture and amazement . . . Never shall I forget the impression I felt at the first glimpse of them which we got as the carriage passed over the hill that overlooks them. We were not near enough to be agitated by the terrific effects of the scene; but saw through the trees this mighty flow of water descending with calm magnificence and received enough of its grandeur to set imagination on the wing; imagination which, even at Niagara, can outrun reality. I felt as if approaching the very residence of the Deity; the tears started into my eyes; and I remained for a moment after we had lost sight of the scene in that delicious absorption which pious enthusiasm alone can produce. We arrived at the New Ladder and descended to the bottom. Here all its awful sublimities rushed full upon me. But the former exquisite sensation was gone. I now saw all.
>
> The string that had been touched by the first impulse, and which *fancy* would have kept ever in vibration, now

rested in *reality*. Yet, though there was no more to imagine, there was much to feel. My whole heart ascended towards the Divinity in a swell of devout admiration which I had never before experienced.

Oh, bring the atheist here and he cannot return an atheist! I pity the man who can coldly sit down and write a description of these ineffable wonders; much more do I pity him who can submit them to the measurement of gallons and yards. It is impossible by pen or pencil to convey even a faint idea of their magnificence. Painting is lifeless; and the most burning words of poetry have all been lavished upon interior and ordinary subjects. We must have new combinations of language to describe the Falls of Niagara.

Moore, another Irishman, wrote this in 1804, while spending "a delightful fortnight" as the guest of Lieutenant-Colonel Isaac Brock, then regimental commander at Fort George, who would become Canada's hero of the War of 1812. He entertained his host with songs at the piano, including one he had just written, "The Canadian Boat Song."

In 1807 a parched American traveler, Christian Schultz, made the poignant observation that there wasn't a single pub on the American bank of the river. All the action was on the Canadian side, which provided a better view and places to eat, drink, and put your feet up. He suggested some enterprising person build a "convenient house" for the accommodation of lady visitors and a ladder with handrails leading down into the gorge. He estimated the ladder could be built for $25 and added "surely no person, after travelling 200 to 1,000 miles to view the Falls, would hesitate to pay one, or even five dollars for a safe and easy conveyance to the bottom."

A couple of years later, an enterprising person did open a

tavern at Lewiston—the redoubtable Mrs. Thomas Hustler. She was less interested in lady visitors than the thirsty boatmen and carters who operated the portage, so Schultz's genteel hostelry had to wait; but she is credited with Niagara's most popular invention: the cocktail. According to local legend, this was a concoction of fruit, sugar, and rye whiskey stirred with a quill from a rooster. It's hard to picture her roughneck clientele sipping anything so elegant, but that's the story. Mrs. Hustler was also the model for Betsy Flanagan in James Fenimore Cooper's novel *The Spy*. Cooper frequented her pub while serving as a midshipman on the sixteen-gun brig *Oneida*, the first American warship on Lake Ontario.

In 1810 De Witt Clinton, a future governor of New York, visited the embryonic village of Niagara Falls, New York, and found there several houses, a gristmill, a sawmill, a tannery, a tavern, a post office, and a ropewalk 360 feet long. The walk used hemp grown in the Genessee Valley, and supplied all the rigging for lake ships. That hemp was a legacy of the Senecas, who had brought seeds up from the Carolinas 150 years before and cultivated them for pot-smoking. This was strictly an Indian vice; the whites stuck to rum and Mrs. Hustler's cocktails.

Clinton made the astute observation that Niagara was the best place in the world for "hydraulic works," but he was thinking of small mills and light industries powered by water. Since electricity had not been invented, he couldn't have imagined the colossal dynamo that Niagara would become.

Despite this progress on the American side, the Canadian bank was still busier and more efficient, thanks to the new military roads Simcoe had built in his anticipation of the "inevitable" next war with the United States. The Ca-

Mrs. Hustler Invents the Cocktail

nadian portage route used handsome new wagon trains, escorted by cavalry. The trains ran on time, so they attracted American business away from the old Crawl-on-All-Fours. This enraged the American portage master, successor to Joncaire and Stedman, and was one cause of the "inevitable" War of 1812.

6
Came the Apocalypse

Black Rock, December 1, 1812. A brass band hooted shakily through the gathering gloom and falling sleet as General Alexander "Apocalypse" Smyth urged his reluctant troops into a fleet of small boats to cross the upper Niagara River and invade Canada.

"Hearts of War!" he intoned. "Tomorrow will be Memorable in the Annals of the United States!"

Smyth was the kind of orator who spoke in capital letters and exclamation points, and his speeches to the Virginia House of Delegates were recorded that way. He had earned his nickname by his interpretation of the Book of Revelations. That night he was apocalyptic as ever, but nobody listened. Two weeks before, he had told the same men: "Companions at Arms, the Time is at Hand when you will Cross the Stream at Niagara to Conquer Canada and Secure the Peace of the American Frontier."

It hadn't worked out that way. They had crossed the

stream which, at its inlet from Lake Erie, was a considerable river, and briefly secured a foothold near Fort Erie. But after a tussle with Canadian militia, they had rowed back. This time, the general boomed, there would be no return. His words were larger than ever, but lacked conviction.

When a third of his 4,500 men were in the boats, huddled under their soaking coats, volunteers from Pennsylvania began shouting that they'd come to defend the States, not fight on foreign soil.

At dawn the damp band was to play "Yankee Doodle" to signal a swift pull across the river, but that signal never came. The clouds lifted; the general peered through his telescope at the defenders on the other side. With mutinous rumblings around him, he called a council of war, which voted to abandon hostilities for the year. The men scrambled happily out of the boats, fired some shots in the air and a few at their general's tent, and then marched off to winter quarters.

One officer spluttered with rage and accused Smyth of cowardice. He said it so loudly that the general was forced to challenge him to a duel.

The officer was militia Brigadier Peter Buell Porter, a "war hawk" congressman who had preached invasion of Canada so long and successfully that his enemies called the 1812 debacle "Peter Porter's War." His motives went beyond securing the peace of the frontier; he wanted control of the profitable Niagara business.

He and his brother Augustus were Connecticut surveyors who had bought lots from the state of New York that included the American falls, the shoreline of the rapids above, and part of the gorge below. They took over the American portage trade and built the mills that impressed

Came the Apocalypse

De Witt Clinton with their uses of water power. War, they hoped, would win them control of the bothersome Canadian portage as well—a monopoly of the throatway to the West. So when the apocalyptic general called off his invasion, Peter was furious.

The businessman in uniform faced the Bible scholar in a clearing on Grand Island. They raised their pistols, aimed, fired, and missed. Honor and military incompetence being satisfied, they dined together, then went home.

The scene typifies the War of 1812, which was misdirected, venal, unsuccessful, and at times comic.

As in 1775–76, the prologue to the Revolutionary War, when Americans led by Richard Montgomery and Benedict Arnold occupied Montreal and besieged Quebec, the 1812 invasion was preceded by congressional assurances that fighting would hardly be necessary. "We have the Canadas as much under our command as Great Britain has the oceans," declared Henry Clay, Speaker of the House of Representatives and leader of the western war hawks.

"We can take Canada without soldiers," added President Madison's Secretary of War, William Eustis. "We have only to send officers into the province and the people, disaffected by their own government, will rally round our standard!"

The sparse settlers in Upper Canada were mostly displaced Americans considered unlikely to fight their former countrymen. The Lower Canadians were French with no love for the king. The latter had almost, but not quite, joined the Montgomery-Arnold invasion. The war hawks reckoned that by now they must have seen their mistake.

The odds were overwhelmingly in favor of the United States, which had more than fourteen times the population of British North America—7,250,000 compared to about

500,000. Without even raising militia units, the United States could field 7,000 regular troops against the 4,500 British and Canadian regulars. And Britain, busy fighting Napoleon in Europe, was not expected to send reinforcements.

Despite these rosy prospects, a great many Americans wanted no part of the war. Although it was touted as "a war for free trade and sailors' rights," caused by highhanded British interference with American ships at sea, the maritime states were against it and the landlocked ones supported it. New England talked of quitting the Union. Lovers of liberty were shocked to find the land of the free on the side of the dictator Napoleon. The war hawks, who came mainly from the frontier states, were lovers of land. They saw Britain's involvement in Europe as a shining opportunity to clear the remaining British out of North America, ending their tacit support of the western Indians —who had risen again under Tecumseh—and opening up the West. To them the war was the inevitable sequel to the revolutionary struggle.

Samuel Eliot Morison calls 1812 the most unpopular war ever waged by the United States, not excluding Vietnam.

The war hawks got their way. But by the time "Apocalypse" Smyth had made his about-face and retired in disgrace to Virginia, their cheerful prophecies were shriveling in the light of a startling new development: the emergence of a national spirit among the former Americans of Upper Canada.

The Brock Monument on Queenston Heights towers over the escarpment where the falls were born, surmounted by an enormous statue of the hero who died below. It was built between 1853 and 1856, replacing an earlier pillar

Came the Apocalypse

blown up by pro-American revolutionaries in 1840. Unlike Wolfe, whose plinth at Quebec City is toppled regularly, Brock has been blown up only once. Wolfe conquered Canada for Britain. General Sir Isaac Brock conquered the apathy of the British Canadian—an equal, if not greater, feat. If dynamite be the tribute of posterity he should be blown up more often.

On the eve of war, morale in Upper Canada was zero. Brock wrote in his capacity as lieutenant-governor:

> My situation is most critical, not from anything the enemy can do, but from the disposition of the people—the population, believe me, is essentially bad—a full belief possesses them that this Province must inevitably succumb. . . . Most of the people have lost all confidence—I, however, speak loud and look big.

Brock *was* big—a massive man of forty-three with fair, curly hair, rearing tall in his scarlet frock coat, blue eyes sparkling curiously in a keen hatchet face. He would use every inch of his height and every strand of the gold braid that bedecked him in the show of bravado that convinced his queasy settlers the Americans could be beaten.

When U.S. General William Hull and his Army of the West bungled their first attack on Canada and retired to Detroit, Brock could have bolstered his defenses and awaited the next invasion. But more dramatic action was needed. At a midnight meeting with Tecumseh on an island in the Detroit River, he decided to invade the States.

The Indian, whose name meant "Shooting Star" in his Shawnee language, had brought 600 warriors to join Brock's 700 infantrymen. The year before, General William Henry Harrison had destroyed the confederacy of western tribes which Tecumseh and his brother The

Prophet had founded at Tippecanoe, Indiana, slaughtered most of their followers, and burned their settlement. They drove the epileptic, half-blind Prophet into the wilderness, shattering his mystic power over the tribes. (He kept a bag of beans at his belt which he said had grown out of his body and protected him from harm. This magic didn't work at Tippecanoe.) Harrison's Long Knives, as the Indians called the Americans because of their rifles with bayonets, missed Tecumseh, who was away at the time of the attack, but the general vowed to get him. With the discrediting of The Prophet, Shooting Star was the last symbol of hope for the western tribes.

At the midnight meeting with Brock, he laid on the table letters written by Hull which he had found during a raid on Detroit. The general was sixty, a creaky relic of the Revolutionary War. Although he had an army of 2,500, the letters showed that he was unsure of himself and distrusted by his men, who believed they were surrounded by hordes of savages.

The numerical odds against Brock and Tecumseh were hopeless, but if odds were to be trusted, Canada was finished anyway—and so were the Indians. Brock studied a plan of the American positions scratched by Tecumseh's scalping knife on a piece of elm bark. He ordered an attack across the Detroit River.

"Ho-o-o!" the Shawnee shouted. "This is a man!"

So early on August 16, 1812, Hull was treated to the spectacle of the two leaders, side by side, riding up the Ohio road toward Detroit. The British regulars marched behind them while the Indians whooped from the woods on either side. The two men were a match in size and dignity—the general in his red and gold, and the chief in neat, fringed deerskin, a silver medal hanging from the strings of

Came the Apocalypse

colored wampum around his neck, and three small crowns in his great nose. They rode stiffly erect in the saddle, looking grim and confident.

Hull panicked. Shells from a British battery and an armed schooner in the river were crashing into his fort. One killed three officers. The 600 Indians were making a hellish din—enough noise for 6,000. Hull had women and children to protect; his officers had brought their families to watch their grand entry into Canada. His own daughter and two grandchildren were in the fort. Any minute the redcoats would descend on him, charging behind the two huge horsemen, and the Indians would scream in from the flanks. He ordered a white flag, rode out to meet the invaders, and surrendered Detroit and the territory of Michigan.

His militiamen were allowed to go home after promising not to serve again in the war, but General Hull and his regulars were taken to Quebec as prisoners of war. On that long journey they were paraded through every accessible small town and village as living proof that the war was not so hopeless as Brock's citizens believed. Morale improved and there were stirrings of pride.

As the Union Jack was hoisted over Detroit, Brock took off his tasseled red sash and tied it around Tecumseh's waist, honoring the man he called the most gallant and sagacious of warriors. It was no empty gesture, like so many of the ceremonies the Johnsons and Joncaires had been through in the past. Without the Indians, whom the king's men always managed to woo more successfully than the republicans, Brock could not have attempted his grand gesture. In return, the Shawnee gave him his own sash, patterned with arrowheads.

The next day, Tecumseh appeared without the general's

sash, and explained: "I have given it to Round Head of the Wyandots, who is older and a more valiant chief." Tecumseh had the modesty that goes with greatness.

Brock hurried back to Niagara, where U.S. General Stephen Van Rensselaer was massing men for the main American thrust across the lower river from Fort Niagara, the old French House of Peace. He had 7,000 men facing a mere 1,700 Canadians on the opposite bank but, as at Detroit, the American strength was not all it appeared to be. The army that trounced Burgoyne and Cornwallis had rusted away, and there were no generals of Washington's caliber left.

Van Rensselaer dithered while "Apocalypse" Smyth, in command above the falls, fought his own cautious little war and refused to join the main offensive. Brock's superior, Governor-General Sir George Prevost, was no better. He arranged a temporary cease-fire in the vain hope that Congress would call off the war. This prevented the daring Brock from making another preemptive strike, this time across the Niagara, and allowed Van Rensselaer plenty of time to line the east bank with troops.

Just before dawn on October 13, the dithering ceased. The calm river waters echoed the boom and crump of artillery as the guns of Fort Niagara hurled their missiles at the village of Queenston. American boats slipped across the 200 yards of dark water.

Brock was at Fort George, seven miles upstream, when a messenger rode in to tell him the enemy was landing in force at Queenston. The garrison there—350 men with three cannon—had held the first landing party on the flatlands, but more and more boats were splashing across the river, bringing regulars in their blue coats and white trousers.

Brock left his infantry to follow him and galloped ahead on his gray charger, Alfred, a black cape over his scarlet coat, Tecumseh's sash streaming out behind him. The sun rose as he raced through the russet farmlands, shouting the alarm. At Queenston village he paused just long enough to collect a few men, then spurred Alfred up the heights to a crest where eight of his gunners were frantically swabbing, loading, ramming, and firing one 18-pound gun. As long as he held the high ground, he could roll the Americans back into the river.

Brock did not know that the invaders had with them a civilian guide who knew an old smugglers' path that led around the cliffs and up the back of the hill he was standing on. Suddenly he found 200 Americans charging him from behind. The gunners rammed a spike into the touchhole of the 18-pounder and ran downhill. Brock scrambled with them, leading his horse.

At the village, he patted Alfred and left him. He would lead a charge on foot, uphill, with 100 men against 200 to try to retake the gunpit and the heights. It was the sort of military madness the British indulge in from time to time. Magnificent, but not war. Like Braddock and Wolfe before him, Brock would flaunt his colorful figure before the enemy at point-blank range. That was expected of a commander. Brock rallied his men, drew his sword, and advanced toward death at a dignified speed.

An American rifleman took careful aim at his gleaming chest and shot him through the heart. He died instantly and wordlessly. The charge collapsed, and his redcoats carried him back down the hill.

Brock alive was a competent, if impetuous, leader. Brock dead, and having died with such style, was an inspiration. Captain John Macdonell took command and led a second charge that was almost a repetition of the first. It failed and he was fatally wounded. Soon there were 1,000 bluecoats and buckskinned militia on the crest of Queenston Heights. General Van Rensselaer sent a messenger to Albany announcing victory. Then Brock's infantry arrived from Fort George—1,000 men, mud-spattered from their march but fresh and eager to avenge their general.

They avoided the steep, open ground that had meant death to Brock and Macdonell and skirted inland through the damp woods. They had 50 Indians with them. When they were within reach of the American outposts on the heights, the Indians gave the shrieks that had demoralized the defenders of Detroit. The effect was the same. About 1,700 militiamen were still on the American shore, waiting to cross, when the chilling sound reached them over the water. They refused to go.

"The name of Indian or the sight of the wounded or the Devil or something petrified them," said a gunner in the Lewiston battery.

Brigadier General William Wadsworth, commanding on the heights, looked in vain for his reinforcements. He was running out of ammunition. When the British rushed the crest with fixed bayonets, his ranks broke. Men ran, fell, and rolled down the 200 feet to the river, to find their boats gone. As the Indians moved in with their scalping knives, Colonel Winfield Scott raised a white cravat on his sword-point and the battle was over. Wadsworth surrendered, with 73 officers and 885 men, having lost 200 killed and wounded. The British casualties were about half that.

It was a tiny battle by American standards, but a great event in the history of Upper Canada, which until then had no history to speak of. The mouse had fought off the eagle. If Brock had waited until his 1,000 men followed him from Fort George, he might still have won and lived to talk about it. But British Canada needed a hero. The man who spoke loud and looked big knew this and, by his mad little charge, fulfilled the need. Death is the meat on which patriotism feeds.

The next year, Canada acquired a heroine—Laura Secord, whose name is engraved forever on stone monuments and candy boxes. She is Canada's Paul Revere, although she walked a cow instead of riding a horse and her warning "The Yanks are coming, the Yanks are coming!" was stale news by the time she delivered it.

By June 1813 the U.S. forces had recovered from their fiasco at Queenston. American flotillas patrolled Lakes Erie and Ontario. Commodore Isaac Chauncey had destroyed the Upper Canadian capital at York (Toronto)—an act that would be used as an excuse for the British burning of the White House and most of Washington, D.C. An American army had taken Fort George and Fort Erie, securing both sides of the Niagara frontier. They had pushed westward but been surprised at Stoney Creek, near Hamilton, Ontario, and driven back to Queenston. They were still being harassed by a British and Indian force lurking at Beaver Dams on the road to Hamilton.

Laura was thirty-three, a "late Loyalist" who had moved with her family from Massachusetts in 1793 and married James Secord, an early Loyalist of Huguenot descent. At their farm near Queenston, they overheard American soldiers chattering about a forthcoming raid on Beaver Dams. Since Secord had been wounded at Queenston Heights and could not walk any distance, she undertook to warn the British. (She had personal reasons for disliking her former countrymen; they had looted her home a few weeks before.)

According to the popular Niagara story, she set off early in the dewy June morning, barefoot, carrying a milking pail and leading her cow past an American camp. No doubt the sentries were farm boys—but while enjoying the innocent scene, it didn't occur to them that you usually bring cows in to be milked, rather than taking them out into the forest. Anyway, Laura got away, abandoned her cow and pail, and walked twenty miles by a circuitous route through the woods. A war party of Mohawks leaped out at her. She cried, "The Long Knives [Americans] are coming!" and they waved her on. At last, torn by brambles and faint from the sticky heat of the afternoon, she stumbled onto a redcoat patrol led by Lieutenant James Fitzgibbon and told her tale.

He knew it already—he had been warned by Canadian spies at Queenston. But in the field of heroism, it's the effort that counts rather than the results. The approaching Americans were ambushed and terrorized by Indians. Fitzgibbon offered them British protection and they surrendered.

The ambush saved the Beaver Dams camp and freed a raiding party from the camp to cross the Upper Niagara, burn Fort Schlosser, and the new U. S. Navy yard at Black Rock (now part of Buffalo). But they were too late to destroy the five ships that had been built or refitted there. They had slipped away to join Captain Oliver Hazard Perry in the safe harbor of Presque Ile, now Erie, Pennsylvania.

Perry, a twenty-eight-year-old blue-water sailor from Rhode Island, was subcommander to Commodore Chauncey, under orders to build a fleet and beat the British on the Upper Lakes, while Chauncey swept Lake Ontario. Erie became his principal shipyard because it was relatively safe from attack by land and protected by a sandbar on the

Came the Apocalypse

lake side. It was too well protected, as it turned out. 1813 was a dry year. The lake level fell, and no craft with a draft of more than five feet could cross the sandbar. So the two 20-gun brigs *Lawrence* and *Niagara* and three schooners that Perry's carpenters were hastily hammering together from green lumber would be bottled up. Still, Perry worked with the optimism of a home handyman who builds a boat in his basement, hoping he'll get it out somehow.

Across the lake at Amherstburg, at the mouth of the Detroit River, the British naval commander, Captain Robert Barclay had assembled five lake craft ranging from the *Queen Charlotte*, a schooner of nine guns, to a gunboat with one. His flagship *Detroit* was still on the stocks at Amherstburg with no guns at all. Twenty-four had been ordered, but were still lying at Burlington, on Lake Ontario. Barclay was thirty-two, a gallant officer who had fought with Nelson at Trafalgar and lost an arm. He was, if anything, too gallant. A chivalrous gesture may have cost him his fleet.

From the deck of the *Queen Charlotte*, Barclay kept watch outside the Erie sandbar. To get his new brigs out into the lake, Perry would have to strip them of their guns and tie barges to their sides to lift them over the bar. They would be helpless targets for the British schooner's guns.

On July 30 Barclay abandoned the watch and sailed away. Apparently he took advantage of high winds, which he believed would keep Perry in port, to visit his supply base at Port Dover on the other side of the lake. Rumor has it that, on the way, he called in at Amherstburg to pick up an attractive young lady whose officer husband had just died and take her and her baggage to Port Dover, where she could get a carriage to York. Throughout the history of the more gentlemanly wars, officers keep vanishing at critical moments to visit beautiful women.

High winds or not, Perry seized his chance. The brig *Detroit* was towed out to the sandbar. Large barges were placed on either side of her and filled with water until they were barely floating. They were lashed to the brig's hull and attached to oak beams projecting from her empty gunports. Pumped and baled out, they rose, heaving up the 480-ton vessel until her normal waterline was six feet in the air and whaleboats could tow her, creaking and groaning, over the bar to deep water. They repeated the process with the *Niagara*. Perry was loose in the lake with a fleet superior to anything Barclay could muster.

The news reached Amherstburg, driving British Army commander General Henry A. Procter to desperation. If he lost control of the lake, he lost his supply ships, and without fresh supplies he had no hope of holding off General Harrison, the scourge of Tippecanoe, who was approaching with 4,500 men. Procter was twenty-six, inexperienced, and alternately reckless and prudent. He ordered Barclay to go out and attack Perry's fleet, knowing the odds were heavily against him but hoping the Trafalgar veteran would somehow outmaneuver the American.

Guns from the shore batteries at Amherstburg were levered from their mountings and hoisted aboard the *Detroit*. They were not naval guns and lacked the quick-firing mechanism needed to launch a concerted broadside but they had a long range. Makeshift crews of nonsailors were rounded up. Barclay had only 55 trained British seamen to man his six ships, so these were augmented by 100 Canadians and 250 soldiers of various kinds. Nelson would have wept at the sight of them.

Perry had nine ships and 60 percent of his crews were

trained navy men, including expert gunners from the famous U.S.S. *Constitution* and the rest sharpshooting Kentucky riflemen. Barclay's one advantage was his long-range guns. Close in, the Americans had twice his firepower. So when the two columns of ships approached each other near Put-in Bay, off Sandusky, Ohio, Perry put on all sail to close the gap.

Perry's flagship *Lawrence* lumbered at the head of the column, flying at her masthead a blue pennant with the slogan *Don't give up the ship!*—the dying words of Captain James Lawrence who had been killed on his frigate *Chesapeake* a few months before. The *Detroit*'s long guns smashed her bow, but she lurched on. Both flagships turned and pounded each other with broadsides, while the smaller ships circled and staggered with the force of their cannonades. After two hours, the *Lawrence*'s last gun was silenced, her hull shattered, and her main rigging torn away. Perry gave her up. A longboat took him through the flying shot to the *Niagara*.

The first lieutenant of the *Lawrence* hauled down the flag from her shaky mainmast, and for a moment it seemed the British had won. But Barclay was badly wounded. His remaining arm had been ripped off. The *Detroit*'s rigging was falling around him, and he could spare no men to take the surrendered American ship. The matches supplied to his gunners wouldn't work, and they were firing the guns by snapping pistol locks at the touchholes. Perry raised his pennant on the *Niagara* and carried on the fight.

The *Detroit* ran into the *Queen Charlotte*, tangling in her rigging. As the two British vessels clung together, unable to move, the *Niagara* moved in on them to rake their decks with grapeshot. The Kentucky riflemen volleyed through the smoke, and the battle was over.

Barclay's two brigs surrendered, followed by two schooners that had been badly holed. The remaining two little craft tried to run for it but were caught. The battle had lasted three hours and ruined the fruits of a year's shipbuilding by both sides. The smoke cleared to reveal a cluster of splintered, soggy hulks, masts broken and sails shredded, trailing their torn cordage in the now-placid lake.

Perry sent his famous note to General Harrison: "We have met the enemy and they are ours"; and Procter, at Amherstburg, decided to destroy his forts and retreat. Tecumseh raged at him before his assembled chiefs, calling the young general "an old squaw" and "a fat dog who carries his tail on his back but drops it between his legs and runs away when he is afraid." The Shawnee demanded that Procter hand over the fort and its remaining ammunition to the Indians, who would defend the frontier themselves. Tecumseh still dreamed of regaining the lost hunting grounds in the West and he wanted Harrison's scalp in revenge for Tippecanoe.

It took Procter two weeks to persuade Tecumseh to join the retreat, and he had to promise to stand and fight along the way. This he did, reluctantly, at Moraviantown, an Indian village on the Thames River, some 50 miles east of Detroit. His tired column of redcoats, flanked by Indians and accompanied by boats and wagons, had limped along the river, its rearguard savaged by Harrison's advance guard of hard-riding Kentucky horsemen, its strength sapped as some of Tecumseh's less enthusiastic followers changed sides.

One charge by the Kentucky riders broke the British line and the battle of the Thames ended in minutes. Tecumseh was killed and his tribesmen dragged his body away to bury it in the woods. It was never found, although the Ken-

John A. Roebling's railway suspension bridge. It opened in 1855. (Ontario Hydro)

Building the new suspension bridge, 1868. (Niagara Falls Gazette)

Collapse of the Honeymoon Bridge, 1938. (Niagara Falls Gazette)

Right, Honeymoon Bridge before being swept downstream. (Niagara Falls Gazette)

Building the Rainbow Bridge, 1941. (Niagara Falls Gazette)

Clifton House, on the Canadian side, where Confederates plotted during the Civil War. (Earl Brydges Library, Niagara Falls, N.Y.)

Cataract House, on the American side, where the Niagara Parks plan was conceived. (Earl Brydges Library, Niagara Falls, N.Y.)

A family group at Table Rock, circa 1890. (Ontario Archives)

Bridge to the Three Sisters islands, 1890s. (Earl Brydges Library, Niagara Falls, N.Y.)

On the Ice Bridge: a late Victorian scene. (Ontario Archives)

The Ice Palace, 1898. This fantastic structure was built with blocks of ice. (Earl Brydges Library, Niagara Falls, N.Y.)

Industry comes to Niagara Falls, New York: the early days of Shredded Wheat. (Earl Brydges Library, Niagara Falls, N.Y.)

The American side in the early 1900s: the Great Gorge Railway and the Niagara Falls Power Company Station. (Earl Brydges Library, Niagara Falls, N.Y.)

tuckians carved up the corpse of another chief, whom they took to be Tecumseh. They made razor strops of the skin and presented them to war-hawk congressmen.

Just before the American charge, the great warrior had made his peace with Procter. "Father, have a big heart," he said, and shook hands.

But Procter's heart was with his wife and little daughter, whom he had hidden in a village nearby. He escaped from the battlefield, picked them up, and rode east to face a court-martial.

Procter was cleared of cowardice but suspended for six months because of the way he had conducted the retreat. Staff officers, safe in Montreal, said he should have died with Tecumseh. This wouldn't have changed the course of the war, but it would have brightened their dark dispatches to London. They needed another Brock. The victorious Harrison, who would become president of the United States, said his old foe Tecumseh was right. Procter should have made his stand at Amherstburg.

On Christmas Day, 1813, General Joseph McClure, commander of U.S. forces on the Niagara, sat in Batavia, New York, a safe 50 miles from the smoldering wreckage of his command. With only the festive aroma of turkey in his nostrils, he composed a letter to his Niagara Indian agent, explaining why he couldn't return to Buffalo.

It was not safe, he wrote, "for me or any that accompanied me to stay there or travel the road. The numerous mob that we met all cried out 'shoot him, damn him, shoot him.' . . ."

And well they might, for the whole American side of the frontier from Fort Niagara to Buffalo was a scorched wasteland of burnt-out buildings and deserted farms and it was all McClure's fault.

The afterglow of Perry's victory and the rout of Procter faded when an American drive on Montreal failed and the British made a probing stab at Fort George. Probe or not, it was enough to persuade McClure, then commanding the fort, to get out and back to his own side of the river.

Before leaving, he had obtained permission from Secretary of War John Armstrong to destroy Newark, because Winfield Scott's troops had used the village as a cover when they captured the fort from the British the previous spring. McClure feared the British might try the same trick. But he did not destroy Newark until the night he abandoned the fort, so it would be argued that it was more use to the Americans standing than flattened if, in the seesaw war, they tried to take it again.

Armstrong had directed McClure to "invite" the villagers to remove themselves and their effects before the destruction began. The general gave them two hours to get out—after dark at the height of a howling December snowstorm. The able-bodied men were taken across the river to be locked in Fort Niagara while the old men and 400 women and children were left to stand in the snow and watch their homes burn.

This senseless vandalism set the frontier afire—literally. A week later, the British struck back. Some 500 men crossed the river near Youngstown and sneaked up on Fort Niagara by night. An advance party killed the sentries and opened the gate; then the rest rushed the old House of Peace, bayoneted seventy-nine Americans, and captured 344. Hardly a shot was fired.

Upstream, another 500 troops with 500 Indians crossed from Queenston and overwhelmed the militia at Lewiston.

The Indians were turned loose to loot and burn everything in sight along the river. Ten days later, another force burned Black Rock and Buffalo.

McClure never returned from his Christmas "holiday" in Batavia. There was nothing to return to but homeless mobs howling for his head.

Brigadier General Winfield Scott was up early on the morning of July 5, 1814, planning a belated Fourth of July celebration on the banks of Street's Creek, near Chippawa, a few miles above the Canadian falls. He would parade his brigade of regulars in their new gray uniforms (the quartermaster's stores had run out of regulation blue cloth), review them under an American flag firmly planted on Canadian soil, then declare a holiday.

Scott had come a long way since the day, two years before, when he had raised a white flag on his sword at Queenston Heights. He had been taken prisoner, then released in a prisoner exchange; he had led the successful attack on Fort George, been promoted from colonel, and given a brigade in General Jacob Brown's new invading army. The lean, six-foot-two-inch Virginian, now twenty-eight, represented the new type of American officer forged by two years of war—hard, cool, and professional. The old blusterers and blunderers were being weeded out—the United States now had enough discredited generals to fill a museum—and panic-prone militia units elbowed aside.

Scott's graycoats were almost as well disciplined as British regular redcoats and they were better shots. Two days earlier, they had floated across the Niagara, part of Brown's army of 5,000, and taken Fort Erie with a few cannon rounds. Independence Day had been spent on the march toward Chippawa Creek. Behind the creek, on the outskirts of what is now Niagara Falls, Ontario, lay 1,500 British regulars with 300 Canadian militia and 300 Indians under the fierce but nearsighted General Phineas Riall. Riall would be crazy to attack, so celebration was in order.

Scott's benign thoughts were shattered by the blast of trumpets and the distant rumble of horsemen crossing the log bridge over the Chippawa—a troop of the 19th Dragoons, the only British cavalrymen in Canada.

Riall *was* attacking, but he was not so much crazy as misled. His aide, the swaggering Marquis of Tweeddale, had seen the gray uniforms and reported that the invaders were only a swarm of ill-clad militia. Riall, who couldn't see that far, took his word for it. A clanking cavalry charge, however small, followed by trotting lines of redcoats with bayonets, would soon rout these raw lads and chase them back to their farms.

They did, in fact, rout part of a brigade under Peter Porter, now a general, who was still fighting his private war of conquest along the Niagara. But when they reached Scott's solid gray line of veterans, they realized that their general had blundered.

The redcoats halted their charge and formed a line across a hayfield. Both sides faced each other, fired, reloaded, advanced three paces to clear their smoke, and fired again. It was classic European field warfare. As the front ranks fell, the men behind them stepped over their bodies, fired, reloaded, advanced, and so on.

When the lines were 60 yards apart, the British broke and ran. A swift summer thunderstorm soaked the Americans' powder and covered Riall's retreat.

It would not have been a good day for a parade. Riall lost 515 men; Winfield's brigade beat him at a cost of 275. The Americans then marched triumphantly along the western portage road to Queenston, where things began to go wrong for them. The professional generals Brown and Scott found themselves bedeviled by forces beyond their control: their own militia and the U. S. Navy.

A militia officer calling himself Brigadier General Swift was killed in a skirmish with a Canadian militia patrol near the Niagara village of St. Davids. Colonel Stone, of the New York militia, called this "murder" and destroyed every home in the village. This ended any hope of a peaceful American reoccupation of the west bank. The settlers had not forgotten the sack of Newark, and this new depredation inflamed them once more. How could you "murder" an enemy officer during a battle in time of war? Soldiers were paid to kill one another.

A U.S. regular officer wrote:

> The whole population is against us. Not a foraging party but is fired on, and not infrequently returns with missing numbers . . . the militia have burned several private dwelling houses and on the 19th inst. burnt the village of St. David, consisting of 30 or 40 houses. This was done within three miles of the camp and my battalion was sent to cover the retreat. My God! What a service! I have never witnessed such a scene and had not the commanding officer of the party, Lieut. Col. Stone been disgraced and sent out of the army I should have handed in my sheepskin.

The U. S. Navy, in the person of Commodore Isaac Chauncey, was impossible to deal with. After his raid on Toronto the previous year, Chauncey had retired to his haven of Sackets Harbor, New York, at the eastern end of Lake Ontario, to build more ships. He had no intention of sailing them until he had the finest battle fleet the inland waters would ever see. Leviathans. He had laid the keels of two first-rate ships of the line—three-deckers of 120 guns. These would not be the leaky, green-lumber tubs Perry had fought in, but magnificent vessels—the largest warships in the world.

Chauncey was obsessed by big ships and so was his British counterpart at Kingston, Sir James Yeo, who had eight warships, including a sixty-gunner, but was building more. His carpenters were carving the deck rails of the *Saint Lawrence*, which was bigger than Nelson's *Victory*, pierced for 102 guns and requiring a crew of 700. The two fleets ventured out occasionally, avoiding each other as far as possible, but for most of the war the bathtub admirals sat in their shipyards, separated from each other by 30 miles of water, and planned the colossal naval engagement they would fight one day—if they could preserve their fine ships from the pesky demands of the military.

At the outset of the 1814 campaign, Secretary of War Armstrong ordered Chauncey to ferry General Brown's army from Sackets Harbor to Kingston to assault the British headquarters there and choke off the supply route to Niagara. Before doing so, Chauncey was to deceive the enemy into believing the attack would come via Niagara. Instead, he deceived Brown, who tramped off to cross the Upper River at Fort Erie, and headed for Queenston. When Armstrong learned that his army had gone to the wrong place, he told Chauncey to sail to the mouth of the Niagara River, pick up Brown's army, and proceed with the attack on Kingston. The army had muddled his orders and the navy had disobeyed them. It was typical of this blundering war.

When Brown reached Queenston, he sent scouts ahead to scan the river mouth for Chauncey's fleet. They scanned in vain; Chauncey wasn't coming out. He had had a bad

Came the Apocalypse

scare when Sir James Yeo made a halfhearted raid on his port at Oswego and even dared to blockade (briefly) his precious shipyards at Sackets Harbor. There had been a fight between parties of sailors in small boats—the nearest thing to a naval engagement between the admirals—and both of them needed to rest up and get back to serious shipbuilding.

Brown sent a message to Chauncey: "Meet me on the lake shore north of Fort George with your fleet and I have no doubt to settle a plan of operations that will break the power of the enemy in Upper Canada." He added pleadingly, "At all events let me hear from you," and, accurately, "Sir James will not fight."

The admiral bristled, snorted, and penned his reply:

> I shall afford every assistance in my power to cooperate with the army whenever it can be done without losing sight of the great object for the attainment of which this fleet has been created—the capture or destruction of the enemy's fleet. . . . I shall not be diverted from my efforts to effectuate it by any sinister attempt to render us subordinate to, or an appendage of, the army.

Thus ended the plan to attack Kingston, and Brown and Winfield Scott and their men were left adrift on the increasingly hostile Canadian side of the Niagara with no clear goal in mind. They retreated to Chippawa, then advanced again to the falls where, by accident, they ran into the nearsighted Riall once again.

So began the carnage at Lundy's Lane—the worst battle of the war.

Neither army had planned to fight there. Throughout the war, opposing commanders had been kept remarkably well informed of each other's movements through scouts, spies, Indians, and friendly amateurs like Laura Secord. Like the War of Independence, it was a civil war between relatives, so loyalties sometimes swayed from side to side. On July 25, 1814, the intelligence networks broke down, and the armies blundered into each other at the junction of the portage road skirting the Canadian falls and the track William Lundy used to reach his farm, two miles to the west.

When they saw Scott's graycoats approaching, Riall's men climbed through an orchard, up a small hill overlooking the crossroads, and took up positions around an old frame Presbyterian church on the summit, mounting their guns among the tombstones of the first Loyalist settlers. They were joined by General Gordon Drummond's force, which had come by ship and road from Kingston when the British learned that Scott and Brown were loose on the Niagara frontier.

Scott was outnumbered, 1,800 to 1,200, but he attacked, knowing that Brown, with his army of 5,000, was on his way to join him.

At 6:30 P.M. he sent his first wave storming up the hill. They were shredded by musket volleys, rocket shells, and cannonballs bouncing down from the churchyard. A second and a third wave were hurled back, bleeding, into the orchard. As the sun went down, Brown's bluecoats arrived, and the Americans surrounded the hill. The battle became a wild melee of shooting and stabbing in smoky blackness, pierced by shafts of fitful moonlight and the orange flash of rockets. Brown and Scott were severely wounded; the British general Riall, who was taken prisoner, was also wounded.

The Americans took the hill, stabbed the British gunners

Came the Apocalypse

as they loaded, and silenced the batteries. Drummond retook it with fresh troops from Queenston. For six hours men died for the position. Sometime after midnight, both sides were too exhausted to continue, and the fighting stopped. The Americans left the battlefield and limped back to Chippawa, knowing they would not be pursued. The British slept on the hill amid the dead and the moaning wounded.

The next day, 84 British and 210 American bodies were burned on a huge pyre of fence rails beside the church. For years no grass would grow on the site, which is now occupied by the old manse of Drummond Hill Presbyterian Church.

For half a century, the Lundy's Lane battlefield was the most popular tourist attraction in Niagara next to the falls themselves. American and Canadian visitors mingled in the graveyard, poked around under the scarred trees for bullets and uniform buttons, and paid their 25 cents to climb one of the five towers built by local tourist operators to provide a panoramic view of the killing ground.

When the American Civil War came along to provide bigger and gorier battlefields, the tourists abandoned Lundy's Lane, the 25-cent towers fell down, and the orchard was choked by weeds and creepers. In 1895 Lundy's Lane was tidied up. The bones of the dead that had turned up over the years were collected and placed in a vault under a 40-foot granite monument commemorating "the victory gained by the British Canadian forces on this field." Much of the battlefield is now a built-up area, and Lundy's Lane a busy street.

The Americans claimed victory, too. In fact, neither side won. Like the war, the battle ended in a stalemate. Hostilities were called off at the end of 1814, leaving the border between Canada and the United States just where it had been and still poisoned with bitterness.

A million chickens have died to feed luncheon speakers prating about "the longest undefended border in the world—undefended since 1814"—but they died in vain, for the border was stoutly defended on both sides until the 1870s. The only disarmament agreement reached in the aftermath of 1812 was the Rush-Bagot Treaty (1817), which limited naval forces on the Great Lakes to four ships per side, none larger than 100 tons or carrying more than one 18-pound gun. The freshwater seadogs Yeo and Chauncey lost the wooden monsters they had built and preserved so jealously. Yeo's mighty *Saint Lawrence*, which cost half a million pounds to build, rotted at anchor until 1832, when she was sold for £32 to become part of a dock. The even mightier *New Orleans* remained on the U. S. Navy list until 1882—but never sailed.

7
The Colonel Invents the Tourist Trap

Brutality lingered after the war ended. A gawking army of spectators watched a shipload of live animals pushed over the Canadian falls to die in the cause of tourism.

This first and probably worst stunt of the Niagara circus was the brainchild of William Forsyth, a hustling Canadian hotelkeeper. In the 1820s Canadians were grabbing the burgeoning tourist trade while Americans lined their river bank with factories. Manchester (Niagara Falls, New York) had not yet achieved the ugliness of its English namesake, but was getting there. Stamford (Niagara Falls, Ontario) was sedately pretty by comparison, but housed some ugly characters, the most notorious of which was "Colonel" Forsyth.

Forsyth was a small, thin man who looked as if a light breeze would blow him away; but his scrawny frame had been toughened by years of rowing smuggling boats across the upper Niagara to his cave, "Smuggler's Home," which runs back from the river on the Canadian side. He was the first king of the Niagara smuggling industry, which began in 1796 when the border was established and has flourished ever since, and he used his profits to become the first king of tourism. His Pavilion was the principal hotel on the Canadian side—a three-story clapboard erection, the balconies of which commanded the finest view of the falls. He built the first stairway down to the gorge below Table Rock and operated the first tours behind the falls. Forsyth's ferries took visitors across the lower river. Forsyth's stagecoaches brought them from Newark and Fort Erie to stay at the Pavilion and use the stairs and the ferry.

If a tourist managed to avoid Forsyth's stagecoaches, he would probably end up in a hackney cab whose driver had been bribed by Forsyth, and end up at the Pavilion just the same. The "Colonel" invented the tourist trap. Later entrepreneurs would develop his system of payoffs to cabdrivers which ensured that tourists were delivered to the fleecing grounds, until Niagara Falls became the most efficient trap on the continent. The cunning mind that had outwitted the customs men was constantly churning out schemes to render the natural wonders of Niagara less natural and more profitable.

In 1827 Forsyth staged his great stunt. With the help of John Brown, a rival Canadian innkeeper, and General Parkhurst Whitney, proprietor of the Eagle Hotel on the American side, he bought a rotting Lakes schooner and printed broadsheets which papered much of western New York State and Upper Canada:

> The Pirate, Michigan, with a cargo of ferocious wild animals, will pass the great rapids and falls of NIAGARA, 8th September, 1827, at 6 o'clock . . .

The Colonel Invents the Tourist Trap

The Michigan has long braved the billows of Erie, with success, as a merchant vessel: but having been *condemned* by her owners as unfit to sail long proudly *"above"*; her present proprietors, together with several publick spirited friends, have appointed her to carry a cargo of Living Animals of the Forest, which surround the Upper Lakes, through the white tossing and the deep rolling rapids of the Niagara and down its great precipice, into the basin *"below."*

The greatest exertions are being made to procure Animals of the most ferocious kind, such as Panthers, Wild Cats and Wolves; but in lieu of these, which it may be impossible to obtain, a few vicious or worthless dogs, such as may possess strength and activity, and perhaps a few of the toughest of the Lesser Animals will be added to, and compose, the cargo. . . .

Should the vessel take her course through the *deepest of the* Rapids, it is confidently believed that she will reach the Horse Shoe unbroken; if so she will perform her voyage *to the water of the Gulf beneath* which is of great depth and buoyancy, entire, *but what her fate will be* the trial *will decide.* Should the animals be young and hardy and *possessed of great muscular power* and *joining their fate* with that of the Vessel, remain on board until she reaches the water below, there is a great possibility that many of them will *have performed the terrible jaunt, unhurt!*

To add even more zest to the execution, the "publick spirited proprietors" dressed up the schooner as a pirate ship and tied a crew of dummies to her decks. Captain James Rough, said to be the oldest navigator on the Upper Lakes, undertook to tow her from Black Rock to Navy Island, using the paddle-steamer *Chippawa,* and point her at the falls. For half a dollar each, visitors could board the

Michigan and view the condemned animals before the ship departed.

These turned out to be less ferocious than advertised—a buffalo, two small bears, two raccoons, a dog, and a goose—but an eager multitude turned out to watch. The crowd was estimated at between fifteen and thirty thousand, an amazing assembly even at the lower figure and bigger than all the armies that fought at Niagara in the War of 1812.

Captain Rough knew his currents. After he set the *Michigan* adrift, she was holed in the rapids and half filled with water but kept going. The bears, which were running loose on deck, jumped ship and swam to Goat Island. The other animals were caged or tied aboard. To gasps and shouts of approval, the schooner, decks awash, slid over the center of the horseshoe and dived, splendidly vertical, to shatter on the rocks below with a crash heard above the thunder of the waters. There was one survivor. The goose struggled ashore and was caught by a Mr. Duggan.

Among the spectators was a tiny man with fierce blue eyes and a red wig perched on his large head—William Lyon Mackenzie, editor and publisher of the *Colonial Advocate*, who had come from Toronto to report on the happening. He wrote:

> The day was very favorable, and every steamboat, schooner and stagecoach which could be procured within many miles of the Falls were in motion, as well as waggons and other vehicles beyond calculation—the roads to the Falls in every direction were like the approaches to Yorkshire fair, and perhaps there were eight or ten thousand persons on the spot by one o'clock, including show men with wild beasts, gingerbread people, cake and beer stalls, wheel of fortune men etc.
>
> The two hotels and the galleries were crowded with peo-

ple dressed in the pink of fashion—the banks of the river above and below Goat Island—the British and American shores, trees, houses and house tops, on waggons and waggon wheels—every place and every corner and nook was filled with human beings—bands of music enlivened the scene—and the roar of the African Lion in the menagerie and the din of the passing multitude, joined to the crash of the cataract, were almost too much for human organs.

Mackenzie was well known along the Niagara as a muckraker, scandalmonger, and a hater and baiter of the rulers of Upper Canada whom he called "a few shrewd, crafty, covetous men." They called him a tiny reptile. He had launched the *Colonial Advocate* in Queenston in 1824, while the first Brock monument was being built on the heights. Somehow a copy of the first edition, in a whiskey bottle, found its way into the masonry around the cornerstone. The enraged lieutenant-governor had the monument torn down so that the offending objects could be removed. Soon after, Mackenzie had moved his press to Toronto to be closer to his political targets and plot a rebellion against them.

As Mackenzie watched that first ship go over the falls he could not know that the second ship would be his own.

Two years later, Forsyth tried to stage an encore. The original Table Rock stuck out level with the lip of the falls on the Canadian side. According to John Howison in *Canada, 1821*:

> Any person who has nerve enough (as I had) may plunge his hand into the water of the Great Fall, after it is projected over the precipice, merely by lying down flat, with his face beyond the edge of Table Rock, and stretching out his arm to its utmost extent. The experiment is truly a horrible one, and such as I would not wish to

repeat; for even to this day I feel a shuddering and recoiling sensation when I recollect having been in the posture described.

For several years before Howison did his horrible trick, chunks of the rock underneath had been falling. By 1829 the rest was unsafe, and Forsyth, ready to cash in even on the loss of a tourist attraction, planned a "blasting-off fete" at which he would dynamite Table Rock. For some reason the explosion did not come off so, as alternative attraction, he and other local promoters booked Sam Patch.

Sam, a jumper, became the first human stunter to perform at the falls. He built a platform out from Goat Island, between the two cataracts, and plummeted from it feet first into the gorge 80 or 100 feet below. Unlike a high diver, he could not see where he was going, which was probably just as well. He kept his arms stiffly by his side, legs straight and eyes staring forward as he fell and cleaved the water at 60 miles an hour.

Mackenzie, who enjoyed stunts almost as much as the politics of rebellion, was there to record the scene:

> While the boats below were on the lookout for him he had in one minute reached the shore unnoticed and unhurt, and was heard on the beach singing as merrily as if altogether unconscious of having performed an act so extraordinary as almost to appear an incredible fable. Sam Patch has immortalized himself—he has done what mortal never did before—he has precipitated himself eighty-five feet in one leap; that leap into the mighty cavern of Niagara's Cataract; and survived the romantic feat uninjured!!!

The feat did not pay off for Sam. He left Niagara feeling that he'd been swindled by the hoteliers, tried a 100-foot jump into the Genessee River at Rochester—and drowned.

The Colonel Invents the Tourist Trap

Travelers who rested at Forsyth's Pavilion or General Parkhurst Whitney's new Cataract House across the gorge were becoming increasingly critical of developments in the area. In 1832 E. T. Coke, a young British officer, mourned:

> The die then is cast and the beautiful scenery about the Falls is doomed to be destroyed. Year after year it will become less and less attractive . . . 'Tis a pity that such ground was not reserved as sacred in perpetuum; that the great forest trees were not allowed to luxuriate in all the wild and savage beauty about a spot where the works of man will ever appear paltry and can never be in accordance.

A year later, Charles Joseph Latrobe reported: "Hotels with their snug shrubberies, outhouses, gardens and paltry establishments stare you in the face; museums, mills, staircases, tools and grogshops, all the petty trickery [that he had seen in English resorts] greet the eye of the traveller. . . . In short, Niagara is now . . . hackneyed."

Visitor Mrs. Anna Jameson objected violently to the Terrapin Tower, the first tourist see-the-falls structure on Goat Island: "It is such a signal, yet puny monument of bad taste, so miserably *mesquin* and so presumptuous, that I do hope the violated majesty of nature will take the matter in hand and overwhelm or cast it down the precipice one of these fine days, although indeed a barrel of gunpowder were a shorter if not a surer method."

She turned her wrath on the "City of the Falls," a proposed Canadian development:

> Fancy if you can a range of cotton factories, iron foundries, grist mills, saw mills—where now the mighty waters rush along in glee and liberty—there the maple and pine woods now bend and wave along the heights. Surely they

have done enough already with their wooden hotels, museums and curiosity stalls; neither in such a case were red brick tenements, gas-lights and smoke chimneys the worst abominations to be feared. There would be a moral pollution brought into this majestic scene, far more degrading; more than all those rushing waters with their "thirteen millions of tons per minute," would wash away.

Two British Congregationalist ministers, Andrew Reed and James Matheson, wrote (with one voice):

> I am sorry . . . that I cannot say much for the taste either of the visitors or the inhabitants of this spot. The visitors seem to regard the Falls as an object of curiosity rather than otherwise and when they had satisfied their curiosity (which in most cases was very quickly done) and could report that they had seen them, the duty was discharged.
>
> With the residents I am half disposed to be angry. On the American side they have got up a shabby town and called it Manchester. Manchester and the Falls of Niagara! On the Canadian side a money-seeking party have bought up 400 acres, with the hope of erecting "The City of the Falls"; and, still worse, close on Table Rock some party has been busy in erecting a mill dam. The universal voice ought to interfere and prevent them. Niagara does not belong to them; Niagara does not belong to Canada or America. Such spots should be deemed the property of civilized mankind; and nothing should be allowed to weaken their efficacy on the tastes, the morals and the enjoyments of all men.

The conservationists were already in full cry, but the depredators were only getting started. The river waters were still daisy-fresh and drinkable. There was practically no industrial pollution, and the moral pollution was small by later standards.

A certain Mrs. Boyle Corbett took one glance at the falls from her hotel window while dressing for dinner, then resolutely ignored them for the rest of her stay. Francis Abbott looked at them and spent the rest of his life looking. He was a young English Quaker, a linguist, world traveler, and musician who arrived in 1829, built a shack on Goat Island, and withdrew from the world to contemplate the waters.

Sir James Edward Alexander painted Abbott, the "Hermit of Niagara" hanging from a plank bridge at Terrapin Point that jutted from the island to the brink of the horseshoe. He wrote in his *Transatlantic Sketches* (1833):

> On the bridge it was the daily practice of the hermit to walk, either when alone or when there were visitors there, whom he often alarmed by his strange appearance in his dark gown, hair streaming in the wind, and bare feet. With a quick step, he would pass along the bridge, advance on the timber to the extreme point, turn quickly but steadily on his heel and walk back, and continue thus to walk back to and fro for hours together. Sometimes he would stand on one leg and pirouette with the other round the end of the log; then he would go down on his knees and gaze in seeming ecstasy on the bright green and snow-white water of the cataract. "But the worst of all," said the ferryman to me, "was when he would let himself down by the hands and hang over the Fall. Lord! Sir, my flesh used to creep and my hair stand on end when I saw him do that."

In June 1831 the hermit succumbed to the bright lure of the waters. He went swimming in the gorge and drowned. His body spun for two days in the whirlpool and was finally recovered at Fort Niagara.

In his shack were found books, music, a guitar, a flute,

and a violin. Sheaves of writing paper lay on a table—all blank. The man who might have written the greatest hymn of praise to Niagara never put his thoughts down on paper. Or if he did, he destroyed them before he took his last swim.

Two years later, twenty-three-year-old Harriet Beecher expressed what may have been in the hermit's mind: "I felt as if I could have *gone over* with the waters; it would be so beautiful a death; there would be no fear in it. I felt the rock tremble under me with a sort of joy. I was so maddened that I could have gone, too, if it had gone."

Fortunately for the slaves of America and unfortunately for all the victims of the Civil War, Harriet didn't go over. She returned to Niagara a decade later, as Mrs. Harriet Beecher Stowe, to gather material for *Uncle Tom's Cabin, or Life Among the Lowly*, from the original "Uncle Tom," the Reverend Josiah Henson, who was smuggling runaway slaves across the Niagara to Canada. That book helped bring on the War Between the States.

Harriet wanted to surrender herself to the falls; Captain Frederick Marryat wanted to boil them dry. The creator of *Mr Midshipman Easy* and popular chronicler of life under sail seems to have been obsessed with steam.

"I wished myself a magician," he wrote, "that I might transport the falls to Italy and pour their whole volume of waters into the crater of Mount Vesuvius; witness the terrible conflict between the contending elements, and create the largest steam-boiler that ever entered into the imagination of man."

Nathaniel Hawthorne (*Twice-Told Tales*) postponed visiting the falls until he was thirty, and when he finally got there, could hardly bring himself to look. "I had lingered away from it," he explained, "and wandered to other scenes, because my treasury of anticipated enjoyments, comprising all the wonders of the world, had nothing else so magnificent, and I was loath to exchange the pleasures of hope for those of memory so soon."

On the stagecoach from Lewiston to Manchester, Hawthorne was trembling with dread and closed his eyes to the sights of the gorge. At his hotel, he spent a long time dressing before venturing forth. "My enthusiasm was in a deathlike slumber. Without aspiring to immortality, as he did, I could have imitated that English traveller who turned back from the point where he first heard the thunder of Niagara, after crossing the ocean to behold it."

Hawthorne was made of sterner stuff. Although he lingered at souvenir shops on his way to Goat Island, buying a walking stick allegedly made by an Indian, he at last forced himself to walk to the hermit's plank bridge, then down to the foot of the precipice:

> Oh that I had never heard of Niagara till I beheld it! Blessed were the wanderers of old who heard its deep roar sounding through the woods, as the summons to an unknown wonder, and approached its awful brink in all the freshness of native feeling. Had its own mysterious voice been the first to warn me of its existence, then, indeed, I might have knelt down and worshipped. But I had come thither, haunted with a vision of foam and fury, and dizzy cliffs, and an ocean tumbling down out of the sky—a scene in short, which nature had too much good taste and calm simplicity to realize. My mind had struggled to adapt these false conceptions to the reality and finding the effort vain, a wretched sense of disappointment weighted me down. I climbed the precipice and threw myself on the earth, feeling that I was unworthy to look at the Great Falls and careless about beholding them again. . . .

Perhaps the novelist had read too much Hennepin. That night in the hotel his dreams mingled with storm and whirlwind until the noise of the falls woke him up. This happened night after night, but each morning he arose with fresh enthusiasm for another look. Like writers before and since, he had to find his personal Niagara.

> Gradually, and after much contemplation, I came to know, by my own feelings, that Niagara is indeed a wonder of the world, and not the less wonderful because time and thought must be employed in comprehending it. Casting aside all preconceived notions and preparations to be dire-struck or delighted, the beholder must stand beside it in the simplicity of his heart, suffering the mighty scene to work its own impression.

It took Hawthorne a long time to get around to this, but it is still the best advice to offer to tourists, whether at the falls or anywhere else; form your own impression and make up your own mind. But the romantic had to add to it. On his last day at Niagara, Hawthorne walked down to the ferry dock half a mile below Table Rock to fix a last picture in his mind:

> The golden sunshine tinged the sheets of the American cascade, and painted on its heaving spray the broken semicircle of a rainbow, heaven's own beauty crowning earth's sublimity. My steps were slow and I paused at every turn of the descent, as one lingers and pauses who discerns a brighter and brightening excellence in what he must soon behold no more. The solitude of the old wilderness now reigned over the whole vicinity of the falls. My enjoyment became the more rapturous, because no poet shared it, nor wretch devoid of poetry profaned it; but the spot so famous through the world was all my own!

Well, of course, it wasn't. The only man who tried to make the view of the falls literally his own was the smuggler-hotelier William Forsyth. While pioneering tourist attractions above, below, and behind the Canadian falls, he ignored the fact that the area was still a military reserve. Because he had not consulted the military about his operations, he eventually lost the ferry service to competitors. In retaliation, he built a high spite fence around his Pavilion hotel property that shut off access to Table Rock and the best view from the Canadian side. This landed him in a legal battle with the Canadian authorities that eventually bankrupted him. He was a great entrepreneur, but a little too greedy.

The journalist William Lyon Mackenzie returned to Niagara in December 1837. He came swiftly and by night, disguised as an old woman, for he was now a rebel leader with a price of £1,000 on his head and the troops and sheriffs of Upper Canada on his heels. Six days before, he had led a few hundred ill-armed supporters against the might of British Canada and seen them scattered by a burst of musketry on Yonge Street, Toronto. He fled on foot for the Niagara River and reached the home of a sympathizer who lived on the banks near Chippawa. As a troop of dragoons approached, hunting him, he launched a boat, rowed furiously, and reached the sanctuary of Grand Island, New York. He was safe, for a time at least, in his philosophic home, the United States.

Mackenzie, a Scots peddler's son, had come to Canada loyal to the king but had rapidly become disillusioned with the king's representatives, such as Lieutenant-Governor Sir Francis Bond Head and the Family Compact—the ruling junta of British officers, Anglican clergy, bankers, and land speculators, which was the result of Simcoe's attempt to create an aristocracy from his tent at Navy Hall in Newark. "Not to gain the wealth of the Indies," Mackenzie wrote, "could I now cringe to the funguses I have beheld in this country, more pestilential in the Town of York [Toronto] than the marshes and quagmires with which it is environed."

The Loyalist settlers who had fought off their American relatives in 1812 often felt powerless in the land they had saved. New immigrants from Britain, unless they belonged to the Compact or were smiled upon by its members, found less freedom in the colony than back home. So American-style republicanism sprouted even among those who had rejected the American Revolution, and Mackenzie provided its shrillest voice.

"First he wrote," reported Lieutenant-Governor Head. "Then he printed and then he rode and then he spoke, stamped, foamed, wiped his seditious little mouth and then spoke again; and thus, like a squirrel in a cage, he continued with astonishing assiduity the centre of a revolutionary career."

The Family Compact laughed at Mackenzie's small stature, but Head was about the same size. When the king's representative and the rebel sat down to exchange insults, their legs were too short to reach the floor.

Mackenzie's supporters were mostly farmers. The townspeople wanted none of his libertarian vehemence. A Toronto mob threw the *Colonial Advocate* press into Lake Ontario. He plotted his republican uprising in country taverns and in John Doel's country brewery. There, in July 1837, he drew up his Canadian version of the Declaration of Independence:

4TH JULY
AT NIAGARA FALLS

THE GREATEST WONDER OF THE AGE

MONS
BLONDIN

Will repeat his Wonderful Feat of

CROSSING

THE NIAGARA RIVER
UPON A TIGHT ROPE & RETURN
ON MONDAY
THE 4th OF JULY

Between 3 & 4.15 P. M. He will cross from the American Side to the Canada side

TIED UP IN A SACK

Mons BLONDIN, will also repeat his World-Renowned Exercise on the

TIGHT ROPE!

On the Ground, previous to the Terrific and Sublime Trip across Niagara River

PRICE OF ADMISSION 25 CENTS

Splendid Seats have been erected for the occasion, price 25 Cents Extra
TIGHT ROPE Performances to begin at 3 P. M.   GENERAL ASCENSION at 4 P. M

A Blondin broadside. (Buffalo and Erie County Historical Society)

Blondin carrying Harry Colcord on his back across the gorge. (Earl Brydges Library, Niagara Falls, N.Y.)

Left, Blondin in later life. (Buffalo and Erie County Historical Society)

Blondin's challenger: Signor Farini. (Portrait: Ontario Archives. Poster: Buffalo and Erie County Historical Society)

Daring Dixon dances on his tightrope.
(Niagara Falls Gazette)

Left, Maria Spelterini walks with baskets on her feet.
(Buffalo and Erie County Historical Society)

Clifford Calverley, fastest man on the tightrope. (Earl Brydges Library, Niagara Falls, N.Y.)

"Professor" Jenkins on his velocipede. (Earl Brydges Library, Niagara Falls, N.Y.)

First barrel artist, Carlisle D. Graham, came safely through the rapids. (Buffalo and Erie County Historical Society)

Mrs. Annie Taylor is helped from her barrel after dropping over the falls, 1901.
(Niagara Falls Gazette)

Right, Annie won fame but not fortune with her barrel.
(Niagara Falls Gazette)

Bobby Leach, the cheery Cockney. The drop broke his jaw. (Buffalo and Erie County Historical Society)

Chief River Rat "Red" Hill. He rode barrels through the rapids but never over the falls. (Niagara Falls Gazette)

The Colonel Invents the Tourist Trap 131

> Government is founded on the authority, and is instituted for the benefit of a people; when, therefore, a Government long and systematically ceases to answer the great ends of its foundation, the people have a natural right given them by their Creator to seek after and establish such institutions as will yield the greatest quantity of happiness to the greatest number.

The heady atmosphere and the froth of newborn beer nourished the delusion that a handful of farmers with clubs, homemade pikes, and fowling pieces could mount a revolution on the American scale. Mackenzie's Patriots were in touch with Louis Joseph Papineau's *Patriotes*, who were planning a similar revolution in Quebec; and, encouraged by exaggerated reports of their strength, Mackenzie timed his uprising to coincide with Papineau's. But by the time he had mustered his shabby little force of untrained freedom fighters, Papineau had tried and failed.

On December 5, 1837, about 700 rebels met at Montgomery's Tavern, four miles north of Toronto, and straggled downhill to attack the town. The tiny fanatic led them, perched gnomelike on a white farm horse, bobbing and weaving in the saddle while shouting contradictory orders and waving his top hat.

At Gallows Hill they met a messenger from the lieutenant-governor. Mackenzie imperiously demanded the surrender of the capital. As his rebels waited for a reply Mackenzie "went on like a lunatic," according to one of his followers. He rushed into a nearby house that belonged to a banker and set it on fire. He hated banks.

The gallows on the hill was not used for hanging men. It was a wooden bar over Yonge Street from which ropes and pulleys were slung to drag carts up a particularly steep part of the muddy road. But its shape was ominous.

After dark, with no reply from Head, the rebels slithered down the slope to the outskirts of the town, where they ran into the sheriff with 26 militiamen. Both sides fired some shots blindly in the dark, then both sides ran away, leaving one rebel dead on the street. Mackenzie's men ran back to the beery fug of Montgomery's Tavern, sweeping their leader along with them. About 200 kept going northward and scattered in the countryside.

Two days later the might of the king and the Family Compact marched on the tavern: 1,200 volunteers, as ill trained as the yokel Patriots but with plenty of muskets, bayonets, and two cannon. They were led (from the rear) by the cautious Head, and urged on by the toots and thumps of two bands and the cheers of the townspeople. Several hundred followed the troops up Gallows Hill to watch the battle.

It lasted about twenty minutes—a non-event in military history but a landmark in the Canadian story. A few cannonballs rolled through a line of rebels in a wood below the tavern. Others smashed through the pub itself. Outflanked and vastly outnumbered, the farmers fled. Only one was killed, but 100 were captured. Eleven would be sentenced to death, and the rest exiled to an Australian penal colony.

When the shooting was over, Sir Francis Head emerged from the rear ranks and ordered the tavern burned to the ground "to mark and record, by some act of stern vengeance, the important victory."

The owner, old John Montgomery, when sentenced to hang for treason, told his judge and jury: "You think you can send me to the gallows, but I tell you that when you're all frizzling with the devil I'll be keeping tavern on Yonge Street."

The Colonel Invents the Tourist Trap

As far as the tavernkeeping goes, he was right. His sentence was reduced to exile, but he never reached Australia. He and some other prisoners tunneled their way out of prison and escaped to the States. Montgomery kept a pub in Rochester for some years, then was pardoned. He returned to Yonge Street to open a new Montgomery's Tavern on the old site.

Only Samuel Lount, the genial blacksmith who made pikes for the Patriots, and Captain Peter Mathews, a Mackenzie lieutenant, were hanged. Mackenzie could never be hanged or drowned, according to Scots superstition, because he had been born with a caul—a piece of womb membrane—on his head. In his case, the lucky omen worked.

Six days after his rebellion collapsed, Mackenzie began a new one at Niagara. On December 13 he stood under a large, strange flag on Navy Island and proclaimed himself chief of state of a new Republic of Canada.

Mackenzie was back on Canadian soil, but only barely—as the Canadian island was a comfortable distance from the Canadian mainland and only a stone's throw from the U.S.-owned Grand Island. The flag was Mackenzie's new Patriot tricolor with two stars representing French and British Canada. Although most of Mackenzie's original Patriots were hiding out in barns or being escorted through Toronto, roped together and at musket point, a new troop of Britons living in the States gathered beneath the new banner. And, what was more important, Americans in the Niagara region and beyond felt a tingle of enthusiasm for yet another attempt on Canada. Here was a genuine British North American raising the standard of liberty and firing up the still-smoldering notion that the other half of the continent was eager to join the Union. He was no

Washington in appearance, and he talked like Jefferson in a fit; but he was a leader, of sorts, and could always be replaced if his wild crusade succeeded.

The citizens of Buffalo had turned out in the thousands to hear the little rebel speak and to roar their approval. A visitor to Rochester wrote: "There is excitement here . . . 40 soldiers marching the streets today under drum and fife; two pieces of cannon went off this morning and three-fourths of the people here, I learn, are encouraging and supporting the cause of the patriots."

The small skirmishes on Yonge Street were blown up into second Bunker Hills and Lexingtons as Mackenzie described them. Boatloads of volunteers rowed over to the pinewoods of Navy Island, which had taken over from Montgomery's pub as the capital of the Canadian republic. Mackenzie talked and talked, but couldn't survive for long without seeing his words in print. He set up a new press on the island and began churning out handbills. When not printing or orating he was designing a Great Seal for the republic—a new moon breaking through the darkness of Family Compact oppression—and issuing his own currency.

He received letters addressed "Dear General" from West Point graduates, relics of the Prussian and French armies, fathers anxious to send their sons to war, and surgeons eager to try their skill on the wounded. The United States had been at peace with its neighbor for twenty-three years but old soldiers still dreamed of war and young men looked for lands to conquer. In two weeks the new republic had 200 supporters on Navy Island, each promised land in Canada once the war was won; it also had a one-boat navy, the paddle-steamer *Caroline*. And it had a military commander: Rensselaer Van Rensselaer, black sheep of an old patroon family and son of General Stephen Van Rensselaer, who had fought Brock at Queenston. He had the backing of those Americans who were content to use Mackenzie as a figurehead but wisely distrusted his abilities as a general. Van Rensselaer was no general either, although he had invented some yarns about his military prowess, but he had the sense to hold Mackenzie back from an immediate invasion of Canada. The "President pro tem," who believed his own handbills, was ready to go.

The *Caroline* brought a cargo of muskets and cannon, some of which had been stolen from the U.S. arsenal at Buffalo, and Mackenzie's wife, Isabel, who had followed him from Toronto. The new troops dug in on the frozen island while Isabel sewed cartridge bags from flannel sheets. Then the steamer churned her way through floating ice back to Schlosser Landing (Niagara Falls, New York) to take on more arms and adventurers. On December 29 she tied up with 100 men aboard, ready to sail back to Mackenzie's republic at dawn the next day. All this activity was strictly illegal, a violation of U.S. neutrality laws and the treaty that ended the War of 1812, but no American official stepped forward to stop the military preparations or reclaim the stolen weapons.

What followed was even more illegal: an act of war by Canada against the United States.

Colonel Allan MacNab, Canadian commander at Fort Chippawa, had spent the day watching the *Caroline* through his telescope. He had planned to seize her in midstream on her return trip, but when he saw her boiler fire banked down for the night, he decided to strike across the watery border. It had been done before; it would be done again—but always at the risk of all-out war.

At 10:00 P.M. seven whaleboats loaded with Canadian militiamen nosed out from Chippawa for the dangerous run across the upper river. Two of them missed the gap between Grand and Navy islands and were swept down to the rapids. Desperate rowing saved them from the precipice. The other five, under Captain Allen Drew, reached Schlosser Landing. Soldiers leapt over the *Caroline*'s deck rail, killed the solitary watchman, an American citizen, and took the ship. The crew and the volunteers, asleep below, were hauled out and thrown ashore. Captain Drew then prepared one of the most spectacular stunts in Niagara's history. He had the steamer's boilers stoked, waited till she had built up a head of steam, then sailed her into midriver, towing his five boats. When she reached the main current he pointed her at the falls, lashed the steering wheel, set fires below decks, and abandoned ship. He and his men jumped into their boats and cut their towlines.

About 1:00 A.M. Mackenzie was awakened on Navy Island by explosions out on the water and saw a glare of flames over by the American side. As the fire grew, he could make out the outline of his ship.

The *Caroline* sped downstream, a spitting, crackling fireship, torn by roaring blasts as the powder kegs in her hold blew up—an angry sight, matched only by the fiendish rage on Mackenzie's choleric features. On her final surge toward the Canadian falls the rapidly sinking steamer grazed the rocks of Goat Island, then stuck in a shoal a hundred yards from the brink, where she broke up and went over in pieces. Her figurehead was found down at Lewiston.

When Mackenzie the rebel had calmed down and recovered from his loss, Mackenzie the journalist exploited the drama of it. His broadsheet, *The Caroline Almanac*, carried a startling artist's reconstruction of the scene. It showed the steamer, ablaze from stem to stern but still in one piece, dipping her bows to plunge over the brink while

The Colonel Invents the Tourist Trap

terrified passengers clung to the rails, staring at the awful fate that awaited them. Mackenzie well knew that there was nobody aboard on the final stage of her last voyage, but he was not a man to let facts get in the way of a great story. *The Caroline Almanac* fueled American outrage at this barefaced invasion of U.S. territory and the murder of a U.S. citizen. The border states wanted war, and so did some Canadian newspapers. For a few weeks, it seemed as if Mackenzie might win his republic with the help of the United States. But the old war hawks of Congress were dying off, and President Martin Van Buren had problems enough without tackling the British Empire. The country was in a depression, unemployment was rife, and banks were collapsing all around him. He therefore sent General Winfield Scott, the veteran of Queenston Heights, back to Niagara once more to preserve American honor on the one hand and American neutrality on the other.

Scott trod carefully. He ordered that no U.S. vessel be sold or leased to the rebels, who were exchanging badly aimed cannon shots with Colonel MacNab's men on the mainland. As both sides were on Canadian territory, Scott saw no need to interfere. But on January 14 Mackenzie took his flag and his forces over to Grand Island, and MacNab occupied Navy Island. The shooting between the two islands resumed, transforming the tiny war into an international conflict.

Scott, deciding that Mackenzie had to be removed, dispatched a platoon of troops to Grand Island aboard the steamer *Barcelona* to bring the rebels to Black Rock. He sent a message to MacNab, explaining the *Barcelona*'s mission, but received no reply. Three armed Canadian schooners appeared in the upper river, and Scott feared they would try to sink the steamer. He placed artillery batteries along the shore, ready to bombard Canada if the *Barcelona* was attacked. He stood beside them in his full-dress uniform, ready to signal a barrage. The governor of New York was also there in top hat and tailcoat. If war was to start, it would start formally.

The American watchers tensed as the *Barcelona* chuffed toward the Canadian schooners, but she passed them without incident and blew her whistle at the Grand Island dock. The rebels argued among themselves, then came quietly aboard. The artillery watch continued as the steamer headed back to the U.S. mainland. The gunners on the Canadian schooners lit their fuses, but nobody fired.

As the *Barcelona* cleared Grand Island, Scott took off his tricorn hat, held it to his chest, and raised his right arm in salute to the Canadians. He ordered his gunners to extinguish their fuses. The crisis was over.

Mackenzie and his patriots were released at Buffalo, and the leader pawned his gold watch to pay for one-way coach tickets to Rochester for himself and Isabel. There he set up still another printing press and was soon churning out more inflammatory pamphlets and haranguing the patrons of John Montgomery's Rochester tavern.

By the summer of 1839, Mackenzie had become as much of a nuisance to the American authorities as he was to the Family Compact. He was put on trial at Rochester for inciting Americans to make war on a friendly neighbor. In truth, the neighbors were still none too friendly. Mackenzie's stirring speech in his own defense claimed that the liberation of Canada had always been an American goal. The courtroom audience and the press were sympathetic. But the jury found him guilty and he was sentenced to eighteen months in the town's damp little dungeon.

Mackenzie served a year before President Van Buren,

The Colonel Invents the Tourist Trap

swamped by petitions from his supporters, ordered his release. While in Rochester, Isabel gave birth to a daughter who would become the mother of William Lyon Mackenzie King, the most durable and certainly the strangest of Canadian prime ministers. King lived in the shadow of his mother, consulted her ghost on how to run the country through mediums, and treasured relics of his rebel grandfather, including the poster offering £1,000 for his capture.

Mackenzie himself lived to be pardoned and return to Upper Canada, where he was elected to Parliament and watched the crumbling of the Family Compact. He should have rejoiced in his vindication; instead, he became disillusioned with the responsible form of government he had helped to create. The older he got, the more radical he became. His press denounced whoever happened to be in power.

When Mackenzie died in 1861, the Canadian provinces were lumbering toward the nationhood they would achieve six years later, prodded by the border troubles with the United States that Mackenzie had stirred up. This earned him schoolbook status as a quirky grandfather of Canadian confederation. But, as his biographer William Kilbourn says: "He is not the cornerstone, but the chief gargoyle on the edifice of our public history."

The tiny rebel has several monuments to mark his place in Niagara's history. There should be one at the spot on Navy Island where he watched the fiery ruin of the *Caroline* sweep toward the abyss, carrying his wild hopes with her.

8
A Boy with a Kite

President Martin Van Buren, a New Yorker who dressed impeccably and fancied himself as something of a dandy, was an early victim of Niagara's expanding transportation system. He landed upside-down in a pile of yelling passengers when his rail car fell off the track about a mile from the falls. According to a construction foreman on the Lockport and Niagara Falls Railroad: "The President crawled out without a scratch and didn't look as if he was mad any. He helped tip the car back up, climbed in, and they went on just as if nothing had happened."

Such spills were fairly common, for although the line had converted to steam power in the late 1830s, it continued to use the original rails laid for horse-drawn trains. These were wood, with straps of iron spiked on top, and the straps had a way of coming loose and curling up over the car wheels. The foreman, Stephen Sult, remembered "seeing a passenger considerable surprised once by having the end of a rail come up through the floor and knock off his hat."

The early railways were built to bring ship passengers from the Erie Canal to the falls. The canal, linking Albany on the Hudson River with Buffalo, had been completed in 1825. It made the town of Buffalo, and the toughs who built and traveled it turned Canal Street into what Rudyard Kipling called "the wickedest street in the world." The Niagara promoters, hell-bent for profit and not averse to a little wickedness, determined to cash in. In just two hours, including stops, passengers could cover the 23 miles from Buffalo to Niagara Falls, New York. The 24-mile trip from Lockport took about an hour and forty minutes. Despite howls of protest from the canal and shipping interests, the small American railroads merged, eventually forming the New York Central.

The first line built in Upper Canada, the Erie and Ontario from Queenston to Chippawa, was completed in 1841 and plodded along under horse power until 1854. It operated only in summer because the cost of clearing snow off the track was prohibitive. But it was soon followed by the ambitious, steam-powered Great Western Railway—229 miles from Windsor, Ontario, via Hamilton, to Niagara Falls.

The logical next step was to link the Canadian and American railroads by a bridge across the Niagara Gorge. It was a Canadian canal promoter who proposed it—William Hamilton Merritt, whose Welland Canal, opened in 1832, bypassed Niagara on the Canadian side and now carries big ships between Lakes Erie and Ontario. It had to be a suspension bridge, for even if pilings could be driven into the eroding riverbed, the broken ice of spring would sweep them away. And no one had yet built a suspension bridge that would bear the weight of a train. But Merritt was a man of great stubbornness and determination. If he could make ships climb over the Niagara escarpment (using locks) he could make trains fly across the Niagara Gorge.

By 1846 he had persuaded the governments of the United States and Canada to permit the construction of a bridge, to be financed jointly by private companies established on both sides of the border. As the guiding force behind them, he invited the world's best engineers to study the problem. Most of them either declined politely or recoiled in horror. Only Charles Ellett, of Philadelphia, and John Roebling, a German immigrant to the United States, were prepared to try.

Ellett was awarded the first contract. At the time he was stringing the world's first long-span cable bridge across the relatively peaceful Ohio River (it collapsed in a storm after five years' service). He inspected the Niagara and chose as the site for his bridge the narrowest part of the gorge, above the beginnings of the Whirlpool Rapids. His first problem was how to get a cable across that fierce water and up the cliff on the other side.

It should be childishly simple—a single rope could haul the first cable across. Even a string could haul the first rope. He pondered the problem over a drink with his friend Judge Thomas Huellet at the Cataract House in Niagara Falls, New York. Childish! That was the answer. Get a boy to fly a kite across. Better still, a great many boys. So the two men staged a kite-flying contest with a prize of $10 for the first lad to get a kite string over from the American bank to the Canadian. Dozens of boys turned out on the first day of the competition but the wind was wrong and the kites fluttered above the international boundary. On the second day, Homan Walsh, an American teen-ager, joined the ranks of Niagara pioneers by snagging his kite in a tree on the Canadian cliffs. Its string pulled a light rope across, the light rope pulled a heavy one, and so on until Ellett had 1,160 feet of iron cable suspended from wooden towers on either side of the 700-foot gap.

Judge Huellet built an ornate iron basket that looked part sleigh and part bedstead and seated two passengers. It was slung from the main cable and hauled back and forth by ropes. On May 12, 1848, Ellett and Huellet crossed in it, to the cheers of spectators who were soon clamoring for a ride. Although the basket was intended to carry workmen who would get on with the job of building the big bridge, its creators didn't hesitate to pick up a few tourist dollars during construction. At Niagara, nobody ever hesitated. Bridge building took a back seat to tourism. At $1 a ride, the basket brought in up to $125 a day. Records show that three quarters of the riders were women. At least one husband took a look at the contraption and left his wife to try it while he walked to the ferry dock below the falls, took a rowboat across, and walked back to meet her.

Soon a footbridge, three feet wide, was slung across beside the basket cable and opened for business at 25 cents a round trip. Bridge crossing on this narrow, shaky platform, open to the winds and dwarfed by the torrent below, became the new thrill. It was by no means safe, as a near-tragedy demonstrated a month after the first footbridge opened. Workmen were building a second one when a sudden gale funneled down the gorge, sent the first bridge lurching wildly, and turned the new one upside-down. Two men managed to crawl along the tangle of twisted wires and broken boards to the bank. Four others were stranded in the middle to ride out the windstorm.

According to a newspaper report:

The unfinished structure was torn and wafted backwards and forwards like a broken web of a spider and four helpless human beings, two hundred feet from shore, supported by two tiny strands of wire, were in constant expectation of a headlong plunge into the raging waters far below. Oh, who can tell those men's thoughts just then? But the tiny threads which held them to existence proved strong enough to outlast the gale.

When the wind died down, a workman carrying a ladder went out in the basket. He ran the ladder out to the footbridge cable and one man at a time crawled along it and into the spare seat in the basket, to be towed to safety. It was the first aerial drama over the gorge and may have inspired all the others that followed.

Ellett then built an 8-foot-wide, 762-foot-long carriageway, planked with heavy oak, and on July 26, 1848, personally drove a team of horses over it. The bridge was officially opened on August 1. It was his last achievement at Niagara, for he got into a row with the directors of the bridge companies over who should keep the windfall dollars from the basket rides and footbridge walks, and he resigned at the end of 1848. It was left to John Roebling to build the great railway bridge Ellett had pictured as he watched young Homan's kite soar over the river—the first successful railway suspension bridge in the world.

Roebling, a graduate of Berlin's Royal Polytechnic School, had been forced to leave Germany because of his antimonarchist views. Before tackling Niagara he had built six smaller suspension bridges in the United States for horse-drawn traffic. His idea that a structure hanging from wires could support a massive iron train was untried and deeply suspect, but Roebling went ahead and designed one that would carry both trains and horse traffic at the same time—a double-decker bridge with a carriageway and footpath 18 feet below the railway tracks. A wild idea, said the critics. Roebling declared that his bridge would be "unique and striking in its effect and quite in keeping with the surrounding scenery." And so it was—a wild bridge in wild territory, a man-made marvel to match the natural spectacle.

Four limestone pillars supported the ten-inch main cables. The two decks, 821 feet long, were connected by wooden trusses. Two workmen died when a scaffold collapsed and they were hurled into the gorge. The rail deck carried a single track but required four rails to fit the various gauges of the Great Western Railway of Canada, the New York Central, and the Canandaigua and Niagara Falls Railroad—66 inches, 56½ inches, and 72 inches, respectively. It was many years before the railroads got together and settled on 56½ inches; in the meantime they shared the bridge.

On March 8, 1855, the locomotive "London," weighing 23 tons, ventured out from the Canadian side to the center of the span, paused there while official parties from the United States and Canada waved flags and gave three hearty cheers, then chuffed to the United States and back. Roebling rode in the tender, following the tradition that bridge builders be the first to test their creations. The locomotive reached a speed of eight miles an hour and bent the bridge down by three and a half inches at the center. Quite tolerable. Ten days later, a twenty-car freight train crossed. Roebling's triumph was complete. He reported to his directors that the total cost of the bridge was only $400,000 and thanked them for their support of his plan in face of constant opposition. "When engineers of acknowledged talent and reputation freely expressed their doubts as to the success of this work," he wrote, "a wavering of confidence on your part would have been but natural."

Roebling went on to design the famous Brooklyn Bridge, but not to build it. His foot was crushed during the final survey, and he died of tetanus before construction began. His son finished the work according to his plans.

Delighted as they were with the strength of their bridge, the directors took precautions. Notices were posted at the entrances:

> a. Fine of $50.00 to $100.00 will be imposed for marching over the bridge in rank and file or by keeping in regular step. Bodies of men or troops must be ordered to keep out of step while passing over this bridge.
>
> b. No musical band will be allowed to play while crossing this bridge except while seated in wagons or carriages.
>
> c. $5.00 fine for every horse driver over this bridge at a canter, rather than a walk.
>
> d. $5.00 fine for allowing buggies or horses to stop on this bridge longer than absolutely necessary.

In addition, not more than twenty head of cattle and two drovers were allowed to cross at one time.

Neither the tramp of marching legions nor the sound of music brought about the replacement of Roebling's bridge, but a combination of weather and increase of loads and traffic. By 1877 the cables were corroded, their anchorages loosening, and the wooden framework weakening. The American engineer Leiffert L. Buck was brought in to revamp the master's work. He replaced the limestone pillars with heavy steel towers and the wooden trusses with steel frames. The original cables and anchorages were overhauled but left in place. By 1886 the bridge was completely refurbished, but ten years later the directors decided to replace it with a steel arch on the same site. Buck was given the challenge of erecting the new bridge while the old one was still in service.

Construction began in 1896, and the arch arose while trains and carts rumbled just above it. Its halves nosed out from the new stone footings at either side of the gorge. Bets were laid on whether they'd meet exactly in the middle. (This is the trickiest part of bridge building. Engineers have shot themselves when their halves missed by a foot or so.) When their supporting cables were slackened off, Buck's ribs came together with a gentle clunk, forming an impeccable bow. But the flat girders on top were half an inch short. Adjustments were made and the gap shrank to a quarter of an inch. Not much of a gap in an 800-foot span, but a gap nonetheless. The whole bridge had to be jacked apart again while one-quarter-inch metal shims were inserted in the top chords to insure that it was properly stressed. Buck sighed happily as the final rivets were placed to lock it all together. The railway floor and tracks of Roebling's bridge were kept, supported by the new arch, but the cables and towers were removed. All work was completed by August 1897—a record time for such a major job—and not one train was canceled during the entire construction period; the carriageway below was closed for just two hours a day during a brief period. The bridge still stands today carrying rail and road traffic. From it you can see the clearing where Homan Walsh flew his kite and the sites of two other less fortunate bridges that collapsed and now lie at the bottom of the river.

The Falls View bridges, two miles upstream, were built to give tourists a grandstand view of the cataracts, which they did. And they provided an equally spectacular sight when they fell down.

The first bridge was begun in the winter of 1867. A cable

was carried across the ice that spanned the river and manhandled up the cliffs. This suspension bridge was all wood, with towers made of twelve-by-twelve-inch posts strapped together in clusters of four. Guy wires spidered out to anchorages on shore to hold it steady in gales. It was fairly steady but, as it was only 10 feet wide, it could only handle one-way traffic. Lines of cabs driven by the notoriously ill-tempered Niagara hackmen waited for a bell to ring that would allow them their turn to cross in convoys. The hackmen complained in the colorful manner that made them detested on both sides of the border, and so did their fares, who had come to see more than the back end of a stationary horse. So, in the fall of 1887, work was begun to widen the bridge and change it from all wood to all steel—again without halting traffic. The new steel bridge was completed by June 1888, but it swayed more than the wooden one and had a sickening habit of rising and falling in ripples.

One January night in 1889, a severe storm tore the entire span loose from the cliffs, cables, guy wires, and all, and dumped it into the river. Fortunately, nobody was on the bridge at the time. It is still rusting under 150 feet of water. It was replaced in amazingly short time because the steel mills still had the patterns for the parts. Work began in late March, and by early May a new bridge was opened for traffic. It lasted ten years, until the coming of the electric streetcar persuaded the owners that they needed a stronger structure to carry these heavy new vehicles. Plans were made to build the Upper Steel Arch Bridge to replace the old Falls View Bridge.

As with the railway bridge, a steel arch was sprung out under the existing bridge, which was then removed, bit by bit, and taken downstream to provide the first crossing between Queenston and Lewiston. The new arch, which became known as the Honeymoon Bridge, had a span of 840 feet and when it opened in 1898, it was the biggest steel arch in the world. Niagara's reputation for superlatives was preserved, and lovers and others could walk or take a cab or a streetcar across while admiring the view or each other.

The honeymoon of bridge and falls lasted nearly forty years, although there were dire predictions that it couldn't last forever. The bridge swayed uncomfortably. In 1925 several thousand people, as well as cars and streetcars, were out on it when it started to heave from side to side. Lights swung, cars rocked, and people staggered on the shifting walkway. There was a mass rush for the exits. No one was hurt, but the bridge had given a warning.

The second warning came on a rainy day in the early '30s when a motorist skidded on the wooden roadway, smashed through the railing, and plunged to his death. At the inquest the railing was described as "rotten enough to cut with a penknife."

It was the Niagara ice bridge—the phenomenon that permitted the original builders to carry their cable across—that finally brought down the Honeymoon span. In 1899 a spectacular buildup of ice around the abutments had reached 80 feet above the normal river level. Gangs of men on both sides had dynamited the ice and saved the bridge. Walls had been built to protect the abutments.

In January 1938 the ice broke up early. There had been a long mild spell, and blocks the size of houses were bumping their way from Lake Erie through the upper river. A sudden windstorm whipped them into roaring, crashing life; they toppled over the falls, and within twelve hours the upper gorge was blocked and filled like a cocktail-party ice bucket. The grinding, straining mass of ice tore at the pinions of the bridge and broke the arch itself. The bridge still clung weakly to its cliffs, but there was no hope of saving it.

The deathwatch began. Trainloads of the curious piled into the seasonally empty hotels and spent their days lining the top of the gorge as the bridge groaned its agony. News photographers from all over Canada and the United States picked their positions, set their focus and apertures, and waited for the fall. They waited for four days, freezing and impatient. By the afternoon of January 27, they were convinced that the bridge would go slowly, giving plenty of warning. All but one were in restaurants, getting warm, when the end came. Only Frank O. Seed, of Niagara Falls, New York, was there with his finger on the shutter when it happened. The Honeymoon Bridge split, fell, and crashed down on the ice in seconds, sending a curtain of mist up the height of the cataract, as Seed's picture showed.

The show wasn't over. Although the huge wreck was dynamited into three pieces in the hope that it would somehow go away and save its owners the cost of removing it, the center section lay on the ice for six weeks.

A crane was set up on the Canadian side to haul bits of wreckage away, but because of the danger to the men working on the shifting ice, only a few scraps were retrieved. Sections of bridge railing became garden fences for local homes.

More tourists arrived to see the bridge sink. Early one April morning half the arch on the American side vanished "with a gurgle magnified by thousands," as a reporter put it, to join the wreck of Falls View Bridge Number One. The big piece on the Canadian side was expected to do the same. But no. At 3:25 P.M. on April 13, the ice floe on which it rested cracked loose, turned and pointed the section of the bridge downstream, then slowly sailed toward the whirlpool.

It gained speed as it went, and spectators and press ran along the banks to keep up with it. The strange funeral cortege proceeded for nearly a mile. Then, at 4:05 P.M., the floe broke up under its enormous burden. Loud cracks were heard; the bridge rose, turned over, and sank in one of the deepest parts of the gorge, leaving only planks from its flooring to float down to Lake Ontario.

The Honeymoon had performed for the tourists to the very end. Of all the stunts tried at Niagara, the sailing bridge event has to be the most unexpected.

By the 1850s the trains were bringing 60,000 visitors a year to the towns perched on the cliffs and a new word had entered the language: "Niagarization."

"One becomes here, indeed, utterly Niagarized," wrote the formidable Lady Emmeline Stuart-Wortley in a letter in 1849. "The great cataract goes sounding through all one's soul and heart and mind."

"Everybody is Niagarized," added visitor George William Curtis (1851), "and flies to the centre as filings to a magnet. Before the train stopped . . . a crowd of men leaped from the cars and ran like thieves, lovers, soldiers or what you will to the Cataract."

Not the watery cataract, Curtis explains, but the Cataract House Hotel. You had to be quick to get a room there, but if you missed out, there were fourteen other hotels, good, bad, and indifferent, on the American side. Each had its paid band of touting hackmen. Niagara Falls, New York, now had 2,000 residents, six churches, a bank, an orphanage, two mills, twenty-eight stores, and five railway terminals. It also had its first full-time guide, a Mr. S.

A Boy with a Kite

Hooker, a dignified figure with top hat and cane who refused money for his services but accepted "gifts." He was said to be, "despite his name, an upright, intelligent and worthy man who has resided at Niagara Falls for 26 years."

The wooden Terrapin Tower was built on the rocks off Goat Island, right on the brink of the Horseshoe Falls in 1833. It offered the most exciting view from the U.S. side and was an instant success. It was advertised as a dangerous climb, but no one seems to have been deterred by this. Unlike other Niagara structures that were advertised as being perfectly safe, but fell down, the Terrapin stood until 1873, when it became rickety and was pulled down.

Still, the real action was on the Canadian side—on the notorious Front which ran from the splendid Clifton Hotel to Table Rock and was choked with peddlers, souvenir hawkers, drunks, gamblers, whores, and some of the most skilled con men on the continent. British artillery officer and historian George Warburton wrote in 1847: "Now the neighborhood of great wonder is overrun with every species of abominable fungus—the growth of rank bad taste, with equal luxuriance on the English and American sides— Chinese pagoda, menagerie, camera obscura, museum, watch tower, wooden monument, tea gardens and old curiosity shops."

Sir Richard Bonnycastle, a British officer who commanded the Engineers in Upper Canada in the 1830s, complained that "pedlars and thimble-riggers, barkers and the lowest rulls and vilest scum of society congregate to disgust and annoy the visitors from all parts of the world, plundering and pestering them without control." He observed that you couldn't get to the cave behind the Falls without passing through a bar. This clever stroke of commercialism was the culmination of years of exploitation of the thunder god's lair.

The cavern was discovered by a Jean Carmine Bonnefons in 1753. It took him an hour to climb down to it, holding on to roots, branches, and narrow ledges. The cavern, as he described it, was 40 feet long.

Over the years, various entrepreneurs enlarged it. By 1827, when Captain Basil Hall measured it, it had grown to 153 feet, and thirty years later, when visitors were being provided with "official certificates" to prove they had made the journey behind the Sheet of Falling Water, the distance was given as 230 feet.

In 1829 the English naturalist Charles Waterton hobbled down the covered stairway William Forsyth built and stuck his sprained foot under the cascade to see if the waters would cure it. Apparently they didn't.

He wrote:

> I remember once to have sprained my ankle very violently many years ago, and that the doctor ordered me to hold it under the pump two or three times a day. Now in the United States of America all is on a grand scale except taxation; and I am convinced that the traveller's ideas become much more enlarged as he journeys through the country. This being the case I can easily account for my desire to hold my sprained foot under the fall of Niagara . . . I tried to meditate on the immense difference there was between a house pump and this tremendous cascade of nature . . . Perhaps indeed there was an unwarrantable tincture of vanity in an unknown wanderer wishing to tell the world that he had held his sprained foot under a fall of water which discharges 670,250 tons per minute. A gentle purling stream would have suited better.

Table Rock became a battleground for rival promoters

Tunneling for the Toronto Power Plant at Niagara, 1905. (Ontario Hydro)

Ice jams the Ontario Power station, 1909. (Ontario Hydro)

Sir Adam Beck, father of Ontario Hydro. (Ontario Hydro)

Beck's "traveling circus" sold Ontario farmers on the advantages of electricity. (Ontario Hydro)

Toronto Power Plant, 1922, with the scow stranded near the lip of the falls. (Ontario Hydro)

The giant power complex, Adam Beck Stations One and Two. (Ontario Hydro)

The collapse of the Schoellkopf plant, 1956. (Niagara Falls Gazette*)*

The Big Picture: an aerial view encompassing the American falls, Luna Falls, Goat Island, and the Horseshoe Falls. (Ontario Hydro)

Above: the dry crest of the American falls when water was turned off in 1960. Below: five years later a mystery "creature" appeared beneath the falls. The thunder god? (Niagara Falls Gazette)

A hard winter at Niagara. (Niagara Falls Gazette)

Two Maids of the Mist *burn at their moorings, April 1955. (Niagara Falls Gazette)*

Marilyn Monroe and Joseph Cotten on the set of Niagara. *(Courtesy of Corky McKenzie)*

Escape artist the Amazing Randi frees himself from a straitjacket over the falls (Insight Productions)

A Boy with a Kite

Thomas Barnett and Saul Davis, each of whom operated his own stairway to the cave and his own bar and souvenir stall above. The United States consul reported in 1866 that visitors were told the cave trip was "quite free" unless they chose to reward their guides. However,

> when the visitors are ready to depart they are reminded that they have bills to settle and exorbitant prices are charged for the use of oil cloth clothing, pictures etc. In case of refusal to comply with these demands, the proprietors and employees take the law into their own hands, the visitors are falsely imprisoned—not allowed to depart without paying every cent it is thought fit to demand—insulted, assaulted and quite frequently knocked down, dragged out and otherwise maltreated.

According to another account: "Visitors were systematically swindled and blackmailed. Derby-hatted gents sold imported pebbles from England as congealed Niagara spray. Tourists who bought bottles of water later found that they did not burn, as claimed by sharpie salesmen."

Barnett sold such souvenirs—and paid a commission on sales to the hackman who had brought in the buyer—but also displayed genuine curios in his Niagara Falls Museum. This began in a wooden shanty but expanded into the first stone house at Table Rock, a magnificent building that cost $150,000 and became known as the Cave of the Forty Thieves. To attract customers, Barnett staged an Indian burial, using live Indians imported from the Mid-west and a buffalo hunt, with buffalo procured by Buffalo Bill Cody and Wild Bill Hickock. These events paled beside the natural drama of the fall of Table Rock.

Bits of it had fallen before, but in June 1850 a saucer-shaped chunk 200 feet long, 100 feet wide, and 60 feet thick suddenly broke off like a piece of biscuit. A hackman who was washing his cab there jumped to safety as the crack opened beneath him. The cab went down with the rock.

Despite this, business boomed on what was left of the rock. The visitors book records the names of Abraham Lincoln, the Prince of Wales, and an anonymous lover who wrote:

> On Table Rock we did embrace
> And there we stood both face to face.
> The moon was up, the wind was high
> I kissed her and she kissed I!

Into the hustle of sharks, cardsharps, elegant English gentry, moaning beggars, and yelling hackmen strode the great Charles Dickens. He found something there that few had noticed before—tranquillity.

He arrived by train from Buffalo in 1841 and was rowed over to the Canadian side by ferry. Strangely enough, these boats provided the safest of all Niagara's transportation systems. Visitors complained that the ferrymen were usually drunk and always rude, but they never drowned anyone.

At first Dickens was "stunned and unable to comprehend the vastness of the scene" but he soon recovered.

> It was not until I came on Table Rock and looked on, Great Heavens, on what a fall of bright green water!—that it came upon me in its full might and majesty. Then, when I felt how near to my Creator I was standing [the rock on which he was standing would collapse nine years later] the first effect and the enduring one was . . . Peace. Peace of Mind. Tranquillity: Calm recollections of the Dead: Great Thoughts of Eternal Rest and Happiness: Nothing of Gloom or Terror. Niagara was at once stamped upon my heart, an Image of Beauty; to remain

> there, changeless and indelible, until its pulses cease to beat forever.

Dickens stayed at the falls for ten days, brooding and writing.

> Always does the mighty stream appear to die as it comes down, and always from its unfathomable grave rises that tremendous ghost of spray and mist which is never laid; which has haunted this place with the same dread solemnity since Darkness brooded on the deep, and that first flood before the Deluge—Light—came rushing on Creation at the word of God.

Walt Whitman came in 1848 and scribbled: "Got in the cars and went to Niagara; went under the falls, saw the whirlpool and all the other sights." It was a poor effort for the greatest American poet of his time. Whitman must have realized this, for he returned thirty years later and tried again.

Meanwhile the novelist Anthony Trollope entered the contest for superlatives by describing the falls as "more graceful than Giotto's tower, more noble than Apollo . . . the peaks of the Alps are not so outstanding in their solitude. The valleys of the Blue Mountains of Jamaica are less green." This put less-traveled scribes in their place.

Later, William Howard Russell, the great foreign correspondent of the London *Times*, complained that he couldn't get a drink. Russell, who had watched the charge of the Light Brigade from the heights at Balaclava and recorded the slaughter with his quill pen, found "an American tout with Van Dyke beard, fur collar, ruffled shirt, watch chain and cigar" who told him all the big hotels were closed for the winter. He was taken to

> a hostelry of the humbler sort [where] the barroom was

closed. In a tawdry foul-odoured eating room swung a feeble lamp: it was quite unreasonable to suppose that anyone could be hungry at such an hour and we went to bed with nourishment supplied by an anticipation of feasting on scenery. All through the night the door and window frames kept up the drumlike roll to the grand music far away.

He said the cataract looked like bog water.

A *Pictorial Guide to the Falls of Niagara Giving an Account of This Stupendous Natural Wonder and All Objects of Curiosity in the Vicinity* (1845) begins modestly: "The author disclaims any attempt to describe the Falls of Niagara simply because they are indescribable." The author then goes on to describe them in 200 pages. On his second visit Whitman, too, labored to describe the indescribable. He found:

> Niagara, its superb severity of action and color and majestic grouping in one short indescribable show. We were very slowly crossing the Suspension bridge—not a full stop anywhere but next to it—the day clear, sunnystill—and I out on the platform. The falls were in plain view about a mile off, but very distinct and no roar, —hardly a murmur. The river tumbling green and white far below me; the dark high banks, the plentiful umbrage, many bronze cedars, in shadow; and tempering and arching all the immense materiality, a clear sky overhead with a few white clouds, limpid, spiritual. Brief, and as quiet as brief, that picture—a remembrance ever afterwards.

As his train crawled across the bridge Whitman must have resolutely avoided the view ahead of it and behind it —the tawdry carnival on the Canadian side and the stinking factories on the American. For at that period, around

A Boy with a Kite

1880, Niagara looked its worst, and governments were being urged to clean it up.

The landscape painter Frederick Church led the way. His immense painting of the Horseshoe Falls—seven and a half feet by three and a half and brilliant with sparkling light—had created a sensation when it was first shown in New York in 1857. "The greatest painting of the grandest subject of nature!" exclaimed the New York *Daily News*. Revisiting the scene twelve years later, Church was dismayed at the mess around him. If an artist could no longer enjoy nature's grandest subject, what hope was left? He persuaded his friend W. H. Hurlbutt, editor of the powerful New York *World*, to run a series of articles on the ruination of Niagara. A petition signed by 700 of the great names of the English-speaking world—including Longfellow, Carlyle, Whittier, Emerson, Ruskin, and Parkman—demanded action. Hurlbutt appealed for support to his friend Lord Dufferin, Governor-General of Canada. Dufferin mobilized the Ontario Society of Artists and pressured the premier of the province, Sir Oliver Mowat, to introduce legislation to preserve the river banks for the people. But under the old Military Reserve Law, the federal government of Canada still controlled all the land one chain (66 feet) deep along the gorge. The federal and provincial governments did not see eye to eye, so it was not until 1885 that Ontario acquired the land. "Worthless" buildings were torn down, and the Queen Victoria Park opened in 1888.

The industrialists on the American side lobbied strenuously against the park idea. Visitors to Niagara, they claimed, were nothing but "second-class tourists and excursionists." It was a rare thing to find any of the "best people" there. So why should they have a park?

Letters to the editor took a high moral tone in defending the hideous blots on the landscape. Young people, the writers claimed, obtained no moral benefit from the beauties of nature. When they visited the falls, they spent all their time at rollicking dances.

A conservationist replied:

> I have each week attended the "hops" at the various hotels, which are conducted by the guests, people of the highest social position and character, and have also looked on at the dances in Prospect Park and there were only slight differences observed at the different entertainments. Young people cannot sit in silence gazing at the Falls through all of a long summer day, thinking of aesthetic sublimities or communing with the Absolute and Infinite.

As governor of New York, Grover Cleveland pushed park legislation through, but he went on to become president of the United States before signing the bill. His successor postponed signing it until 1885. But the two countries, in their different and devious political ways, finally agreed that the exploitation of Niagara had to stop. The year 1885 was the turning point. Since then the trend has been toward controlled growth and a return to the tranquillity Dickens found and millions have sought since.

9
Blondin the Great

"I verily believe," wrote London *Times* reporter Nicholas A. Woods in 1859, "that at least half of the crowds that go to see Blondin go in the firm expectation that he must fall off and be lost some day or other. . . . When once he begins his feats you can never take your eyes off him (unless you shut them from a very sickness of terror) until he is safe back on land."

On the day of the great tightrope walker's first show at Niagara more than half the crowd were convinced he wouldn't venture out on his rope. Despite the efforts of bandsmen and barkers to liven them up, they were sullen and cynical. The advance publicity had been poor. Newspapermen sneered when Blondin announced that he would walk across the gorge. Some didn't bother to send the story to their papers. It was another piece of Niagara flackery. No man could perform such a stunt and live. No man—not even a Frenchman—was crazy enough to try.

Several thousand people did turn out, expecting either a letdown or a fall-down, but the audience was far short of the promoters' expectations.

Jean François Gravelet, who used his fair-haired father's nickname "blondie," walked his first tightrope, a clothesline strung between two kitchen chairs, at the age of five. He fell off. That was his last accident, although he walked ropes until he was nearly seventy. He took to the stage at eight, billed as "The Little Wonder," and soon achieved star billing in British and French music halls and circuses. Showman P. T. Barnum brought him to America with a troupe of aerialists called The Revels. He was well known, but hardly a world figure when he came to Niagara in 1859. He couldn't afford his own rope, so 1,300 feet of two-inch manila, with guy wires to hold it steady, was bought for him by a Mr. Hamblin. It was stretched across the gorge about three-quarters of a mile below the Canadian falls, from White's Pleasure Grounds, below Prospect Point on the U.S. side, to a spot above the present *Maid of the Mist* dock on the Canadian. It was actually a "slack rope," sagging in the middle of the 1,000-foot section that stretched 150 feet above the water.

At 5:00 P.M. on June 30, the band at the Pleasure Grounds struck up "The Marseillaise." Blondin, shimmering in his silk suit, picked up his 35-foot balancing pole, sprang onto his rope, and headed out over the gulf. As the Toronto *Globe* described it:

> ... although the sun was shining in his eyes he tripped forward and almost before the people were aware he had cleared the American land and nothing intervened between him and destruction but a two-inch rope. The band struck lively airs and the spectators on the Canadian shore were about to greet the daring adventurer with a cheer

when they were stilled by the men in Blondin's employ. Blondin marched on at a lively pace, his toes hardly appearing to touch the rope. After walking out about 150 feet he suddenly sank down on the rope and took a short rest. An involuntary shudder passed through the crowd as he thus fearlessly threw himself on his face on the cable, while several of the ladies gave a *petite* scream and clung more firmly to their protectors.

On arriving about a third of the distance across, Blondin sat down once more and waved his hand for the Maid of the Mist to steam up under the rope. It had been found impossible to anchor the craft at the point assigned for her, owing to the strength of the current. After a delay of about five minutes, the steamer was brought directly underneath the rope and by her paddles being set in motion and her head up the stream she was kept almost stationary. Blondin then, from his giddy elevation, lowered a piece of twine, which fell on the deck of the steamer, and a bottle containing some liquor was fastened to it which Blondin drew up and having drank of the liquor he tossed the bottle into the river and in a twinkling was pursuing his perilous journey.

So far the walk had all been downhill. He looked tired and was sweating as he faced the uphill stretch on the sagging rope, but that was probably acting. He plodded the last few steps and landed to a tremendous cheer from both banks. The crossing had taken fifteen minutes. He was wined and dined in Canada, then said he was off back to the States and would get there quicker than any pedestrian could by taking the bridge. He marched back by rope in seven minutes.

That first, incredible performance made Blondin's name. He eclipsed the falls themselves. Trainloads, coachloads, and steamerloads of thrill-seekers hurried there to watch the tiny figure on the rope rather than the famous view. Blondin walked, danced, and leaped again and again, and never the same way twice. The artist never repeated himself. He crossed with a sack over his head, he pushed a wheelbarrow, he walked on stilts, he performed backward somersaults on the rope. He took a stove out to the middle of the rope, cooked a full meal on it, and lowered portions down to passengers on the *Maid of the Mist*. He stood on his head and he struggled along with his arms and legs in chains. He stood, holding out his hat, while marksman John Travis shot a rifle bullet through it from the paddle steamer below. He walked at night, by lamplight.

Each show had its moments of calculated terror when it seemed certain he would fall, but after two months of shock upon shock, his audiences believed he was a superman, impervious to harm. So he offered to humanize his performance by carrying an ordinary mortal on his back. He offered a large prize to anyone who would volunteer. There were no volunteers. Then, in August, he announced that he would carry his manager, Harry Colcord. This caused the biggest sensation yet. The crowds could not imagine how Blondin felt as he danced over the abyss, since he was a professional and obviously fearless. But they could readily identify with the ordinary earthbound passenger who was going to cling, helpless, to his shoulders. They knew how Harry must feel: terrified.

There is some doubt whether Harry volunteered or was pressed into service under threat of losing his $125-a-month job. Certainly he was no superman. When his fateful day arrived—August 19—he was seen to be shaking in his buckskin shoes. He was thirty-five, the same age as Blondin, and born in Chicago. He was about the same height—five feet eight inches—and weighed 148 pounds to Blondin's 142.

Blondin the Great

The biggest crowd yet seen at Niagara clung to vantage points on the banks or paid exorbitant prices for seats in viewing stands. Estimates of the attendance ranged up to 250,000. Allowing for the usual Niagara exaggeration, there were probably 100,000 present.

Blondin warmed up by turning somersaults on the rope, then running across and back without his pole. Trains blew their whistles in encouragement. The aerialist took a fifteen-minute rest to allow the tension to build up. Harry Colcord was tense enough already.

Blondin told him: "Harry, do not undertake to balance yourself. Rest like a dead weight on my back. Even if you think we are falling, do not try to adjust yourself." Sound advice, no doubt, but hardly reassuring.

The manager put his arms around his performer's neck and slung his legs into hooks fitted around his waist. Blondin strode out from the Canadian side, over some pine tops and on out over the void. Colcord had been told not to look down, but risked a peek. He said that first glimpse of the trees below was as bad as anything that followed.

Before he was halfway across, Blondin stopped to rest. He was not faking this time. The extra weight had caused the rope to sag down almost 50 feet, making the descent steeper and the climb fearful. He stood while Colcord very carefully unhooked his feet from their stirrups and slid down to balance on the rope, hanging on shakily to Blondin's waist. After a few minutes he climbed up again and the pair progressed a little farther. Colcord dismounted six times altogether. There were no guy wires to hold the rope in midstream, and the new weight caused it to sway more than usual. On one sway Blondin lost his balance and yawed to one side. Colcord clung, frozen, to his back—"Even if you think we are falling, do not try to adjust yourself." Blondin corrected himself with the pole and made a dash for the nearest guy wire on the American side. He put a foot on it to steady himself and the wire broke. The rope jerked violently, but he remained upright. There was a terrible silence among the crowd. Blondin unloaded Colcord once more and rested. His silk costume was damp and clinging to him.

On the last stage of the climb to the American bank, a new danger loomed. People were crushing forward to the brink, crowding the rope and holding their arms out, liable to topple both men into the gorge.

"You can't get through that mob," Colcord muttered. "You'll have to charge them."

Blondin gathered his strength, hitched his passenger higher, then rushed along the remaining yards and lunged into the crowd. Men wept with relief. The band crashed forth discordantly because the players were too tense to blow the right notes. Blondin and Colcord were carried shoulder high to a waiting carriage and the great thrill was over.

Colcord claimed the broken guy wire had been weakened deliberately. He said: "A dastardly attempt has been made to kill us, probably by some unscrupulous and murderous gamblers who had adopted this method in trying to secure their miserable stakes." Blondin remained unperturbed.

The following year, Blondin moved his rope downstream to the site of the present Whirlpool Rapids bridge and again carried a man on his back. Not Colcord—he had had enough. He offered to carry the greater bulk of the young Prince of Wales (later Edward VII) but the prince graciously declined. So he took Romain Mouton, one of his assistants.

Blondin the Great

The trip did not go smoothly. Blondin unloaded Mouton in the middle of the rope, so that he could take a rest. Mouton refused to climb up again and Blondin threatened to leave him to get back as best he could. High above the rapids, the two men raged at each other in French as the Prince of Wales watched, thunderstruck. "The attempt is so full of sickening terror that not many can bring themselves to witness it," wrote Woods of the *Times*. "Those who do remain cold, trembling and silent till the dreadful venture is safely passed." When the row was over, Mouton had remounted, and the pair were back on firm ground, the prince cried, "Thank God. Never try it again!"

For his last stunt at Niagara, Blondin wore a pair of three-foot stilts with hooks on them and not only walked on them but hung the hooks from the rope and dangled upside-down from them. The Prince of Wales brought him to the new Crystal Palace in London where he performed 170 feet up in that vast iron and glass case. He gave his last performance in Dublin in 1896 at the age of seventy and died peacefully in London a year later.

There was never another Blondin, but he had many imitators. When he was carrying Mouton, another walker with a man on his back was crossing the gorge.

Willie Hunt, aged twenty-two, took his fiancée from Lockport, New York, to watch Blondin at the height of his fame. While thousands gasped and shuddered, he remained unimpressed. "I could do that," he said. His girl laughed, but that night he quit his job at her father's store —at which she broke off the engagement—and set out to challenge Blondin. He took the name "Signor Guillermo Antonio Farini" and would use it for the rest of his ninety-one years. He had practiced tightrope walking in the barn of his father's farm at Port Hope, Ontario, and made his first public walks across the little Ganaraska River at Port Hope and over the main street of nearby Bowmanville, from the dome of the town hall to the roof of a liquor store. He had studied medicine, but decided there wasn't enough money in it, and became a professional strongman instead. He lifted weights and had local blacksmiths smash rocks on his chest with sledgehammers.

"Farini" bought ten 1,000-foot coils of rope and strung them across the Niagara at Blondin's original site. In his attempt to outdo Blondin, he aped and mocked the Frenchman, who took his art very seriously.

Blondin had lowered food to the *Maid of the Mist*. Farini lowered himself on a rope, dunked himself in the river, then used his strongman's muscles to haul himself back up. Blondin had taken a stove out on his wire and cooked a meal. Farini took a washing machine. His advertisements proclaimed:

> In his wonderful and laughable character of Biddy O'Flaherty the Irish Washerwoman, by carrying out upon his cable a new Patent Washing Machine! Standing over six feet high and weighing nearly 100 pounds, he will Draw up water from the river and do his own washing. Hanging his clothes out to dry upon his guys where he can leave them out all night without fear of having them stolen. If anyone doubts their being washed clean they can go out and examine them!

Sure enough, Farini washed ladies' handkerchiefs in pails of water hauled up from the river. He also duplicated nearly all of Blondin's 1860 stunts, usually an hour or so after Blondin performed them. He carried a man on his back. He stood on his head, lay on the rope, and hung from it.

Blondin the Great

The Toronto *Globe* reporter, who by this time considered himself a qualified critic of tightrope walking, noted: "He is not quite so active on the rope as Mons. Blondin but he will no doubt improve by practice."

The *Newark Advertizer* declared: "Blondin has met a rival worthy of him. Farini has already outdone Blondin."

He carried on his back Rowland McMullen, a tailor's son from Port Hope who seems to have appeared from nowhere, volunteered for the trip, then vanished immediately afterward. "The performance eclipsed anything ever done at Niagara Falls," said the Niagara Falls *Gazette*. "We trust Signor Farini will be satisfied with his hard and well-earned laurels and never undertake to repeat such a daring and truly frightful performance."

Farini's night performance outdid Blondin's when the firecrackers and giant roman candles that were supposed to light his way set fire to one another and exploded in a burst of flame all along the rope, singeing his costume and leaving him to make his way back in pitch darkness. The one feat Farini could not duplicate was Blondin's final walk on stilts. He brooded over this for four years, then returned to Niagara to try something less difficult but as madly reckless as any high-wire act.

This was his downfall. On August 8, 1864, he put on stilts and walked into the shallow rapids just above the American falls. As the crowd egged him on, he walked nearer and nearer to the brink. When he was less than 200 feet from it, one stilt stuck in a crevice on the bottom. Farini tugged, but it would not come loose. He could have unbuckled it and left it but that would have left him hopping on one stilt. If he took both stilts off, he would be swept over the precipice. So the great aerialist stayed, helplessly wedged for several hours while the crowds, who had gasped and cheered for so long, laughed and jeered at him. Farini, the clownish daredevil, had become a figure of fun. Eventually he was dragged ashore at the end of a rope. Farini left Niagara, deflated and defeated.

He went on to become a showman; an explorer—he crossed the Kalahari Desert in southern Africa—an inventor of, among other things, the tip-up theater seat and the circus cannon that fires daredevils through the air; painter; writer and sculptor; but he never forgot his humiliation at Niagara.

The funambulist (rope-walking) fad continued. Harry Leslie trotted the wire as "The American Blondin" while "Professor" I. F. Jenkins paraded as the Canadian one. Jenkins got a poor review in the Niagara Falls *Gazette* of September 1, 1869:

> We have been pretty reticent in regard to the proposition of Jenkins, the "Canadian Blondin" to cross the Niagara on a velocipede. Somehow there appeared an air of humbug about the fellow, and our suspicions have been realized.
>
> The "great feat" came off last Wednesday and a good many spectators were pretty well jenkinsized. His velocipede was just no velocipede at all but a sort of machine so attached to the rope that it could not fall, and the rider was reasonably secure from accident. The "feat" was about equal to that of the son of Erin who runs a handcar.
>
> Jenkins' performance bears about as much resemblance to Blondin's as a poor counterfeit does to the genuine. If our Canadian neighbors can't turn out better performers than this one they had better keep them for some more useful purpose.

When Henry Bellini slung his rope across in 1873, the *Gazette* reported "considerable apathy." Tightrope walkers had done wonders for business, but they were now old hat. They had done everything but fall off. Tightrope walking was safer than going by train. So Bellini fell off.

He tied a 12-foot stretch of rubber, $1\frac{1}{4}$ inches in diameter, to the center of his tightrope, grasped a short handbar attached to its loose end, and dropped.

"His fall was very swift," said the *Gazette*, "though, of course, his descent was somewhat retarded by the precautionary contrivance, which sprang upward to the rope the instant he released it. Going under the water for an instant, he quickly rose to the surface and was taken to a boat in waiting for him and rowed to the Canadian shore where his wife was waiting to meet him."

He dropped again a few days later. Again he bounced back up. But on his third fall the rubber broke with a great *ping!*, contracted, and whipped itself around the jumper's legs. Bellini crashed into the water, hopelessly entangled, but his boat crew picked him out before he drowned.

Bellini's young assistant, Stephen Peere, cashed in on his master's fame by borrowing his rope and balancing pole. For some reason he was allowed to make only a one-way trip from the Canadian bank. He could land on the American side but was not permitted to start from there. The immigration men had caught up with the funambulists.

Young Stephen took off at a trot, stopped in the middle to do Blondin-style tricks, then trotted on. Bellini felt upstaged. He was furious. When Stephen repeated his performance the rubber-cord jumper tried to cut the rope. This caused an uproar among tightrope fans and Bellini left Niagara under a cloud. He started a new career jumping off bridges without a rubber band and was drowned in the Thames at London.

Stephen Peere returned in 1887 to walk a rope across the

gorge between the two railway bridges. The walk was a success, but soon after, his body was found on the rocks below the Canadian end of his rope. He was wearing street shoes instead of his performer's slippers, so it was assumed he tried to walk at night while drunk. He became the only fatality among all Niagara's tightrope walkers, and he did not die during a performance.

The only one to fall accidentally before a crowd was "Professor" de Leon, who proved that even an aerialist could lose his head for heights. The professor was prancing happily on his wire on August 15, 1887, when, suddenly and unaccountably, he stopped and looked down. The cheers of the crowd died away. He shook, wobbled, then dropped his pole and leaped for the nearest guy wire anchoring the rope to the Canadian shore. He slid along the wire, tearing his hands, then dropped, plummeting into a mass of thorn-apple bushes.

The spectators, who had been yelling "Bravo!" minutes before, booed as a sorry, scratched figure crawled out of the thicket. Professor de Leon ducked back under cover and hid in the foliage until the crowd went away.

Wire walking continued until 1890. Sprinter Clifford Calverley set the all-time speed record by running across in 2 minutes, 32.4 seconds. Sam "Daring" Dixon, a Toronto photographer, wrested his pole away from his weeping wife, who was trying to hide it to prevent him from walking. He crossed Niagara, but collected only $56 in tributes. That was the actual end of the craze, but the grand finale had taken place in 1876, when Maria Spelterini showed that a woman could copy Blondin.

Maria was a genuine Italian and a very pretty one—twenty-three and splendidly built, weighing 150 pounds in her flesh-colored tights, scarlet tunic, sea-green bodice, and green boots. She walked sedately but proved she was as surefooted as the men by wearing peach baskets on her feet. She also walked with a paper bag over her lovely head. Once she made the trip walking backward.

After Maria, the air above the gorge had been well and truly conquered. There remained only the waters below and the cataract itself.

In the summer of 1850 a somber sixty-year-old Negro preacher walked the new suspension bridge across the Niagara back to the land from which he had escaped as a runaway slave twenty years earlier. He was taking a risk, for the U. S. Congress had just passed a law providing a fine of $1,000 and/or six months in jail for anyone helping fugitive slaves, and he had helped 600 of them. But the Reverend Josiah Henson was determined to tell his story. He took the train to Lockport, New York, to meet Mrs. Harriet Beecher Stowe, a popular writer. That story became the basis of *Uncle Tom's Cabin, or Life Among the Lowly* and Henson became "Uncle Tom." The name is chiseled on his headstone at Dresden, Ontario, where he died in 1883. It was, at the time, a great compliment to a great black leader. Henson was no "Uncle Tom" in today's derogatory sense; he was tough, at times dictatorial, and very much in command of the flocks he shepherded along the Underground Railroad to freedom in Canada.

The "railroad" was a network of free blacks and antislavery whites who risked the vengeance of Southern slave-hunting gangs to smuggle escaped slaves by riverboat and wagon and to shelter them in their homes and barns on the long route north. It was a successor to the "Scarlet Pimpernel" channels by which French aristocrats escaped to England from the revolutionary Reign of Terror and forerunner of the escape routes manned by the Resistance movements in Nazi-occupied Europe. It was the stuff of high drama, and Mrs. Stowe did full justice to it.

Her novel, published in 1852, not only stirred up abolitionist feelings in the northern states, it heightened tensions along the U.S.-Canadian border. The smuggling of slaves had been going on since Governor Simcoe's first Parliament of Upper Canada enacted a partial ban on slavery. (No new slaves could be imported into the colony.) About 750,000 Negroes crossed the St. Lawrence, Detroit, and Niagara rivers in the first half of the nineteenth century. Those who slipped by boat across the calm stretch of Niagara water to Queenston or Newark knelt and prayed their thanks on the wharves. When bands of slave hunters made the American banks unsafe for boats, hundreds of slaves swam across. One who tried to float across on a gate was picked up by a Canadian steamer in the middle of Lake Ontario. He knelt on the deck and cried, "Thank you, Lord, for deliverin' me to Canaan."

Uncle Tom's Cabin focused attention on underground operations, which had been going along quietly for years without arousing too much ill feeling along the border. But while abolitionists warmed to the Canadian "Canaan," its heart was not truly with them. When the Civil War came, Canada welcomed slave holders as well as slaves. Escaped Confederate prisoners found refuge there, and the Canadian bank of the Niagara became a hotbed of Southern spies. (Britain, although ostensibly neutral, was betting heavily on the South.)

James Murray Mason, the U.S. senator from Virginia who had drafted the Fugitive Slave Act, took a room at the fashionable Clifton House on the Canadian side of the falls in July 1864. There he met New York editor Horace

Blondin the Great

Greeley, who was attempting to arrange "peace at any price" between North and South.

Mason was the Confederacy's commissioner to Great Britain whose capture on the high seas had nearly caused war between Britain and the United States. The Union Navy grabbed him and another Confederate agent, John Slidell, from the British steamship *Trent* and held them until British threats secured their release. At the Clifton House, Mason gave Greeley the Confederacy's demand to be recognized as a sovereign nation, with borders along the Ohio and Potomac valleys. Greeley telegraphed this to President Lincoln but Lincoln, with victory in sight, would have none of it.

The abortive peace meeting increased United States distrust of Canada. Other treacherous plots were rumored to be hatching at the Clifton House. According to one story, Canadian chemists had been hired to put yellow-fever germs into bales of fur and ship them to northern U.S. cities. Other shipments were supposed to contain time bombs that would go off on arrival and start fires. The U. S. Customs opened all bales crossing the Niagara frontier and searched all Canadian visitors. Nothing suspicious was found.

Canada was blamed for turning a blind eye to the shocking affair of the Sandusky party-girls—probably the strangest naval happening in the history of Lake Erie—but it was never established that Canada was involved.

In September 1864 a dozen Confederate agents who may or may not have come from Canada hijacked the American sidewheeler *Philo Parsons* in Put-in Bay, scene of Commodore Perry's 1814 triumph. They ordered the captain to head for nearby Johnson Island, where 3,500 Confederate officers were being held prisoner in a Union stockade. On the way *Philo Parsons* met another steamer, the *Island Queen*, and the rebels boarded and seized her, too.

The pirate fleet anchored off Johnson Island, a few hundred yards from the island's guardian, the U.S. ironclad gunboat *Michigan*. The plan was to seize the gunboat and use its artillery to subdue the fort and liberate officers, whom the South badly needed.

The U. S. Navy of the day was in some ways better provided with creature comforts than it is now. Congress had yet to forbid strong drink to sailors at sea. And women were supplied from time to time—hence the term "son of a gun," meaning the offspring of an encounter on the gun deck. So it was quite in order for Madame Annie Davis, owner of a Sandusky brothel, to bring a boatload of her girls out to the *Michigan*.

Annie was in the pay of the Confederacy and may have been getting her orders from Mason at the Clifton House. One of her girls was a Pinkerton detective working for the Union side. Annie was escorted aboard by a young Virginian, John Yates Beall, playing the role of pimp. The party began while Beall was taken on a courtesy tour of the ship. Annie prepared to dope the crew by slipping chloral hydrate into their punch. But the Pinkerton girl tipped off the skipper. He slugged Beall and his officers pulled pistols on the brothel party. The *Michigan* turned her guns on the *Philo Parsons* and the *Island Queen*, and the conspiracy collapsed.

Angry U. S. Navy men felt that such acts of piracy on the lake could not have taken place if the Canadian Navy patrols had been on their toes. The Union would take its revenge two years later.

When the Civil War ended, Lincoln's Grand Army of the Republic, a fine military machine, was left with nothing to do. To many land-hungry Northerners it seemed logical to turn it around, sound the jubilee once more, and send it marching through Canada. This would repay the British for their tacit support of the rebels and settle all border questions for good. After the Trent affair, Britain had rushed 14,000 regular troops to Canada and 40,000 members of the Canadian Sedentary Militia were ready with shotguns and pitchforks. But they could not have held out for long. Britain was now extremely anxious to patch up relations with Washington, so it appeared that Canada was ripe for the taking. But Lincoln abruptly rejected the scheme. His army was sick of war, and he would have trouble enough putting the United States back together without acquiring new states.

Still, if an official invasion was out, Americans saw no reason to condemn a small, unofficial one. Let private enterprise do the job.

Private enterprise, in this case, was represented by the Irish Revolutionary Brotherhood—the Fenians—who proposed to liberate Ireland from the English yoke by seizing Canada and holding it hostage until Ireland was given independence. The potato-famine Irish immigrants were now a political force in the northern states, particularly around Buffalo, where many had settled after digging the Erie Canal, so the authorities did nothing to stop the "Freedom for Ireland" rallies with their wild orations and waving of green and gold banners. Irishmen discharged from both armies drifted into Buffalo, still wearing their blue or gray uniforms to hear the Fenian leader, John O'Mahoney, tell them all they had to do was cross the border, blow an anti-British trumpet, and the oppressed Canadians would rush to their standard. This was not just the view of a few moonstruck Irish fanatics. Most northern Americans still clung to it, despite the experience of 1812 and the collapse of the Mackenzie rebellion in 1837. John O'Mahoney knew it for a fact because long-dead Celtic kings had told him so in visions.

The visions stretched from coast to coast. A Fenian army would seize Niagara, then march on to Toronto and Montreal while a Fenian navy guarded lakes Huron, Erie, and Ontario. Meanwhile a west coast fleet would capture Vancouver Island. The entire half-continent would become New Ireland. The Fenian navy never came into being— O'Mahoney had to rent boats just to cross the Niagara— but there were supplies aplenty for his army. Rifles and ammunition were being sold off cheap from U.S. arsenals. The countryside was littered with abandoned military equipment. He could draw on a well of cash and sympathy from middle-class Irish who might not quite believe in the visions but loved a vicarious fight. O'Mahoney chose Captain John O'Neill, a twenty-five-year-old Union infantry officer, to command the Niagara assault and, on the evening of May 31, 1866, 1,500 volunteers embarked on two rented tugs and two barges at the Black Rock docks. The U. S. Navy stayed clear of the Upper Niagara River, and the invasion fleet sailed.

Early the next morning, the villagers of Fort Erie awoke to find armed men in the streets demanding breakfast. O'Neill had been told he would find Canadian supporters there with food supplies. There were none. He invited the villagers to join his liberation army—and appeared stunned when no volunteers stepped forward.

One of his lieutenants banged on a cottage door and declared: "We want the enemy." "Who's the enemy?" asked the bewildered cottager. "Queen Victoria!" cried the Fenian.

Red Hill, Jr., poses in "The Thing" before his fatal trip over the falls in 1951. (Courtesy of Corky McKenzie)

The remains of The Thing after it fell, killing young Red. (Niagara Falls Gazette)

Mystery man "Nathan Boya" was the last stunter to go over the falls. (Niagara Falls Gazette)

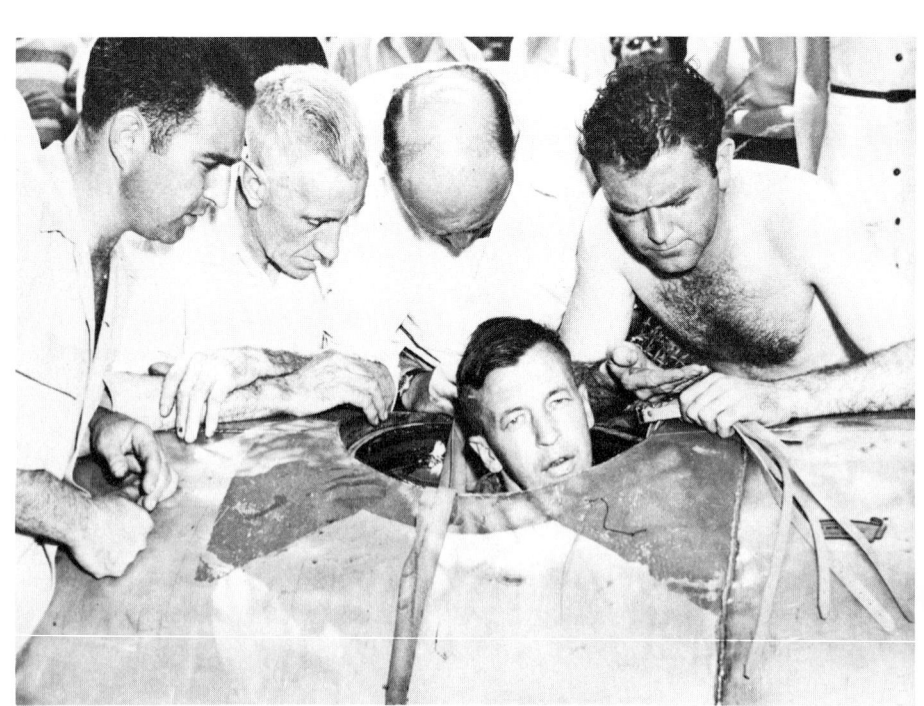

Major Hill, another of Red's sons, tried to go over the falls, but his barrel got stuck at a power intake near the edge. (Courtesy of Corky McKenzie)

A helicopter crashes above the falls during a rescue attempt in 1950. (Niagara Falls Gazette)

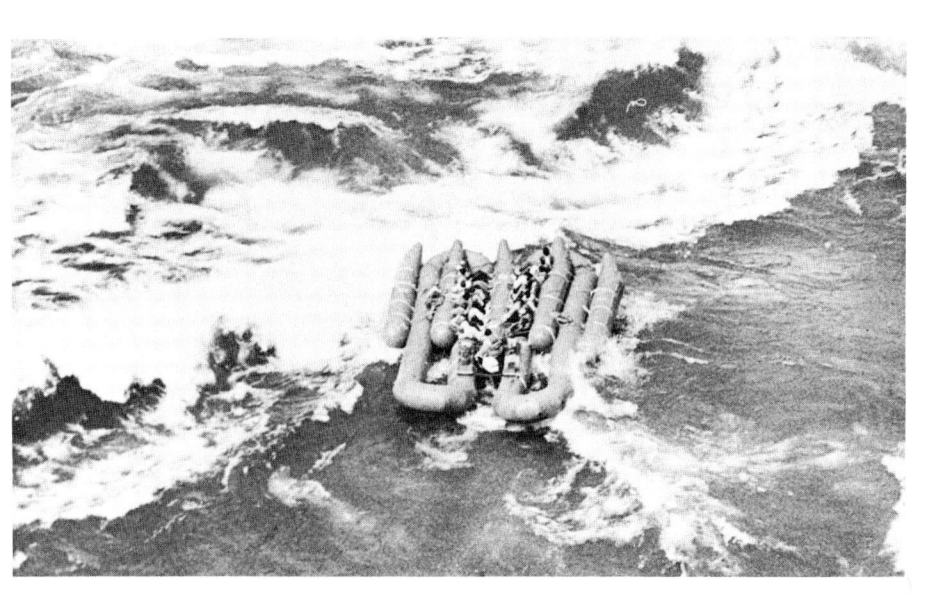

A 1975 attempt to run tourist rafts through the gorge ended when this 37-foot raft overturned on a test ride, drowning three passengers. (Niagara Falls Gazette)

Historical sites: (above) Laura Secord's house; (below) Old Fort Erie, manned by cadets in the summer. (Ontario Ministry of Industry and Tourism)

The much-damaged Brock Monument at Queenston. The general's arm was replaced in 1930. *(Ontario Ministry of Industry and Tourism)*

Killer whales at Marineland, in Niagara Falls, Ontario. (Ontario Ministry of Industry and Tourism)

Ontario Hydro's Floral Clock in Queenston draws large crowds of tourists. (Ontario Ministry of Industry and Tourism)

This picture of the Spanish Aero Car was taken in 1916. It is still a popular tourist attraction. (Earl Brydges Library, Niagara Falls, N.Y.)

The Horseshoe Falls: night illuminations. (Ontario Ministry of Industry and Tourism)

Maid of the Mist *approaching the Horseshoe Falls. (Ontario Ministry of Industry and Tourism)*

In the absence of the queen, the Fenians seized all the food and whiskey they could find, commandeered horses and carts, and lumbered off in the direction of the Welland Canal. O'Neill thought of destroying one of the locks as a gesture before proceeding either forward or back; but before he reached the canal, he was attacked by several hundred ill-led and disorganized Canadian militia. His seasoned troops fought them off, killing 9 and capturing 30. Crowds on the American side of the Niagara cheered when they heard the news. After two days of Fenian indecision and Canadian bungling, a column of British regulars marched toward Fort Erie. The invaders split up, took to their boats, and hurried back across the river.

O'Neill and 700 of his men were arrested for breach of the U.S. neutrality laws, but were released without trial. The U. S. Army commander ordered his forces along the frontier to guard against "further Fenian activity," but the U.S. government refused to accept responsibility for the invasion launched from its territory. Canada received no compensation for the damage done and men killed. The provinces were frightened and humiliated. Their militia had been routed by a bunch of crazy Irishmen who had escaped unpunished, thanks to the conniving Yankees.

There would be other Fenian raids on Canada—all failures—but none had the salutary effect of the Niagara episode. For two years the Fathers of Canadian Confederation had been trying unsuccessfully to father it. They had feasted, drunk, and argued their way from Prince Edward Island to the Niagara peninsula, endeavoring to hammer out a constitution containing sufficient compromises to unite the squabbling provinces and meld them into a semi-independent Kingdom of Canada. At the last moment Nova Scotia, New Brunswick, and Prince Edward Island shied away, and hope faded for the new nation.

O'Neill's raid changed that in two days. Anti-American feeling spurted like sap from the maples; the Maritime provinces swung back toward Confederation and on July 1, 1867, just thirteen months after the Fenians landed, the kingdom came into being. It was called a Dominion to satisfy the antimonarchist French and the former Americans who made up a large part of the small population, but it was united under the monarchy.

Soon it would stretch from coast to coast, fulfilling geographically—if not politically—the vision of John O'Mahoney. The Celtic prophet should be included among the Fathers of Confederation—although the creation of a new British nation was the very last thing he had in mind.

The Fenian raid was the last armed incursion across the Niagara frontier, although tensions persisted for years along that part of the great "undefended border" between the United States and Canada, and both sides maintained defenses until the 1890s. The era of mutual suspicion ended around the turn of the century. Appropriately, the magnificent Clifton House, home of the Confederate plotters, burned down in a sensational fire in 1898.

10
The Awful Eye

The eye of the great whirlpool is the most sinister sight along the river—a dark hole like a gullet leading down to appalling depths and a colossal stomach in which the Niagara would hold and digest its victims of ten thousand years. In fact, the whirlpool is 126 feet deep—less than half the depth of the Devil's Hole—and the boats and bodies it swallows are usually released after a few days. But the horror remains and no one knows just what lies at the bottom.

The river waters, soothed after their leap over the falls, froth into new fury as they enter the Whirlpool Rapids and drop another 52 feet, smashing over blocks of fallen dolomite rock, then career madly, counterclockwise around an 1,800-foot-wide basin, tearing themselves open in the center, the hole. Its ways are capricious. Some small objects are seized upon and sucked under; others following the same course are spurned and tossed aside.

Until June 1861, nobody knew what the whirlpool

would do with a very large object—the seventy-two-foot paddle-steamer, *Maid of the Mist II*—but for $500, Captain Joel Robinson was prepared to find out.

The *Maid*'s voyage was no stunt; it was undertaken out of financial necessity.

The first *Maid of the Mist*, a squat, awkward-looking steam barge of 100 tons, was launched in 1846 and operated from the American side of the falls. The owners hoped she would become a link in a proposed stagecoach route between New York City and Toronto, but coach business fell off when Roebling's railway bridge opened, so the *Maid* was used to carry sightseers as close to the falls as she dared go—the route followed by all subsequent *Maids* up to the present day. She proved that it was possible to get excitingly near, shower in the spray, and bathe in the mist at no greater risk than that of catching a cold.

In 1854 she was replaced by a bigger boat, a single-stack sidewheeler commanded by Captain Robinson who, the Lockport *Courier* said, "is known the world over as one who, above all others, understands the business of navigating the Niagara in this vicinity."

The second *Maid* carried the Prince of Wales and featured in the tightrope wars between Blondin and Farini. Then came the Civil War. Tourists avoided the frontier and the *Maid* had to be sold at public auction. A condition of the sale was that she be delivered to Lake Ontario. The *Maid* had been built and launched at Niagara and spent her career trapped between the falls and the Whirlpool Rapids. No vessel had ever braved the 30 mph current of the rapids, much less the whirlpool, which seemed quite capable of swallowing a 72-foot ship with barely a belch.

Robinson was not out for glory, but needed the $500 bonus. We don't know what engineer James H. Jones and

The Awful Eye

fireman James McIntyre were promised, but they went, too, battened down below decks.

At 1:00 P.M. on June 6, Robinson wheeled the *Maid* out from her dock on the New York side and headed up toward the falls. In midstream he abruptly swung her round and headed downstream until she was caught and dragged into the rapids. The paddles thumped ineffectually, trying to hold her straight. She slewed to one side. Then the first big wave hit her, snapped off the funnel, swept the deck, and seemed to engulf her in seething foam. Down below, Jones was dashed against a wall. McIntyre clung to a rail in the furnace room and prayed. Robinson lost his grip on the wheel and was hurled across the wheelhouse as the *Maid* staggered out of control. But she righted herself, shook the water off her deck, and was still steaming and paddling furiously as she charged the whirlpool. Robinson regained the wheel and tried to nudge her nose outward as she began circling, dangerously near to the eye. She was moving smoothly now. McIntyre piled more wood into his furnace, and Jones urged his 100-horsepower engine to its limit. After three or four circles, she began to answer to her helm and moved farther out from the vortex. Gradually she broke free and sailed, battered but triumphant, for the smooth waters downstream.

Robinson brought her into the dock at Queenston. Since he had come from the American side, a dour Canadian customs man made him fill out entry papers and pay port fees before allowing him to land. The *Maid* was the first and last ship to arrive there from upstream. Robinson's feat remains unique. Apparently he was so shaken that he never again sailed the Niagara. The *Maid* was given a new funnel and paddled calmly on to Montreal, to serve for many years as a St. Lawrence River ferry.

The whirlpool had been beaten for the first time. In view of the senseless tragedies that followed, perhaps it was a pity the *Maid* got through. While the high-wire artists still cavorted overhead, a new series of stunters tackled the river, with much less success.

In June 1883 a squat figure in pearl-colored derby and gray frock coat climbed from his carriage on the Canadian cliff top, made his way down to the river's edge, and eyed the haystack billows that had smashed the steamer's smokestack. "A rum bit of water," he remarked. Captain Matthew Webb was billed as the world's greatest swimmer but, at thirty-five, he had passed his peak. He was five foot eight, weighed 200 pounds, and was thinning on top. Eight years earlier, as the slim, fair-haired master of a British sailing ship, he had astounded Europe by swimming the English Channel from Dover to Calais in 21 hours 45 minutes. Said the mayor of Dover: "In the future history of the world I don't believe that any such feat will be performed by anybody else." Needless to say, it was. Teen-age girls now perform it regularly, and in midsummer the Channel is as crowded as a public swimming pool in a heat wave. Captain Webb, he of the stolid breaststroke, is still hailed as its conqueror. The American Paul Boyton made the swim three months before Webb, but he wore a life jacket, and thus is forgotten.

Captain Webb never returned to his ship. He toured English seaside resorts giving swimming lessons at a time when sea-bathing was in its infancy and few people could swim. He also set endurance records. Once he swam for 74 hours. But by 1881 he had exhausted his appeal and his bank account. He moved to the United States to try his luck anew. He lived at Nantasket Beach, Massachusetts, with his wife and two young children, giving swimming

The Awful Eye

demonstrations to small audiences. A new sensation was needed. He must master another famous stretch of water. His manager suggested Niagara.

Captain Webb told the press how he planned to navigate the rapids. He would let the current carry him downstream, using his swimming strength to make sure he stayed in the middle, away from the rocks. "When the water gets very bad," he continued, "I will go under the surface and remain beneath until I am compelled to come up for lack of breath. . . . When I get through I will try to land on the Canadian side but if the current is too swift I will keep on down to Lewiston on the American side."

On the day of Webb's swim, the crowds on the cliffs and the suspension bridge were sure he'd never come out of the water alive—if he went in at all. There was the same skepticism as on the afternoon of Blondin's first walk. Nobody could be that crazy. Bets were taken that Webb would stay in his boat.

As ferryman Jack McCloy rowed the tubby swimmer down the calmer stretch, he asked Webb if he had any money left over from his Channel triumph. "Most of it is gone," said Webb. "If I was you," said the river veteran, "I'd go ashore and keep the rest."

Webb did not reply. The smooth green water tugged faster, and McCloy pulled against the current to hold his boat back. Then came the point of no return. Whitewater showed several hundred feet ahead. Without a word, the captain stood up on a thwart and plunged cleanly over the side. McCloy hauled his boat back.

The people on the bridge saw the little figure in red bathing trunks, arms sweeping strongly, glide ever faster toward the foam. He shot under the bridge and hit the first great wave. He vanished, reappeared, was thrown from one whitecap to another, then vanished again. For a minute there was nothing but churning water to be seen.

("I will go under the surface and remain beneath until I am compelled to come up for lack of breath.") Two hundred yards nearer the whirlpool, he shot halfway out of the river—alive, or dead, conscious or not, no one could tell. Another hill of water collapsed over him, and Captain Webb disappeared for good. Less than four minutes had elapsed since he hit the first wave.

Webb's body was never seen in the whirlpool, but it must have been sucked down and held there, for it was four days before it turned up on the shore near Lewiston. ("If the current is too swift, I will keep on down to Lewiston.") He lay face down, arms and legs extended as if in his famous breaststroke. There were no bones broken and he had not drowned. Three examining doctors concluded that the force of the water had pressed the life out of him. They added in their report: "No living body can, or ever will, pass through the rapids alive."

This warning failed to discourage others. Nor did a stern editorial in *The Saturday Review*:

> It was unquestionably very appropriate that Mr. Webb should have met his death in America; and in sight of the United States. That country has a passion for big shows, and has now been indulged in the biggest thing of its kind which has been seen in this generation. Nothing was to be gained by success—if success had been possible—beyond a temporary notoriety and the applause of the mob. . . . As long as there is a popular demand for these essentially barbarous amusements, men and women will be found who are desperate, or greedy, or vain enough to risk their lives and ruin their health for money or applause. . . . The death of Mr. Webb is shocking in the last degree; but it

The Awful Eye

will not be wholly useless if it at least awakes the sightseeing world to some sense of what it is they have been encouraging.

The sightseeing world did not awaken and neither did the desperate adventurers. Webb was barely in his grave at Oakwood Cemetery, Niagara Falls, when James Scott, a Lewiston fisherman, followed him into the rapids and met the same fate.

However, the doctors proved to be wrong. Three years later, William Kendall, a Boston policeman, swam the rapids and lived. He wore a life jacket.

After swimmers, the sightseers demanded more and better useless stunts in the whitewater, and the desperate, the greedy, and the vain were ready to provide them. The barrel craze began.

Only a man who made barrels for a living would have thought of them as river vessels. Sure enough, it was a cooper from Philadelphia, Carlisle D. Graham, who built the first navigable barrel. It was made of the strongest oak he could find—seven feet long and equipped with a canvas and string bag inside. Graham fitted himself into the bag and had the barrel tossed into the rapids on July 11, 1886. He came through unscathed, barrel and all, so tried again a month later. This time he left his head sticking out of one end of the barrel and the pounding of the waves made him deaf.

Graham, now called the Hero of the Rapids, gave up coopering for stunting. One Niagara historian has given him credit for designing a barrel that could conceivably be used to save people from shipwrecks, but Graham himself never made that claim. He built barrels to hold beer, which made sense—or to carry passengers through the gorge, which made no sense, but a fair amount of money. He had no higher aspirations for barrels.

Weeks after his first barrel ride, two Buffalo coopers, George Hazlett and William Potts, lugged their super-keg to the river. It was a great two-seater barrel, and its makers rode the rapids crammed inside it. It seemed that the whirlpool had no taste for big barrels and spat them out. Later Hazlett added a romantic touch by taking his girl friend Sadie Allen along with him in the same cask. Barrel riding looked easy.

The first woman to barrel ride all by herself was Martha Wagenfuhrer, who timed her adventure for September 6, 1901, in the hope that President McKinley would watch during his state visit to the Niagara area. It was not a fortunate choice of date. The President was shot and fatally wounded by the anarchist Leon Czolgosz at Buffalo. Martha was slightly drunk when she climbed into her barrel. She got through the rapids very quickly, but got stuck in the outer reaches of the whirlpool. It took an hour to rescue her. When they opened the lid and pulled her out of the barrel, the first thing she demanded was a drink of water.

In the same year, Maude Willard of Canton, Ohio, borrowed her friend Graham's original barrel, now fifteen years old, and took it for its final outing. Unfortunately, she brought her dog along, insisting that it travel with her, and that probably cost her her life because the barrel spun around for six hours in the whirlpool and there was not enough oxygen in it for two creatures. When it was opened, the dog was alive. Maude was not.

That same day Graham, having abandoned barrels, made the first successful swim without a life jacket from the whirlpool to Lewiston. He expected to meet Maude

The Awful Eye

there, but when he was washed up alive at Lewiston she was still whirling around upstream, dead in the barrel he had made. It was one of Niagara's more poignant moments, but few stopped to ponder or weep because the frenzy of activity in the rapids was mounting.

Charles Alexander Percy, a local wagon builder, watched the barrels bouncing in the violent water and figured out a design for an unsinkable boat. It was 17 feet long, strongly made of hickory, covered with canvas, and weighted down with 900 pounds of iron to hold it upright. One day in 1887 Percy crawled into a watertight compartment deep in his boat and launched himself on a course pioneered by the barrel makers. The whirlpool sucked his craft under but did not take it down to its depths. It bobbed up again after 25 minutes, spun out from the whirling coils, and Percy climbed out and rowed ashore.

The dreaded black hole in the water was not as dreadful as had been feared. Or so it seemed.

The following year Robert Flack of Syracuse built a similar boat and challenged Percy to a race around the vortex. He tried his boat out first on an experimental run and the vortex sucked him in. The boat went down the eye of the whirlpool with Flack strapped to it, then was tossed out vertically and fell on its builder, killing him. Percy, who was watching from the bank, swam out to the edge of the whirlpool, but Flack was beyond help.

Undeterred by this, Walter G. Campbell entered the rapids in an ordinary open boat, which he paddled standing up. As might have been expected, it capsized long before it reached the haystack waves. Campbell reached shore, but a black dog he had taken with him drowned.

The craziness continued. Campbell had proved you

could not shoot the rapids in an open boat. Peter Nissen of Chicago decided to start a passenger service through the rapids—using an open boat. It was a 16-foot steam launch, equipped with flotation chambers, and bore the uninviting name *Fool Killer*.

Its maiden voyage in 1900 did little to entice prospective passengers. With only Nissen aboard, it struggled through to the whirlpool, then suddenly nosedived into the hole, heaving its stern in the air. When half its length had disappeared and it seemed to be heading straight for the bottom, the whirlpool abruptly spat it out. It hurled backward into the air, landed right side up, and was steered ashore. Nissen survived to try again the next year. Still no passengers came forward, so *Fool Killer* set off once more with only its owner aboard. It was so badly battered in the rapids that it reached the outer lip of the whirlpool minus rudder, propeller, and smokestack. Not relishing another nose dive, Nissen jumped ship and swam ashore. So ended the first attempt to sell tickets for the world's worst ride. It was not the last.

While madness raged in the gorge, a truly lunatic idea was forming in the mind of a mousy little schoolmistress in Bay City, Michigan. Mrs. Anna Edson Taylor was not the type to frequent Bowery bars but she may have heard the tall tale of famed New York barkeeper Steve Brodie, who boasted that he had gone over the falls in a padded rubber suit. Steve's story has never been taken too seriously but he holds a record as the first person to *claim* to have made the drop and lived.

Mrs. Taylor was the first to actually do it. She was the most unlikely of stunters—a plain, childless widow of forty-three. She had never had an adventure in her life so far as was known; she had seldom ventured beyond Bay City.

The Awful Eye

Yet, beneath her frumpish exterior, beat the heart of a Blondin. True, she needed money. With only her schoolteacher's pittance, she could look forward to a penniless old age. On the other hand, she had no children to support and would doubtless have managed somehow. Fame was the spur that sent Annie over Niagara Falls in a whiskey barrel.

As she explained in a booklet published in 1902, she was reading a newspaper story about visitors to the falls when the idea "came to me like a flash of light. Go over Niagara Falls in a barrel! No one had ever accomplished this feat. I did not think it wrong as there was nothing immodest in the act, nor did it involve the life of anyone but myself. . . . I immediately set to work to shape a barrel, which I did, cutting it out of paper and sewing it together with twine. . . ."

In the fall of 1901, after Maude Willard suffocated in her barrel and the *Fool Killer* made its last voyage, Mrs. Taylor arrived with her barrel, made from her paper pattern. It was an oak cask, 54 inches high, 22 inches in diameter at the top, 34 inches in the middle, and 15 inches at the bottom, and the same weight as the plump teacher: 160 pounds. To test it, she sent it over the brink with a cat inside. The barrel survived but the cat died. This did not stop Annie, who had come for her first and, as seemed highly probable, her last big adventure.

On October 4, 1901, she sat sedately in the sternsheets of a rowboat and was taken to Grass Island, above the falls. The barrel was towed behind the boat. She wore a long black dress with billowing sleeves and a tightly pinched waist, a large black hat, and long gloves. She had refused to dress for the barrel before leaving Niagara Falls, New York, because, she said, a short skirt "would be unbecoming to a woman of refinement and my years."

On the island she made her boatmen turn their backs and went into some bushes to take off her hat and stockings and put on the necessary short skirt (which came down below her knees). The boatmen squeezed her into the barrel through an opening at the top and strapped her into a harness inside. Pillows were stuffed in for padding. "*Au revoir*," Annie said pointedly. "I'll not say good-bye because I'm coming back."

Boatman William Holloran screwed down the lid, then pumped air into the barrel with a bicycle pump for 20 minutes. "We've given her enough gas for a week," he said, then helped roll the barrel into the river. The boat towed it into the main stream leading to Horseshoe Falls. Holloran rapped twice on the top—a signal to Annie that she was on her way—then cut it adrift. It banged from rock to rock, buffeting the woman inside as it entered the shallows near the brink. A 100-pound anvil was tied to the bottom to keep it upright. Apparently this touched bottom in the final rush of smooth water, tilting the barrel forward. It nosed over the brink and vanished in the spray.

Annie remembered falling. The sound of lapping water and bumping rocks ceased. Then the barrel hit the water with an immense crash and she remembered no more. She lay unconscious while the barrel bobbed up below the falls and slowly drifted toward the Canadian shore. Seventeen minutes after it went over the top, it grounded on an outcrop of rock. Rescuers climbed out on poles and planks to haul it ashore. The lid was jammed tight and they had to saw it off. They feared what they might find inside.

The top came off and the first man peered in. "My God, she's alive!" he yelled. The cry was echoed along the

The Awful Eye

shore and cheers went up from the crowds on Table Rock. They spread to the American side, and roars of applause challenged the thunder of the water.

Annie was soaked and bleeding from a cut jaw as they pulled her out. Dazed and slightly delirious, she had to be helped over the rocks. For the first half-hour she could not remember what had happened. Then she changed into her long black dress, smoothed herself down, and smiled in triumph.

The triumph did not last. She toured the vaudeville theaters for a while, but her prim, retiring personality did not make a hit. Once the audiences had seen her and heard her brief, confused tale, there was nothing left to say. She returned to Niagara Falls as "The Queen of the Mist" to sell autographed pictures of herself standing beside a barrel. It wasn't even her barrel, for she lost that. Some accounts say it was stolen; others, that it was left in the water and rotted. Either way, Annie Taylor had nothing left. Twenty years after her one big day, she was buried in a pauper's grave at Niagara Falls, New York.

The sight of the sad Queen of the Mist hawking her postcards discouraged stunters for ten years. Then, in July 1911, they returned to the falls in force. Bobby Leach, a chirpy little Londoner, had the gift of the gab that Annie lacked. Once over the falls, he knew he could talk about it for years. He was a professional circus stunt man and he surveyed Niagara with a cool eye, selecting the stunts to be performed there. He decided to go through the rapids in a barrel, then over the falls in a barrel and, finally, parachute into the rapids from the upper suspension bridge. He used a steel drum, which he entered from a manhole on the side. It floated horizontally most of the time. The drum bobbed through the rapids in fine style, then stuck in the whirlpool, spinning Bobby round and round until he lost consciousness.

He was rescued by the king of the Niagara rivermen William (Red) Hill, Sr., who was to take part in every famous rescue for the next thirty years. The Hill family had lived along the river for a century. When he was five years old, Red was thrown into it by his father and commanded to sink or swim. He swam and from then on he never feared the current or the rapids, although he respected them. No one knew Niagara like Red, Sr. He always seemed to be available when someone required rescue—he won his first lifesaving medal at the age of seven by hauling his aunt from a blazing building—but he earned his living by salvaging the remains of those beyond rescue. Over the years he hauled 177 bodies from the Niagara, at a bounty of up to $25 each because he and his family knew every eddy and every mood of the river.

Bobby Leach recovered his spirits and his steel drum and proceeded with Stunt Number Two. He took the same route over the falls as Annie Taylor, but hit bottom much harder, breaking his jaw and both kneecaps, and spent six months in the hospital. He presented his drum to Red Hill and forced his newly healed limbs into a parachute harness and jumped from the suspension bridge. He did not land in the rapids, as planned, but drifted safely over the river and came down in a cornfield. For the next fifteen years, he lectured on his daredevil exploits and made a fair living. Then, in Christchurch, New Zealand, the apparently indestructible Cockney was skipping happily along a street when he slipped on a piece of orange peel and broke his leg. The fracture became infected, and he died two months later.

Two days after Bobby's barrel drop in 1911, the marvels

The Awful Eye

of aviation came to Niagara. To celebrate the opening of an international river carnival, stunt pilot Lincoln Beachey flew his box-kite Curtiss biplane over the falls and under the Upper Steel Arch Bridge.

Remember, this was less than eight years after the Wright Brothers' first flight. No one had flown *under* anything before. Aviators spent their time trying to keep their machines aloft. Beachey told the Niagara Falls *Gazette*:

> For a portion of the trip my eyes were shut and I cannot now remember whether they were shut or open when I went under the bridge. But I do know this. I dropped so fast that the flow of gasoline was stopped and the engine missed several times. That has happened with me before but never in such a dangerous place. The spray from the falls cut my face like a knife and struck my eyes so I had to shut them.
>
> It was just under the bridge that the machine seemed to go down and down as though it was in a vacuum. The space under the bridge seemed awfully small when I was down there in the river. I was close to the Canadian side because the air currents from the American falls drove me over that way. I wanted to pass under the center of the bridge. There was between six and twenty feet between the top plane and the arch of the bridge, and I was probably twenty feet above the water.

Beachey then pulled hard back on his joystick and just managed to ease the biplane up and over the lower bridges. He got $1,000 for the flight.

The next barrel dropper, in 1930, was another Englishman, Charles Stephens, who had eleven children to support and gambled on either raising them in style or leaving them fatherless. Stubbornly rejecting the advice of Bobby Leach and Red Hill, he used an oak barrel with a

100-pound anvil in the bottom. Annie Taylor had also used an anvil but had not attached it to herself. Stephens tied his anvil to his feet. In the drop the bottom fell out of the barrel, and the weight of the anvil tore him apart. All that was found of him was one arm, strapped inside the barrel.

Red Hill made three successful trips through the rapids in Bobby Leach's barrel but for nearly twenty years, daredevils avoided the falls themselves. Then along came Jean Lussier, a cheery French-Canadian who literally bounced— in a six-foot rubber ball he designed himself. It was a double-walled steel frame covered with 32 automobile inner tubes, interconnected and containing oxygen at 35 pounds' pressure. It was built by a rubber manufacturer in Ohio and proved to be as safe as today's steel-wall radial tires.

On July 4, 1928, Lussier, in his ball, bounced over the Horseshoe, surfaced 65 seconds later, drifted for an hour, and was fished out. Emerging unscathed, he said the drop felt like a ski jump. He said his only fear was that the police might seize it before it went over, for barrel-type stunts were now forbidden. For him, the race with the police was the most exciting event of the day.

Although born in Quebec, Lussier worked as a machinist in Niagara Falls, New York, and was no innocent to the ways of the tourist frontier. He avoided managers and promoters and signed no contracts. He displayed his ball, told his story for a fee, and sold thumbnail-sized bits of the ball to visitors at 50 cents each. Large amounts of rubber were sold over the years, but the ball remained more or less intact. When Niagara locals remarked that his supply of inner tubes was lasting well, the daredevil grinned and said there were plenty to be had at a nearby service station.

"Hundreds of tubes I sold," he told an interviewer. "One day I talked to a fellow from Paris. I showed him my

The Awful Eye

ball and told him all about it. He talked French. I talked French. I winked at a cabbie and said, 'My friend here, he will show you the falls.' '*Non, non,*' he said, 'I got bad heart, I can't stand look down.'

"'Look, *mon ami,*' I said. 'You can't go away without seeing the falls. The falls she is the seventh wonder of the world. I am the seventh son of seven. My father, he is a seventh son. I go over the falls in the seventh month. See? Here, hold this piece of rubber from Jean's ball next the heart—fifty cents please—look at the falls and your heart will feel fine.'"

The Frenchman came back a few hours later declaring that his heart did feel fine and he wanted a *big* chunk of the magic rubber.

"I gave Frenchie a piece so big," Lussier chuckled, indicating the size of his palm. "He gave me ten dollars, the cabbie slipped me three dollars—everybody happy!"

Jean and his ball lived happily for many years, having proved that falling over the falls could be safe and profitable. And despite the police ban on stunts, the barrel craze continued.

George Stathakis, of Buffalo, a Greek chef and religious mystic, went over in 1930 holding his pet turtle. He used the biggest barrel yet—a one-ton wood-and-steel monster that contained sufficient oxygen to keep him alive for 3 hours. But it was trapped behind the foot of the cataract for 22 hours. Stathakis slowly died. The turtle survived.

William (Red) Hill, Jr., should have known better. Like his father, Red, Sr., and his three brothers, he knew the river and lived off it. They called themselves River Rats and when not rescuing stunters and people who accidentally fell in, they recovered the bodies of suicides. They knew exactly where to look for them. Red, Sr., had made three barrel trips through the Whirlpool Rapids and had swum across the river just above the rapids, but knew better than to tackle the falls. Red, Jr., and brother Major (a name, not a rank) had followed their father in barrel rides through the rapids. But young Red determined to do something no Hill had been foolish enough to try. He put together a rubber contraption based on Lussier's ball but flimsily made. It consisted of thirteen inner tubes held together by light canvas straps and fishnet. He called it The Thing. The other River Rats said it would never hold together. Young Red said, "The worst I'll get will be a wetting."

On August 5, 1951, he dodged the police, climbed into The Thing, and drifted off to a terrible death. The Thing was torn and battered in the upper rapids long before it reached the brink. It was upended, tossed in the air, and ripped by sharp rocks. The bindings were coming apart before it went over.

What emerged below was a tangle of deflated tubes, loose netting, and a red air mattress. The River Rats found Hill's mangled body in the river the next day. They knew exactly where to look.

The last barrel stunter was—and remains—a mystery man. Alone among the extroverts, fortune hunters, and desperate souls who dared the awful plunge, "Nathan Boya" seems to have sought nothing for himself—not even death. He did not publicize his drop and did not capitalize on it afterward. He paid $5,000 to have a ball built in the style of Lussier's—Lussier is said to have advised him on the design—and later paid $113 in fines for performing an illegal stunt. Then he vanished without leaving his real name.

On July 15, 1961, the ball suddenly appeared on the Canadian bank below the falls. The man inside was trying to close the hatch when Corporal Sawada of the Niagara Parks Police hailed him and told him he was under arrest. It was a far cry from Annie Taylor's wild applause.

The man inside looked surprised. He told the corporal he was trying to shut the hatch, which had sprung open, before going over the cataract. He didn't know he was already over and down in the gorge. He gave the name "Nathan Boya" but would not give the reason for his adventure. He said it was "very, very personal."

The police found a banner inside the ball inscribed *Plunge-O-Sphere. Step from your Pit of Darkness into light-Dell.* Boya wouldn't say what, if anything, that meant. An International Business Machines official in New York said the ball-plunger was an IBM maintenance man from the Bronx named William Fitzgerald, but Boya denied this.

His story ends in Niagara Falls, Ontario, City Court where he paid his fines, then picked up his ball, and left with his "very, very personal" secret.

Police still keep a lookout for strange objects towed by boat above the falls. Someday, in some new kind of barrel, ball, or whatever, someone will try it again. There is no regular patrol to guard against tightrope walkers because no one is likely to string a rope up overnight. Walks across the gorge are banned, not because of danger to the walker, since all but one artist proved it was safe, but because of the hazard to crowds who line the banks in such great numbers that someone might fall or be accidentally pushed over. The only surviving tightrope is a miniature one outside the Louis Tussaud Wax Museum in Niagara Falls, Ontario, which carries a figure of Blondin. (His bicycle, wheelbarrow, and a piece of his original rope are on display inside.)

So the authorities were caught off guard when yet another tightrope walker appeared in 1975. Henri Rechatin, a French acrobat, didn't bring a rope of his own. He used one of the cables carrying a classic Niagara vehicle—the Spanish Aerocar. This forty-passenger successor to Ellett's iron basket travels 1,700 feet across the Whirlpool Rapids, allowing riders to stare into its awful eye from the air. As it seems to cross the Niagara River, most people think they are traveling from Canada to the United States.

An escaped Canadian convict once made that mistake. He leaped off at the "American" end, only to find he was still in Canada, for the river makes a sharp bend at the whirlpool. And few of the 250,000 who ride on it each season (April to October) realize that it is more than sixty years old and little changed since it made its first journey on August 9, 1916. It was owned by a group of Spanish businessmen and designed by the Spanish engineer Leonardo Torres-Quevedo on the lines of a cableway at Mount Ulia in Spain. The car was built in Bilbao. It travels on six one-inch steel ropes, held taut by a 10-ton counterweight at one end and is hauled by a $7/8$-inch wire driven by a 75-horsepower electric motor. For its first forty-five years, auxiliary power was supplied by an ancient Buick gasoline motor. This has now been replaced along with the original braking system but the original electric motor is purring along. No one has been injured on the Aerocar in its long history, which is some kind of record for any form of transportation—not even Henri Rechatin.

That acrobat sneaked out at six-thirty one morning in the off season with his wife, Janyck, motorcyclist Frank Lucas, of Toronto, a publicity man, and several reporters and photographers who had been tipped off. Lucas drove his tire-less bike along a rope while Rechatin balanced on top and Janyck dangled from a trapeze hanging below it. There was a heart-stopping moment in the best Blondin tradition when one wheel slipped off and Rechatin had to climb down and heave bike, rider, and suspended wife back onto the track. The police arrived when the stunt was over.

That same year, Toronto travel agent George Butterfield tried to revive Nissen's scheme of running tourist rides along the gorge and through the rapids. His 37-foot rubber raft made ten experimental manned trips along the old barrel and lifeboat route, and Butterfield was almost ready to sell tickets to the public when disaster struck. On the eleventh voyage, the raft carried twenty-nine volunteers, including two experienced whitewater pilots. All wore life jackets. It hit a sudden "haystack" wave and flipped over. Although there were rescuers waiting on the banks and helicopters overhead, three people drowned.

The tourist trips were canceled. The river had won.

Still Niagara attracts fools and heroes. In August 1976 tourists on Goat Island spotted flares fired from an object snagged on the rocks in shallow water a few hundred yards from the brink of the Horseshoe Falls. The flares were red, white, and green—the colors of the Hungarian flag—and they came from a six-foot steel cylinder, buoyed up by two beer kegs. A helicopter lowered rescuers to the cylinder. They turned it over to expose its submerged hatch.

Power plants on both sides of the river opened their intake gates to lower the water level and to make sure that the cylinder stayed trapped. The hatch was opened, to reveal Tibor Hetenyi, a twenty-six-year-old Hungarian from Edison, New Jersey, the latest would-be barrel jumper.

"Did I go over?" he asked. No, said the police, and charged him with disorderly conduct.

Since La Salle's *Griffon* first floundered in the currents of the Upper River, there has been real, if remote, danger of boats miles upstream being sucked toward the brink of the falls. The 1953 movie *Niagara*, featuring Marilyn Monroe at the peak of her success and beauty, dramatized a narrow escape and added new dimensions to the spectacle of Niagara. The world's most famous blonde was strangled on film by Joseph Cotten among the bells of the carillon tower on the Canadian side. Cotten was swept over the falls in a cabin cruiser.

A rusted-out iron scow still lies aground in the rapids 300 yards from the falls on the Canadian side. It has been there since August 6, 1918, when it broke loose while being towed by a tug a mile from the brink. The two men aboard, Gustav Loftberg and James Harris, both of Buffalo, spent frantic minutes arguing what to do. Loftberg decided to stay with the ship if it went over and tied himself to a deck rail. Harris tied himself to an empty barrel and prepared to jump, hoping he'd float free and reach shore. However, they had dropped the anchor and opened the dumping doors in the scow's bottom. The anchor slowed the scow, and it settled gradually as it filled, hitting bottom on a rock ledge. Hydro workers and lifesavers shot a rocket line from the top of the nearby Toronto Power House. The stranded men grabbed it and winched in a heavy cable attached to it which a hundred volunteers had heaved up to the powerhouse roof. Attempts were made to rig a breeches buoy but the lines fouled and tangled. Red Hill arrived, fresh from the trenches of World War I and took command, as he usually did in rescue operations. He crawled out on the lines toward the scow and tried to untangle them. Darkness fell, and he struggled with the ropes in the beams of searchlights, wavering a few feet above the boiling rapids. He failed to clear the tangle and climbed back, leaving the two men to spend a terror-filled night, expecting that at any moment the scow would slip off the rock and make its final plunge. At daybreak Hill climbed back out to within 40 yards of the wreck, shouted instructions to the men, and rigged the breeches buoy. At 9:00 A.M. Loftberg adjusted the harness around Harris. More than a hundred men tugged at the rope and he moved, painfully slowly, over and sometimes through the water, then up to the powerhouse roof. The haul took 45 minutes; Loftberg made it in half an hour. They had been aground on the brink of Niagara for 18 hours. Harris lived in Buffalo for the rest of his life, but would never look at the river again. When they helped him out of the breeches buoy, he said, "I'm going back inland somewhere and lash myself to a tree. Then I'll know I'm safe." Apparently he meant it.

The old scow now has bushes growing through it, for the water level has dropped since 1918. In exceptionally low periods in the winter visitors can see the remains of its companion, the World War I U.S. submarine chaser *Sunbeam*. It was bought as war surplus in 1923 by a Chicago businessman, Seymour Lasker, who intended to convert it into a private yacht. With a crew of three, he sailed the *Sunbeam* from New York, along the Erie Canal and into Lake Erie, heading for Chicago; but took a wrong turn and ended at Chippawa—the wrong end of the lake. He and his crew tied the ship up for the night and went ashore. Obviously, they didn't tie her up tight enough. The next morning, she appeared beside the scow. She had drifted downstream, struck a rock, and turned on her side.

Red Hill bought the subchaser for a dollar and made plans to salvage her, but the Niagara Parks Commission demanded that he put up a bond to pay for any damage caused to parklands by the salvage operations. Hill was forced to abandon the vessel and his hopes of making money out of her. Heroes seldom get rich—at least not at Niagara. The *Sunbeam*'s wooden hull has been smashed and carried away by the ice, but her boiler and propeller shaft are still there.

More than a dozen people have been rescued by helicopter in the past ten years after their boats' motors failed in the Upper River, and six others have been swept to their deaths. Rescue methods have improved, but the river remains deadly.

It is also unpredictable. The so-called Miracle at Niagara proved that. It was not a true miracle in the religious sense because there are logical explanations for it, but it was a popular and newspaper miracle: the most amazing escape in Niagara's history. On July 9, 1960, seven-year-old Roger Woodward fell over the Horseshoe Falls and lived.

Roger and his seventeen-year-old sister, Deanne, newly arrived in Niagara Falls, New York, had gone for a boat ride with their father's friend James Honeycutt in the calm waters five miles above the falls. Honeycutt, aged forty, worked with their father, Frank Woodward, on a New York State power project, but he underestimated the power of the river. Deanne sat in the bow of his 14-foot aluminum boat, Roger in the stern beside Honeycutt, who was at the tiller of the 7½-horsepower outboard. The children were in bathing suits, and Roger was wearing a life jacket. All seemed smooth and safe on that gorgeous summer's day as Honeycutt steered the boat downstream and past the Ontario Hydro control dam, which reaches out

The Awful Eye

from the Canadian side, one third of the way across the river. The dam, built to smooth the flow of water and reduce erosion, is generally considered the point of no return for small boats. It is one mile from the brink. Beyond that, the current picks up speed. The boat chugged smoothly on. Tourists on Goat Island saw it approach and wondered.

Half a mile from the brink, Deanne, in the bow, saw the spray approaching and panicked, shouting at Honeycutt to turn back. He swung the boat broadside to the current and tried to head for Goat Island, but they were in the rapids now, where the river drops 50 feet in the last few hundred yards before the big drop. The motor hit a rock and sheared a pin. It tilted forward. The propeller raced uselessly out of the water. Honeycutt dragged out his oars, fitted them frantically into the oarlocks, and began pulling and splashing against the now solid grip of the current. Deanne flung on her life jacket as the boat lurched sideways, taking on water.

Roger screamed, "We're going to die!" Deanne forgot her own terror for a moment as she tried to calm him. "I don't want to go swimming!" he cried. Then a wave flipped the boat end over end. Roger and Honeycutt were thrown ahead of it. It landed upside-down on top of Deanne. She struggled out from underneath and grabbed the wooden gunwale, but the force of the water tore her hands loose. She swam hard for Terrapin Point, where she could see people shouting and waving. The river swept her toward the point, on the edge of Goat Island—almost but not quite to shore. Hundreds stood along the iron railings, only yards away, but no one moved to save her. They seemed frozen with horror at the thought of what was about to happen.

One man broke the collective trance. John R. Hayes, a

black truck driver and auxiliary policeman from Union, New Jersey, broke through the crowd, climbed the guard rail, and stretched out an arm, grasping the rail with the other as Deanne was swept toward him. She was still too far out to reach. Hayes ran along an 18-inch ledge just above the water, then kneeled on it, hooked a foot around the bottom of the guard rail, and leaned out as far as he could above the water. He shouted to the girl to kick harder. She splashed furiously and lunged for Hayes's hand. In her last possible chance, she managed to grab his thumb with one hand.

She lay in the water, just 15 feet from the glassy brink where the waters slid so smoothly to crash on the rocks 162 feet below.

Hayes could hold her, but couldn't pull her in. Only his foot curled around the railing was holding him. He yelled for help but again the crowd gaped and did nothing until John Quattrochi, of Pennsgrove, New Jersey, barged through, climbed the railing, and grabbed Deanne's other hand. Together the two men of action pulled her to safety. "My brother," she mumbled. "Pray for him," said Quattrochi.

Captain Clifford Keech had brought his *Maid of the Mist* as close to the base of the Horseshoe Falls as he normally took her—much farther and she'd be swamped—and was about to turn back when he noticed an orange blob in the white water and peered closely. It was a life jacket with a boy in it—a boy waving and obviously alive. In twenty-three years on the *Maids*, Keech had seen nothing like this. He grabbed his ship-to-shore phone and called the *Maid*'s office to send out another boat while he tried to pick the boy up.

In the water, Roger saw the *Maid* turn away from him,

The Awful Eye

and shouted for help. His shouts were drowned by the thunder of the cataract. But Keech had turned his boat to approach the boy from upstream and keep him away from his propellers. From the starboard bow, first mate Murray Hartling and deckhand Jack Hopkins flung life belts toward the bobbing figure. At the third throw, a belt landed within two feet of Roger; he grabbed it and held on, then clambered up to lie spreadeagled on top.

Safe on the *Maid*'s deck, Roger cried, "Save my sister. She's still in there!" He had a couple of bruises on his right chin and cheek. Nothing more.

Later he told reporters, "I could feel I was falling. I was holding on to Jim [Honeycutt] but I had to let him go. Then I was falling and I hit some rocks."

The sensation of hitting rocks must have been the impact on the waters below. Roger weighed just 50 pounds, so the river above must have tossed him outward over the brink so that he fell clear of the rocks. Honeycutt fell straight down. The River Rats found his body four days later.

Roger now sells medical equipment in New Orleans. He still returns to Niagara from time to time to revisit the scene of the miracle, which was really two miracles because the last-minute rescue of his sister was almost as sensational. It, too, provided food for church sermons for months to come. For, in 1960, the United States was entering a decade of racial turmoil. And it so happened that, of the only two men with the courage to lean out and save Deanne, one was black and the other white. And they rescued her together.

11
Power and Glory

It was Daniel, one of the legendary Joncaires, who first harnessed a minute fraction of the power of Niagara and put it to work for him. As Master of the Portage in the final years of New France, he dug a narrow ditch above the falls on the American side and drew enough water from the river to turn the wheel of a small sawmill. The sawed-up lumber was used to strengthen the defenses of the House of Peace, which his father had built and which fell to the British in 1759. It was the tiny beginning of the immense complex that now provides electric power to millions. Joncaire did not invent the waterwheel, but before he built one, the force of the third mightiest waterfall in the world had been used for nothing more useful than rinsing socks.

There were few, if any, further power developments until 1805, when Augustus and Peter Porter, the Buffalo entrepreneurs who promoted the War of 1812, bought the

American falls at public auction from the State of New York. With them, they acquired the eastern rapids above and below them, and lots along the bank, reaching toward the village of Buffalo. They built a water-powered gristmill and a tannery on Joncaire's old ditch, but these were forced out of business when the Erie Canal opened twenty years later. The Porters held on to their riparian and water-power rights, knowing there was a fortune to be made, but always short of the capital needed to line their river bank with industries.

When no one would back Augustus' first scheme—to use the power of the 50-foot drop of the rapids above the American falls—he thought of a bigger one. He would by-pass the falls with a "hydraulic canal," leading to a large reservoir on the cliffs above the gorge. From this, water would gush down the cliffside to drive turbines connected by belts to industrial machinery. The Porters died before the canal was begun, and the original company went bankrupt building it. The second company ran out of money in 1860 and sold out to a third company, which was almost ruined by Civil War stoppages. In 1875, the first wheels turned in the powerhouse, operating a flour mill, but two years later the third company's creditors closed in and its assets were sold at public auction. Joseph Schoellkopf bought the lot for $71,000—a bargain price for works that had cost $1,500,000—plus the key to the might of Niagara.

Schoellkopf was neither an inventor nor a dreamer, but a successful manufacturer. He had arrived from Europe in 1844 with $800 in his wallet and set up factories in the ugly little canal town of Buffalo. When he took over the "hydraulic canal," he had no thoughts beyond belts and drive shafts. Electricity was a scientific toy with no place in a factory. It was used in telegraphy and the newly invented telephone, but seemed to have little commercial potential. Schoellkopf found several new customers for his water power, and soon the cascades spraying down from his reservoir were a sight to rival the falls themselves. Then Schoellkopf saw the light—electric light—and one of the world's first hydroelectric systems was born.

Illuminations had been a Niagara attraction since 1860, when the falls were lit up by calcium flares to mark the visit of the Prince of Wales. They added new magic to the view and extended the tourist's day. However, flares didn't burn for long, so the illuminations were reserved for special occasions—until 1881, when Charles Brush of Euclid, Ohio, brought his electric carbon arc-lights to Niagara Falls, New York. He brought sixteen of them, with a generator to run them. Schoellkopf offered the services of his water turbines to power the generator—and thus began the great union of natural forces. The waters provided the light that, in turn, lit the waters.

It was the first permanent installation of arc lamps; but, to begin with, it seemed like just another Niagara stunt—fun to watch but of no importance. For the direct current that lit the brilliant lamps could not be transmitted more than a mile or two. It could not travel the 20 miles to Buffalo, which had grown into a city of 250,000 and where it could be used to best advantage. Still, the thought that Niagara could become a gigantic powerhouse intrigued the world's best brains.

Wilhelm Siemens, the steel and electrical genius, estimated that the Horseshoe Falls alone could generate as much power in a year as that produced by burning 266 million tons of coal:

> In other words, all the coal raised throughout the world

would barely suffice to produce the amount of power that continually runs to waste at this one great fall. . . . but it would be impossible to utilize the power on the spot, the district being devoid of mineral wealth, or other natural inducements for the establishment of factories. In order to render available the force of falling water at this and hundreds of other places similarly situated, we must devise a practicable means of transporting the power.

Before that practicable means was found—in fact, before the search got under way—Thomas Evershed, a divisional engineer on the Erie Canal, proposed that 200 new factories be built at the source of the power. His plan was to build a wide-bore ice-proof tunnel, running for two and a half miles under Niagara Falls, New York, to feed thirty-eight vertical shafts containing turbines, which would power the factories by the shaft-and-belt method. A group of New York businessmen seized on the idea and formed the Niagara River Hydraulic Tunnel, Power and Sewer Company—an apt title, for if the original Evershed plan had succeeded, the factories would have turned the river into a sewer. But the company failed to attract enough investment capital, and in 1889 it was reorganized as the Niagara Falls Power Company. Meanwhile, pressure from the conservationists was growing; the move was on to preserve what was left of the beauty of the American side of the gorge. Plans were going ahead for a state park and there was no place in them for 200 industrial plants.

The new company decided to keep Evershed's tunnel scheme, but to use all its water power to generate electricity. Niagara Falls (pop. 3,500) could not possibly use the then-immense amount to be generated. A way simply had to be found to transmit it to Buffalo. The company offered a $100,000 prize to anyone who could come up

Power and Glory

with the answer. When no one did, the company president, New York banker Dean Adams, and its consulting engineer, Dr. Coleman Sellers, sailed to Europe to widen the search.

In Berlin they saw the world's largest generator, a 1,000-horsepower machine producing direct current that traveled only half a mile. In Budapest they looked at a steam-driven generator producing alternating current, but only for arc lights nearby. In Geneva they watched water power being moved along a pipe under pressure, but for less than a mile. Obviously, no electrical or hydraulic plant in Europe held the secret.

Adams and Sellers moved to London, where they set up a think tank to solve the problem. The International Niagara Commission, with headquarters in Brown's Hotel, was headed by the inventor Sir William Thomson, later Lord Kelvin. Its members included the best engineers and physicists of the day. They examined hundreds of proposals for the transmission of electricity or water power but found none worthy of the $100,000 prize. The commission split between the younger thinkers, who favored alternating current, and the older ones, who clung to the first workable electrical system: direct current. Finally, the young won. The commission's report suggested some form of AC transmission, against the advice of Kelvin and the American electrical genius Thomas Edison.

Kelvin and Edison were both wrong. The answer came eventually—not from the commission, but from Nicola Tesla, a Croatian who created an efficient AC transmission system, and George Westinghouse, the American inventor and manufacturer who adopted it. Westinghouse, a late convert to AC, installed magnificent electrical illuminations at the 1893 Chicago World's Columbian Exhibition, which outshone anything yet seen at Niagara. In 1895 the Niagara Power Company plumped for Tesla's system and placed contracts with Westinghouse for power generation, and with the General Electric Company for the lines and transformers necessary to light the city of Buffalo from Niagara.

It was a huge gamble. The largest AC generators in use were 150 horsepower, but Westinghouse undertook to build three of 5,000 horsepower each. The largest transformers carried 10 horsepower, but General Electric contracted to build ones that would handle 1,250 horsepower, while stringing overhead wires that would transmit an unheard-of 11,000 volts.

On November 15, 1896, Mayor Jewett of Buffalo threw the switch that sent this amazing surge of energy along the 20-mile line—the first long-distance transmission of electricity for commercial purposes. The ceremony was held quietly, with only a few officials present, because nobody was certain that the juice would flow. Only one local newspaper reported the event. At an official banquet two months later, Buffalo acclaimed itself the first electric city and gave credit to the combined brains of Europe and America for making this possible. Unlike most statements made at official banquets, this was no exaggeration. The perseverance of the Power Company, its creation of an international brain trust, and its refusal to accept the apparently impossible had brought about an electrical revolution. As Merrill Denison wrote in his official history of Ontario Hydro:

> A little more than a century before, James Watt's reciprocating engine had ushered in the first industrial revolution. The surge of power over the twenty-miles trans-

mission circuit from Niagara marked the dawn of a second, more tremendous in its consequences than the first. Without the long-distance transmission of electricity neither the modern mass assembly-line, nor its offspring, automation, would have been possible.*

Ironically, Schoellkopf, the pioneer of Niagara power, is best remembered today because he gave his name to a Niagara disaster. With the success of the transmission system, new electrochemical and electrometallurgical plants moved into the area and the demand for power soared. Schoellkopf Station Two was built in front of the original plant in 1895. The side of the gorge was walled in, and behind the walls shafts carried water down 210 feet to operate a new set of turbines just above river level. Behind the shafts and the rear walls of the powerhouse were the old scars in the rock, cut by the first open tailraces of the belt-and-shaft-driven mills. Over the years water seeped into them, trickling and then pouring down, eating away the shale of the escarpment and loosening the layers of hard rock.

On the morning of June 7, 1956, workers in the powerhouse noticed water seeping through the back wall. They piled up sandbags to stop it, but the seepage became a flow. By mid-afternoon there were widening cracks in the wall, and part of the floor had buckled. The forty men on the afternoon shift brought in more sandbags and tried to pump out rising pools on the floor. They left the doors open at the south end of the plant—the end nearest to the American falls—in case they had to get out in a hurry. Suddenly there was a rumble from behind the wall. One worker said, "All I know is that the walls and ceiling started to come down, window frames began to pop out, and I ran like hell."

* *The People's Power*, p. 18.

All but two of the men ran for the northern end of the plant, which was dry. Two made for the open south door and faced a raging torrent of water. One jumped across it to solid ground; the other fell short and was swept away and drowned. His was the only life lost.

Watchers on the Canadian shore heard a roar like the sound of a low-flying jet, accompanied by giant blue flashes and showers of intensely bright sparks as the generators blew out. Then the lower part of the cliff slid down toward the river, carrying part of the powerhouse with it, followed by the now-unsupported upper part, which toppled and crashed down on the wreckage. A great cloud of dust blotted out the scene. When it settled, the southern half of the Schoellkopf plant was gone.

The plant had become outmoded long before it collapsed and it was always an eyesore; so there were few mourners. During its half-century of existence, it had been superseded by colossal new hydroelectric plants which, despite their size, managed to blend with their surroundings. The struggle between industry and tourism, power and beauty, ended in compromise. It was fierce while it lasted. The Ontario government of Premier Sir Oliver Mowat was on the side of beauty and controlled power development. Although both Ontario and New York moved to protect Niagara in the same year—1885—the state's effort was confined to Goat Island, some small islets, and the river frontage along the upper rapids, which it acquired as a state reservation. Ontario designated the entire Canadian shore from Fort Erie to Niagara-on-the-Lake as parkland, excepting the towns that were already there. This worthy scheme delayed hydro development on the Canadian side and, although this was not Mowat's intention, ensured that Americans would do the initial developing.

Power and Glory   217

The new Queen Victoria Niagara Falls Parks Commission soon discovered that preserving natural beauty cost more money than it could wring from tourist concessionaires. The Ontario legislature felt that it had done its bit for Niagara by establishing the park and was not inclined to subsidize it with tax dollars. So the commission had to look across the river for money and lease the power of the Canadian falls to American interests.

The first electricity generated came from a 2,100-horsepower plant just above Table Rock, built by the American-owned Niagara Falls Park and River Railway and used to power its electric trains between Queenston and Chippawa. The scenic railway ran until 1932; the power plant still stands.

Two other American companies, later joined by a Canadian firm, were given franchises to generate a total of 400,000 horsepower, but due to financial problems and political wrangles, the first big plant was not completed until 1905. Its output was fed back across the river to the United States. Niagara Falls, Ontario, continued to generate electricity by steam until 1912.

The Canadian Niagara Power Company was incorporated in 1892 but did not begin generating until January 1, 1905, in a handsome stone station with a green tile roof about 500 yards above the Horseshoe Falls. The Ontario Power Company's station, opened later that year, is at the base of the falls, almost at river level. It takes its water from an inlet one mile upstream, bringing it down through conduits and steel penstocks tunneled through the rock. The Electrical Development Company (later Toronto Power Company) plant, which began producing in November, 1906, has the most dramatic outlet tunnel—2,000 feet long and 33 feet in diameter—which runs under the falls and has one exit leading right into the curtain of water. When it was built, it was the biggest storm sewer in the world.

Engineers drilled and blasted their way through the thunder god's lair until they had knocked a small hole in the face of the precipice. A howling blast of wind and dense clouds of spray drove them back. Water poured into the tunnel. For a time it seemed the thunder god was going to keep his domain to himself. Then the chief engineer and three others, roped together like mountain climbers, waded back in, carrying sticks of dynamite. They were battered and frequently swept off their feet by the tremendous force of wind and water, but they went back and forth carrying more and more dynamite, until an enormous charge was ready at the hole. This blew away a pile of broken rock that had been diverting the force of the falls into the tunnel. The tunnel drained, the wind died down, and bricklayers completed a portal only a few feet behind the cataract.

While these three big plants were under construction, a significant meeting was held at Berlin (now Kitchener), Ontario. Twenty-five businessmen put up a total of $45 to pay the expenses, which included lunch, and they certainly got their money's worth. For that gathering on June 9, 1902, became, in effect, the founding meeting of the multi-billion-dollar Ontario Hydro Commission, which would bring cheap electric power to the province.

At the turn of the century, supplies of wood fuel were running out and Ontario's factories depended almost entirely on coal, which was expensive because it had to be brought in from Pennsylvania or Alberta—or even shipped from Wales. Most of the electricity available was generated by coal-burning steam plants, and the plant owners not

Power and Glory

only passed on to the consumer the high cost of the coal, but added a healthy markup. The Toronto Electric Light Company, which had a near-monopoly of the city's electricity supply, not only overcharged, but dictated how much power each industry should get.

The time was ripe for public control of the distribution of electricity, and the businessmen at Berlin set up an action committee to press for it. However, the time for public ownership of the big power plants at Niagara had come and gone. The two American companies and the Canadian company had been granted irrevocable franchises to exploit the waters of the falls. The Parks Commission had even agreed not to generate any hydro power itself except for park purposes.

Niagara power became a key issue in the Ontario election of 1905. Urged on by Adam Beck, the colorful mayor of London, Ontario, who had become leader of the public-control forces, the Conservative Opposition leader James Whitney declared: "The water power of Niagara should be as free as air . . . not the sport and prey of capitalists."

Whitney won the election and promptly announced that no further water franchises would be granted at Niagara—for the time being, at least. He brought Beck into his cabinet to deal with power questions and soon afterward created the Ontario Hydro-Electric Power Commission, with Beck as chairman. It was the world's first public electrical authority. It was viewed with dark suspicion by private enterprise in the United States and Britain, and violently opposed by the private electricity interests in Canada. Beck had to campaign from town to town, persuading local politicians that he could supply power more cheaply than anyone else. He was constantly dogged by agents of the electrical companies, particularly those of the

Canadian syndicate, which owned the Electrical Development Company.

To begin with, Beck could not generate electricity; he could only buy and distribute it; so his first major project was the establishment of a transmission line from Niagara to Toronto and the towns along the way. The syndicate already had a line to Toronto, carrying 60,000 volts, which was the highest voltage then transmitted. Beck's engineers opted for 110,000 volts. The syndicate's men frightened the farmers along the Hydro route by telling them this incredibly high, dangerous, and untried voltage would shrivel their crops or themselves, and that they should refuse to allow Beck's pylons on their land. As a result of these scare stories, Hydro had to pay twice as much as it expected for a right-of-way.

Work on the transmission line began in November, 1908, and in the following spring, when it was half built, Beck nearly lost his main power source. The Ontario Power Company, which had contracted to supply Hydro, had its generators knocked out by an ice jam in the lower river that created an enormous dam, raised the water level, and flooded the powerhouse. It took weeks to clean up the mess, but the machinery was undamaged, and finally the turbines turned once more.

In October 1910 Beck had his triumph. The first public power was switched on; appropriately in Berlin, where the Hydro concept began, to illuminate a large sign across the main street and spell out the words *For the People*. Beck and Premier Whitney were chugged by automobile past cheering crowds to a platform at the hockey rink. There little Hilda Rumpel brought an electric switch on a velvet cushion and offered it to Whitney to press. Graciously, or perhaps cautiously, he gave it to Beck (with the might of

Niagara behind it and 110,000 dangerous volts leaping over 100 miles, you never knew what might happen). Beck pressed—and the rink, the streets outside, and the sign glowed magnificently.

Whitney's speech reviewed the battles of the past eight years:

> We have been attacked, vilified, slandered. Large sums of money have been expended in creating and fomenting prejudice and ill feeling against us. And still larger sums have been expended in conducting a campaign against us outside of Ontario. Our opponents have left nothing undone that could be done, and men and influences from the humblest man in the land up to the Prime Minister of Great Britain were approached in an endeavor to destroy our power legislation and render it impossible for this wonderful new force to be used and enjoyed by the people, except on the terms laid down by private corporations and individuals. Further, we have been told it would destroy the credit of Ontario and indeed of Canada.

Beck pledged to continue the fight until "the poorest workingman will have electricity in his home." At a dinner that evening, a band saluted him with "See the Conquering Hero Comes," and, for a moment, the father of public power lost his voice.

The Berlin *News Record* called it the greatest day in the history of Berlin. The switch-on ceremony at Toronto the following year was somewhat less successful. A miniature Niagara Falls had been built over the city hall steps, where the ceremony took place. When the switch was pressed, the lights went on—but the small falls misbehaved, and the top-hatted dignitaries below got drenched.

By 1914, the year Adam Beck was knighted for his services, Hydro was supplying over 100 municipalities and running short of power. It had been forced to make a deal with the still-hostile syndicate to buy current from its Toronto Power Company generators, but still that was not enough. Beck sent surveyors down the Niagara gorge to find a site for a new publicly owned plant that would use, for the first time, almost the maximum drop of the river. They chose the cliffs above Queenston near the ridge of the escarpment where the falls were born.

Between Lake Erie and Lake Ontario, the Niagara River descends a total of 326 feet, or about twice the height of the falls, and the existing powerhouses used only part of the drop around the falls. By bringing water from Chippawa on the upper river around the falls and along the top of the gorge, Beck could create his own falls—320 feet high—on the Queenston cliff face. With this colossal drop, every cubic foot of water would produce 29.6 horsepower every second—between two and three times as much as the Niagara Falls plants could generate. The new power station, Beck promised, "would be larger than any even contemplated anywhere in the world."

As Hydro was authorized only to distribute electricity, not manufacture it, a change in the law was required and in view of the then-staggering cost of the scheme—$20 million—the matter was put to a plebiscite. Beck campaigned across the province preaching the benefits of electricity and the need for more power for the munitions factories to win the war in Europe. On New Year's Day, 1917, the voters went to the polls and approved the Queenston-Chippawa plant.

Hydro purchased the Ontario Power Company that year, and construction on the new plant began in May and went on for four and a half years. The digging of the canal turned out to be far harder than anticipated. Although it

Power and Glory

was only 12½ miles long, the operation rivaled the building of the Panama Canal in size and difficulty. A ship canal can climb hills through a system of locks; a power canal has to flow downhill all the way, and part of the route from Chippawa to Queenston was uphill. From the intake from the upper Niagara River at Chippawa, the scheme used 4 miles of the Welland River, which had to be widened and deepened to reverse its flow (normally it flowed into the Niagara, not out of it). From there 8½ miles of new canal, 48 feet wide and lined with concrete, had to be excavated, mostly through the escarpment rock. Although the depth of water to be carried was between 35 and 40 feet, some of the canal floor had to be 140 feet below the surface. It ended in a huge reservoir on the cliff top. The total amount of earth and rock to be dug out was estimated at five times the volume of the Great Pyramid. Hydro engineers had to design many special pieces of equipment needed for construction, and new methods were found to deal with problems that seemed impossible to solve. Ten thousand men did the work, at an average wage of $35 a week.

The powerhouse, a cathedral of energy 590 feet long and 18 stories high, was built in sections and extended as new power units were installed. The first unit was tested on Christmas Day, 1921, and went into operation a month later. At the inaugural ceremony, the floodgates opened, the generator hummed, and a huge electric sign flashed on: *The Largest Hydro-Electric Plant in the World.* Sir Adam watched, proud but slightly uneasy, for his accountant told him the cost had risen alarmingly. When the tenth and final unit went into service eight and a half years later, the price tag of the Queenston-Chippawa project had reached

$76 million—peanuts today but an appalling sum at the time.

The eighteen-year war between Beck and the syndicate ended in 1920, when Hydro bought its Niagara power plant, the Toronto Electric Light Company, and other assets for $32,734,000. But Beck had other enemies, and to the end of his life feared that Ontario Hydro, his great creation, might not survive him. In 1925, when he knew he was dying of pernicious anemia, he told an employee: "Remember what I am telling you. They have no cause to raise Hydro's rates. Watch what they do when I am gone." And on his deathbed, he told a group of friends: "I had hoped to live to forge a band of iron around the Hydro to prevent its destruction by the politicians." Beck was barely in his grave before the politicians tried to destroy it, but it survived, thanks to the popular support for "people's power" that he had built up in his years of lobbying and missionary work.

"He was a hard man and sometimes brutal," wrote his friend and biographer W. R. Plewman. "He was anything but pleasant in a number of his personal contacts. But let this be said to his everlasting credit: that a man of greater refinement and tenderness could not have mastered the alliance between predatory interests and pliant politicians and given Ontario the cheapest hydro-electric power system in the world and the greatest publicly-owned power system."

On August 15, 1950, the twenty-fifth anniversary of his death, the Queenston plant was renamed Sir Adam Beck–Niagara Generating Station No. 1—number one, because work was about to start on number two, a super giant three times the size of the first. The way for this project had been cleared by ratification of the Niagara Diversion Treaty between Canada and the United States which spelled out for the first time, not how much water could be diverted from the river, but how much must be left to splash over the falls and satisfy the tourists. It specified that at least 100,000 cubic feet a second go over the brink of the cataracts during daylight hours between late spring and early fall, and at least 50,000 at other times.

This settled, a new battle of superlatives began. Adam Beck 2, on the cliff beside Adam Beck 1, needed three times as much water as its older brother. This, too, was taken from the upper Niagara near Chippawa, but this time it was carried most of the way in twin tunnels, 45 feet in diameter, deep below the city of Niagara Falls, Ontario, then into an open-cut canal to be pumped up into a 750-acre reservoir. The six electric pumps doubled as generators as required. To ensure a year-round water supply that could not be choked off by ice, Hydro walled off 14 acres of the upper river, and drained and excavated it to take two 500-foot intake tubes, each capable of supplying water to the tunnels at the rate of 7,500,000 gallons a minute.

By March 1954 the new water system was ready and 25 tons of explosives were used to tear out the rock barriers between the old and new reservoirs. One charge was set off only 160 feet from the top part of Adam Beck 1 and could have damaged the building, but for an "air bubble curtain" that cushioned the shock. This was produced by forcing compressed air through holes in a line of pipes strung along the bottom of the reservoir. The fizzy water reduced the impact on the building by 95 percent.

When Adam Beck 2 opened, Ontario once again had the world's largest power station. But not for long. Across the river at Lewiston the even larger Robert Moses plant of the Niagara Power Project was under construction. It took the world title when it began operating in 1961. Bigger plants have been built since, but the combined output of the Queenston and Lewiston generators make Niagara the greatest source of hydro power anywhere.

Linked by the international grid system, they supply a quarter of all the power used in New York State and Ontario. They fulfill Adam Beck's dream of providing electric light and comfort to "the poorest workingman" and take much of the drudgery out of his wife's housework.

Niagara has become a great tap, to be turned on or off at will and while the spectacle of the falling waters is preserved, their spate is a fraction of what it was in Hennepin's day, for much of the water is diverted into the power canals, tunnels, and artificial lakes. And at night, when the illuminations are turned off, Niagara shrinks to a comparative trickle.

By international agreement no less than 100,000 cubic feet per second—less than half of Niagara's potential—must be allowed to flow over the falls between 8:00 A.M. and 10:00 P.M. from April 1 to September 15. At night, and during the winter the minimum is cut to 50,000 cubic feet. When the tourists have gone to bed, the generators rev up.

The power developments have also demonstrated that nature is not to be mocked, and that the mightiest of man's works can go wrong. On November 9, 1965, a switch at Adam Beck 2 tripped the wrong way, sending a surge of "wild" current in the wrong direction along the grid, shutting off cutouts, blowing transformers, and causing the great blackout of New York City and much of the East Coast. Niagara took its revenge on those who dared to treat it like a mere faucet.

12

In Fifi's Footsteps

> Here there are no poisonous vapors arising from stagnant pools, no miasma from marshes or swamps, but the moisture with which the air is saturated is driven from the fall of broken waters, not raised by the influences of heat or cold, but, purified and buoyant, it floats away from the clear stream and as we breathe it, charged as it is with ten thousand particles, fresh from Nature's great alembic, we not only see and hear but feel and taste and breathe the falls.
>
> —*The Falls of Niagara, A Tourist Guide to this Wonder of Nature* (S. de Veaux, 1839)

Research into ions—electrically charged atoms in the air—shows that positive ions make you feel seedy and irritable while negative ones cheer you up, invigorate you, and start you thinking about sex. According to experimenters at the University of Surrey, England, they do this by raising or lowering the level of a chemical in the brain called serotonin, which affects the emotions. Hot, dry winds such as the chinook in western Canada, the foehn in central Europe, and the Santa Ana in California, produce positive ions, which increase your serotonin content and cause unpleasant moods. Happy negative ions are produced by falling water. A cold shower will brighten you up and, despite rumors to the contrary, increase your sexual ardor. Niagara Falls is the ultimate cold shower. One and a half million gallons of water fall every second—which may be one explanation for the euphoria that overtakes visitors to the falls and the area's claim to be The Honeymoon Capital of the World.

The first famous honeymooner was Napoleon's brother, Jerome Bonaparte, later known as "Fifi" and The Best-Dressed Man in Europe. He was a nineteen-year-old lieutenant in Napoleon's army when he took part in an ill-fated expedition to Haiti, ducked across to the United States to avoid capture by the British in the Caribbean, and met the ravishing Baltimore beauty Elizabeth Patterson. He was still nineteen and she twenty when they married and headed off by coach to New York, Boston, and then Niagara. That was in 1803. The effect of the falling waters seems to have worn off fairly rapidly, for the couple started fighting soon after the honeymoon. After two years of legal battles, the marriage was annulled by a French council of state in 1805. But they did have a son, who fathered Jerome Napoleon Bonaparte (1830–93), an American soldier and French officer. Fifi left his American fling behind him and went on to become king of Westphalia and later marshal of France.

Millions of happier couples have followed in Fifi's footsteps. The honeymoon tradition really began in the 1830s, when the railroads came to the falls and the huckstering

In Fifi's Footsteps

began. Niagara was an exotic, romantic spot, but not too far away from the big eastern cities. In the days when people tended to stay home—a sea voyage was more likely to wreck your health than improve it—a honeymoon was a once-in-a-lifetime excuse to travel. Now, with the advent of jet planes, package tours, and credit cards, North Americans travel like swarming bees, but still the honeymooners come to the falls.

Jim Moir, manager of the Niagara Resort and Tourist Association (Ontario), hands out 15,000 honeymoon certificates a year to couples who sign his honeymoon register. The certificates allow the bride free admission to nineteen attractions from the House of Frankenstein to the Criminals' Hall of Fame and Castle Dracula, which should guarantee her a few sleepless nights. The bridegroom has to pay. "It's educational for them," says Mr. Moir. "That's the way it's gonna be for the rest of their married life—the old man pays and the wife goes free." You don't have to produce your marriage license to get a certificate. The tourist bureau will take you at face value and besides, Mr. Moir says, one can usually tell a honeymoon couple; there's something special about them.

There was something special about a couple who arrived to sign the register in 1977. They were both men. "The girl on duty was shocked, but she didn't show it and gave them a certificate. No giggles. Everyone in the office was happy it went off as smoothly as it did."

Niagara is a favorite with older honeymooners, some of them on their second or third falls honeymoon with different partners. A couple of eighty-year-olds checked in recently, and Jim Moir's mother, remarrying in her seventies, collected her certificate a couple of years ago.

The twin cities of Niagara Falls, New York and Ontario,

claim over 16 million tourists a year, but this is a figure grabbed out of the negative-ionized air. A tourist "visit" is a stay of eight hours, not necessarily overnight. However, the Canadian side, which has the bulk of the hotel accommodation—7,000 rooms—manages to keep them reasonably well booked, and the American city, which concentrates on conventions and has built a new 12,000-seat hall for them, reckons that delegates and their families spend $26 million a year there. Dick McLeod, president of the Convention and Visitors Bureau, hopes to garner $60 million a year from conventions alone by the mid-eighties.

Obviously, Niagara wouldn't be Niagara without the falls, but it cannot lure and retain customers by water power alone. Its appeal rests on a combination of natural beauty (spoiled and unspoiled), man-made history, and man-made diversions—educational, entertaining, or plain silly. The area today, for practical purposes, extends thirty-six miles along both banks of the river from Buffalo and Fort Erie in the south to Youngstown and Niagara-on-the-Lake at the Lake Ontario end. Considering the years of strife along this particularly violent piece of frontier, the natives on both sides are remarkably cooperative. While rival tourist operators fight for their piece of the action, no one demands, or even suggests, that the visitor stick to his side of the water. To appreciate Niagara you have to see both sides. It can take an hour, a week, or a lifetime. Everyone begins at the falls, so let's start there.

Hennepin Point, a few hundred feet back from Prospect Point, at the northern edge of the American falls is, as far as anyone can estimate, the spot where the tall, gray-robed Great Liar parted some hemlock branches and first gazed upon the tremendous scene, which grew even more tremendous in his telling. At the time, 300 years ago, the falls were nearer Hennepin Point than they are now, and Prospect Point was larger, since big chunks of it have since broken off, a big one in 1954. There the priest fell to his knees to thank his Maker for the sight and there most of the wordsmiths who followed—Dickens, Longfellow, Thomas Moore, Hawthorne, Harriet Beecher Stowe, and Oscar Wilde—plus Lincoln, Lafayette, and Phineas T. Barnum, had their first impressions. Barnum wanted to buy the place; Wilde, the magnificent cynic, said: "[It] is simply a vast, unnecessary amount of water going the wrong way and then falling over unnecessary rocks. The wonder would be if the water did *not* fall."

There are better views of the falls but this was the first—and lasting—one. You can now see them from thousands of feet in the air, from the river below and the caves behind; but it's the first sighting that counts.

"All the pictures you may see, all of the descriptions you may read of these mighty falls, can only produce in your mind the faint glimmer of the glowworm compared with the overpowering glory of the meridian sun," wrote naturalist John J. Audubon, after standing on Hennepin Point.

"I saw Niagara. Oh, God! Who can describe that sight?" added Victorian actress Fanny Kemble. Huge "unnecessary" rocks plug the base of the American falls, breaking the sheer descent of the cataract and sending up less spray than the smoky pillar that often obscures the Horseshoe. The U. S. Army Corps of Engineers considered removing them, and they shut off the falls for several days by diverting water down the power intakes and building a temporary dam while they examined the bare bones below. The engineers decided to leave things the way they were, and turned on the water again.

The fall of most of Prospect Point, in July 1954, was almost a rerun of the fall of most of Table Rock in June 1850; only this time there was no hack driver to leap for his life. The area was roped off after officials noticed an alarming crack and water began pouring into the shaft of the elevator which took tourists down to the *Maid of the Mist* dock below. A great pie-shaped piece weighing 185,000 tons broke off and thundered into the gorge.

From Prospect Park, a viewing platform now juts out like a diving board and a new glass-enclosed elevator drops visitors 160 feet to the flats beside the American wharf of the *Maids of the Mist*. Here the original ferry boats landed. Before the bridges were built, there were forty of them, rowed by raucous, barrel-chested men who were generally insulting and frequently drunk but never lost a passenger. Victorian ladies in hoopskirts would be helped ashore to climb a wet wooden stairway to the park above with its bandshell, its pavilion for "Dancing, Recitations and Singing," and perhaps a view of the great Blondin prancing on his rope.

Today, from the foot of the elevator, oilskinned visitors can reach the rocks at the base of the American falls and revel in the thunder from above. In winter these rocks become glassy hills of ice—the eastern pillars of the Niagara "ice bridge" that spans the gorge with a congealed white stew of lumps, cubes, mounds, and crevices, sometimes garnished with ice towers in fantastic shapes. The American falls have been known to freeze up completely and turn into an enormous wall of icicles, their waters caught in mid-leap, stark and silent. And on March 29, 1848, an ice jam between Buffalo and Fort Erie stopped all water to both great falls, and Niagara went dry for a day. Sightseers walked across the river above the falls and picked up old muskets and swords off Chippawa Creek

—equipment discarded by American troops after the battle fought there in 1814.

The ice bridge used to be the scene of winter fun and games. Boys slid down the icy rocks on the American side on homemade sleds or burlap bags, risking a spill that might throw them into the cataract. Alex Landreth, who became well known for his photographs of the falls, sledded there as a boy in the 1870s, using barrel staves nailed together. A beautiful, fashionably dressed lady asked for a ride, and they whooped off down the slope, falling off the barrel staves and rolling in the snow. The lady regained her dignity, handed the boy five dollars, and said, "Tell your mother Sarah Bernhardt gave it to you." So the ice bridge was blessed by "the divine Sarah," greatest of French actresses.

The Drummondville *Recorder* of February 24, 1888, describes a typical Sunday on the ice:

> The visitors during the day must have numbered twenty thousand. The visitors to the ice bridge amused themselves all day either watching toboggans coast down the ice mound at Prospect Point corner or in trying the fun themselves. What laughing and yelling as some of the unlucky sports came to grief. The seven shanties on the ice bridge were doing a good business in liquor, photographs, and curiosities all day long. The police were on the watch for a gang of gamblers but the light-fingered gentry scented danger and took a back seat somewhere.

These shanties of wood and tarpaper were hauled out from the Canadian side by horse and sleigh and set up on a path of smooth ice, if this could be found, midway between the ferry landings. The international boundary runs along the middle of the river, but it would have taken a surveyor a week to find it in the jumble of ice, so the shanty owners boldly made their illegal liquor sales, knowing that if the Canadian police charged them, they could claim to be on the American side and vice versa. Besides, a drink was always welcome on a cold day and took on added savor when drunk while perched on 40 feet of ice over 140 feet of water.

Amid the fun was danger. On Sunday, January 22, 1899, the ice bridge broke loose without warning and floated downstream, carrying 150 people on it. All managed to reach shore, but the last man was carried as far as the Upper Steel Arch Bridge and had to grab one of the girders, haul himself onto it, and climb to the shore.

The great days of the ice bridge ended on Sunday morning, February 4, 1912. It was seven degrees below zero and visitors were just beginning to arrive when there was a great crack and a crunch. Red Hill, Sr., was in a shack in midriver, talking with his fellow River Rats when the ice beneath him suddenly fell several feet. He ran out and saw several dozen people scrambling for either the Canadian or the American shore as the ice broke into huge rumbling blocks and spray from the water below plumed into the air. Hill leapt the widening cracks and reached the Canadian shore. Turning, he saw tourists still on the ice, panic-stricken and uncertain where to turn; their shrieks could be heard over the mounting roar of the shifting floes.

Hill jumped back, grasped the nearest, forcing them to safety and yelling to the others to follow. All but four reached shore. A honeymoon couple from Toronto, Eldridge Stanton and his bride, and two young men from Cleveland, Burrel Heacock and Ignatius Roth, stayed behind, arguing which direction to take. Hill ran over to them, begging them to follow him. Roth did, leaped a five-foot crevass, and was saved. The others started for the New

In Fifi's Footsteps

York shore. Another crack, and they were trapped on a moving block of ice. Large crowds on both sides of the river who had been on their way to the ice bridge when it broke watched as the three were carried slowly downstream. Thousands more hurried to the lips of the gorge. Fire carts and police wagons raced to the bridges and ropes were hurled down and dangled from the spans in the hope that the victims could catch them. They missed. The floating ice block disintegrated, piece by piece as it left the Upper Gorge and neared the rapids. The Stantons were seen embracing while Heacock knelt in prayer. Then their remaining small cake of ice turned over, and they were gone.

After that tragedy, visitors were banned from the ice bridge. It is still a winter spectacle—but viewed from the safety of the shore.

Goat Island, which separates the two principal falls, was once called Iris Island, a pleasanter and more appropriate name. That was before John Stedman pastured his goats there. Stedman, the English portage master who survived the Indian massacre of his wagon train at Devil's Hole, brought the herd to the island by flat-bottomed boat in 1778. There, he reckoned, they would be safe from the packs of wolves that still roamed the river banks. However, all but one tough old billygoat died of the cold in their first winter on the island.

Despite this, the pioneers of Niagara Falls, New York, Augustus and Peter B. Porter determined to put sheep on the island—again because of the wolves. They first tried to buy it from the New York State Legislature in 1811, but the state planned to build a prison there. There was no bridge to the island, and the deadly currents would have made it a tough pen to escape from, so this seemed a good idea at the time. The legislators didn't care about the beauties of Niagara, which would have been ruined by a big, bleak jail. For that matter, neither did the Porters, who were out to make money. But along came the War of 1812, the prison project was dropped, and the Porters acquired Goat Island in 1815. In 1817 they built the first wooden bridge across the upper rapids to the mainland. It was a marvel of the times. Visitors were happy to pay to use it, so the Porters abandoned the sheep and developed the island for tourism. Some local worthies objected. An Indian named Red Jacket muttered "Damn Yankees!" (meaning Porters) every time he passed the bridge, and an elderly white lady proclaimed that Augustus' increasing deafness was a curse visited upon him for defiling the waters. The waters did get their own back by sweeping down piles of ice that carried away the first bridge, but the Porters built two more.

Today, a choice of stone foot and road bridges connect Goat Island and the small islands around it—Bath, Luna, and the Three Sisters, named for the daughters of General Parkhurst Whitney, keeper of the noted Cataract House. Reminders of old tragedies line the route.

In June 1849 a Mr. and Mrs. de Forest, from Buffalo, walked the log bridge to Goat Island with their little daughter Anna and a Mr. Addington. Addington picked up the girl and playfully made as if to toss her over the rail. Anna screamed in terror, tore herself away from him, and fell from the bridge. Addington jumped after her. Minutes later both were swept over the falls.

On a February day in 1902, Alice Colie, a young Buffalo woman, wrote a message to her fiancé and parents on the back of a visiting card, left it, with her handbag, on the bridge to Luna Island, and jumped. "Goodbye Ray,

Mama, Papa and all the dear ones," she wrote. "Do not think I do not love you, for I do. The waters are calling me." She had a return train ticket to Buffalo and apparently had no intention of killing herself until she saw the falls. The Buffalo *Evening News* blamed her suicide on their "hypnotic influence."

In the rapids halfway between Prospect Point and the first Goat Island bridge lies a jagged rock—Avery's Rock. Seventeen-year-old Samuel Avery clung to a crevice in that rock for a night and most of a day in July 1853. A skiff carrying Sam and two companions had overturned in the rapids. The other two were carried over the American falls, but Sam found his rock and held on to it all night. He was seen in the morning and the villagers of Niagara tried lowering empty boats to him on ropes attached to the bridge. All capsized and were smashed before they reached him. In the late afternoon, a raft came close enough to the rock for the lad to jump for it. But it, too, turned over, throwing him into the torrent. He caught and held onto another rock at the brink, but the current was too strong for him. He was pulled over the crest and disappeared with a cry that haunted the hundreds watching for the rest of their lives.

On Goat Island stood the shack of the Hermit of Niagara, young Francis Abbott. Pause there awhile and you may feel the intoxication of splendor that made him decide to spend the rest of his days there, with his dog, his flute, guitar, and violin, his books and paintings. Pause too long, and you may understand why it brought him to his death. He wandered the small island for three years, drinking in beauty; and when he had drunk his fill, he died. The plume of water between the western end of Goat Island and the first of the Three Sisters, where he bathed, is still known as the Hermit's Cascade. What may be his epitaph was found chiseled on a rock on the island, perhaps by the Hermit himself: "All is change, eternal progress, no death?"

Another elevator slides down behind the blank wall on the falls end of Goat Island from the Cave of the Winds House. A walkway down below leads to the base of the little Luna, or Bridal Veil Falls, the little pure white plume between the two great falls. The cave behind the Luna Falls was first entered by George Sims and Berry Hill White in 1834, found to be safe, and opened to tourists soon after when a tourist named Biddle financed the Biddle Stair, a shakier way down than the present elevator. Again, the might of the falls is best appreciated from below, where the tourist in his borrowed oilskins can imagine himself a turbine blade like those in the power stations around him, but the beauty is above. And beauty was the subject of discussion among Frederick Law Olmsted, William Dorsheimer, and Henry Hobson Richardson as they rambled Goat Island one fall day in 1869.

All were Americans—Olmsted and Richardson architects, and Dorsheimer a lawyer and onetime district attorney for the Northern District of New York. Olmsted had visited Niagara from time to time for thirty-five years and watched the steady ruination of the scene by hideous factories, already polluting the American side of the river and equally awful tourist meccas on both sides, but particularly the Canadian, where a tent containing a five-legged calf was the latest "educational" wonder. The artist Frederick Church, who had painted the falls in better days, had asked for his support in preserving the area as a park. Church realized that this was not something New York State or the United States could do alone. There was no point in clearing up the American mess so that Canadians

In Fifi's Footsteps

could enjoy the view of the American side, while the Canadian honky-tonks survived to hurt the eyes of Americans viewing the scene from their bank. So Church wrote to the governor-general of Canada, the Earl of Dufferin, asking for Canadian cooperation, which he received. However, that came later. The credit for the preservation of the Niagara frontier as public parkland on both sides of the border, according to Ronald L. Way, official historian of the Canadian parks, goes to Olmsted and his associates. And the beginning was that fall day on Goat Island. (Olmsted points out in an 1888 letter to Thomas V. Welch, first superintendent of the State Reservation at Niagara, that, although Goat Island inspired them, they really got down to business that evening at a table in General Whitney's Cataract House.) Their agitation, plus Church's, finally won the day.

Communications were slow in 1869, and the ways of politicians even slower. It took eleven years to organize the remarkable petition signed by 700 leading literary and scientific men of the United States, Canada, and Great Britain, appealing to Canada and New York to "secure and hold for the world's good, the lands adjacent to the Falls of Niagara."

It continued:

> The Falls of Niagara are peculiarly exposed to disastrous injury. The heights of snow, the precipitous crags of great mountains, however they may be disfigured by man, can rarely be applied to uses which would destroy their sublimity. But should the islands and declivities of the Niagara River be stripped of their natural woods, and occupied for manufacturing and business purposes; should even the position, size and form of the constructions which the accommodation of visitors will call for, continue to be reg-

ulated solely by the pecuniary interests of numerous individual land owners, the loss to the world will be great and irreparable. The river's banks are denuded of the noble forest by which they were originally covered; are degraded by incongruous and unworthy structures, made for advertising purposes, wilfully conspicuous and obtrusive, and the visitor's attention is diverted from scenes to the influence of which he would gladly surrender himself, by demands for tolls and fees, and the offer of services, most of which he would prefer to avoid. Objects of great natural beauty and grandeur are among the most valuable gifts which Providence has bestowed upon our race. The contemplation of them elevates and informs the human understanding. They are instruments of education. They conduce to the order of society. They address sentiments which are universal. They draw together men of all races, and thus contribute to the union and peace of nations.

The language was stirring and so were the signatures beneath: the Vice President of the United States, the Chief Justice and seven other members of the Supreme Court, eleven prominent United States senators (but only seven Canadian members of Parliament), and the cream of the literary world. Despite this brilliance, it took another five years—until 1885, before the Ontario and New York park schemes became reality. New York Governor Cornell blocked the park bill. Listening to harrowing descriptions of the awful state of the falls area, he said, "Well, the water goes over just the same, doesn't it?"

At various times the Marquis de Lafayette had tried to buy Goat Island for a summer home; railroader Jim Fiske wanted to put a railway station there; P. T. Barnum wanted it for a showground, and some New York promoters hoped to build a racetrack. Now the state of New

In Fifi's Footsteps

York acquired it, along with Bath Island, the Three Sisters, Prospect Park, and a narrow strip of land along the main shore of the upper river. This first American park at Niagara covered 412 acres, of which only 112 were above water. It was opened with great ceremony on July 15, 1885.

The first Canadian park, now Queen Victoria Park, comprised 154 acres of dry land from Clifton Road on the edge of Niagara Falls, Ontario, south past Table Rock and the Horseshoe Falls to Dufferin Islands, which nestle in a bay beside today's Marineland and Game Farm. Later that year the Parks Commission was given the old military Chain Reserve—a strip of river bank one chain (66 feet) wide, stretching from Niagara Falls to Niagara-on-the-Lake. Three years later, it acquired the southern strip from Chippawa to Fort Erie. The Niagara Frontier State Park Region now has a chain of parks from Grand Island to Lake Ontario. Although commercialism still rears its ugly head, the park makers have succeeded in driving it back from the principal beauty spots. The Goat Island thinkers, and those who followed them, worked well.

The most terrifying view of the Horseshoe Falls was the one from Augustus Porter's original Terrapin Point bridge, a shaky wooden structure, in places without a handrail, that climbed 200 feet across the rocks and then stuck out for 10 feet, unsupported, over the brink. The Hermit used to dangle from it. The view was "terrific," according to a writer in the 1820s, but the experience was "absolutely appalling." In 1833 the Porters replaced it with their Terrapin Tower, which lasted for forty years. Today's view from Terrapin Point is still terrific, but to get the full effect of the Canadian falls, cross to the Canadian side.

Table Rock House, set back from the site of the original

Table Rock, which broke off, nearly taking a hackman with it, offers an elevator ride 125 feet down to the tunnels behind the falls. There, in the thunder god's lair, black-slickered visitors can see the crashing waters from three viewing spots only 25 feet above river level. In two of them, the viewer stands behind the curtain of water, only a few feet from the colossal shower. Table Rock is now operated by the Parks Commission, so tourists no longer have to fight their way to the scenic tunnel through a barroom crowded with touts and peddlers. And after exploring the innards of the falls they can take a gentle stroll along the promenade near, but not too near, the edge of the gorge and get a soothing panoramic view of falls, gorge, and skyline.

The stretch of Queen Victoria Park between Table Rock and Clifton Hill, the main drag of Niagara commercialism, is all leafy loveliness, marred only by the giant viewing towers that loom over the trees from the escarpment behind. There are three: from the smaller Niagara Tower to the Panasonic to the futuristic Skylon, soaring 775 feet above the falls. All are built on the theory that tourism is a form of mountaineering made easy, and the sightseer is not truly content until he can look down on the sight from a dizzy height. They look vaguely incongruous—man's attempt to dwarf the natural splendor, and not what the Duc de la Rochefoucauld envisaged in 1774 when he proposed better vantage points. But they do provide a fine view and if you're looking for the world's largest *indoor* Ferris wheel, the Skylon's got it.

The Oakes Gardens, a stately formal layout of lawns and vine-covered arbors, stand on the grounds of the old Clifton House Hotel, scene of high-level plotting during the Civil War. There, in 1864, Senator Clement Claiborne

Clay, secret agent of the Confederacy, hatched plans and Horace Greeley launched his peace proposals, only to have them circumvented by Lincoln. The gardens belonged to Sir Harry Oakes, whose thirty-seven-room baronial hall stands on the hill above, and is open to tourists. Oakes, a prospector from Sangerville, Maine, was down to his last few dollars when he struck gold in Kirkland Lake, Ontario, in 1912 and went on to develop one of the continent's richest mines. He collected a knighthood in England and moved to Niagara in the 1920s, where he lived the life of a squire. He was hard, unpredictable, and given to unpleasant moods and bursts of generosity. He was horribly murdered in the Bahamas in 1943. His son-in-law was tried for the murder and acquitted, so his death remains a mystery; and the name Oakes, even while attached to this serene, verdant sanctuary, still evokes dark memories.

Next to the Oakes Gardens, on the driveway above the *Maid of the Mist* dock, is a piece of asphalt big enough to park half a dozen cars—where once stood a 50-foot-high stone arch in memory of William Lyon Mackenzie, the rebel of 1837 whose ship the *Caroline* met a fiery end in the upper river before dropping in pieces over the falls. It's an interesting example of history in the unmaking.

William Lyon Mackenzie King, Mackenzie's grandson and Canada's most durable Prime Minister, unveiled the Pioneer Arch in 1938. It bore a bas-relief of the little rebel raising hell in the Parliament of Upper Canada. Nearby were sculpted profiles of his lieutenants Peter Mathews and Samuel Lount, who were hanged for treason in Toronto after Mackenzie got away. There was also a list of martyrs from the 1837 Papineau Rebellion in Quebec. An inscription explained that the arch was erected to honor men and women who were "the pioneers of political freedom and a system of responsible government which became the cornerstone of the British Commonwealth of Nations." Twenty years after Prime Minister King's death, the Niagara Parks Commission discovered that the rebels' memorial was a traffic hazard. Early in 1968 it was dismantled as quickly as one can dismantle a massive stone structure resting on thirty-four one-ton blocks, and the carved slabs were stacked outside a warehouse. Later a local committee was formed to save the stones and erect them somewhere else, but it appears that Mackenzie is no longer one of Niagara's favored sons. In life he was a nuisance; long afterward, his arch became a traffic hazard. However, his stone house downstream at Queenston, where he printed his early, savage broadsheets, is still open to tourists. Only twenty weekly issues of *The Colonial Advocate* emanated from there, but it remains a shrine of North American journalism.

Uphill from the once-hallowed mini-parking lot, is Clifton Hill, a short street rich in horrors, fun, and freaks that worthily maintains the old Niagara tradition of giving the tourist a lot more than water.

The great Harry Houdini never visited Niagara Falls during his lifetime (1874–1926), but the Houdini Magical Hall of Fame on Clifton Hill is his earthly home, if he needs one. Elaborate séances are held there every few years to see if Harry, the greatest escape artist ever, can escape from the dead. Since these events are attended by magicians, something exciting always happens. Lamps suddenly crash to the floor. Books about Houdini pop out from bookshelves, to open at significant pages. But these are tricks that would have been child's play to Houdini in his other role of magician, since he invented most of them. (I attended one Houdini séance with a television film crew,

In Fifi's Footsteps

who kept tripping over lengths of black thread attached to objects that later leapt around the room.)

Houdini never believed it was possible to return from the dead, or communicate with the living through spiritualism, and he spent years exposing phony mediums. But if it could be done, he promised to try. In a famous pact with his friends Sir Arthur Conan Doyle, creator of Sherlock Holmes, who did believe in spiritualism, and Joseph (The Amazing) Dunninger, the world's leading mind-reader, Houdini devised a coded message, which was sealed in an envelope and hidden. Only the three men knew the message. The first to die would try to communicate it from the afterworld. Houdini died in 1926, Doyle in 1930. Although at one séance Houdini's widow, Bessie, claimed to have received part of the message, the complete version never came through, according to Dunninger, who knew it. He died in the mid-seventies, but the séances continue. So far they seem to have proved that Houdini, the skeptic, was right and Doyle, the believer, was wrong. Dunninger didn't believe either, but he was a great showman. "Anything I can do," he said of his astounding mind-reading act, "can be done by a child of five—with thirty years' experience."

The Houdini museum is a treasurehouse of trickery. It displays old boxes used in sawing women in half, mirrors to make them disappear, a large bottle in which Houdini was suspended, upside-down and in chains and his straitjackets, locks, and handcuffs. Escaping from straitjackets while hanging upside-down over main streets was a Houdini specialty. In February 1977 the Amazing Randi, a Houdini disciple, performed the same trick for a film crew while suspended by a crane over the brink of the Horseshoe Falls. It took the film producer six months to convince the parks police that the stunt was perfectly safe. It certainly doesn't *look* safe.

Next door to Houdini's show, Castle Dracula offers its own sanguinary spectacles, and next to that a coffin lid creaks open in the window of the House of Frankenstein and a skeleton peeks out. The world's best murderers are enshrined in the Criminals' Hall of Fame across the way. Crime pays at Niagara and so does religion. The Biblical Wax Museum features the world's largest Crucifixion scene, with computerized lighting and sound system. The oddities the late Robert Ripley accumulated on his world travels—e.g., the Four-Eyed Chinaman—are in Ripley's Believe It Or Not Museum, vying with the Guinness Book of World Records Museum, which has a dummy nine-foot giant in the window. The Movieland Museum has a bigger one—"King Kong, the biggest wax figure ever created"—and Louis Tussaud's Wax Museum displays all the other wax celebrities you'd care to meet, plus an excruciating Chamber of Horrors and Blondin's original wheelbarrow and a piece of his rope.

Tape-recorded barkers shout: "the Greatest, the Tallest, the Shortest . . . See the Boston Strangler . . . I am Houdini, I am Houdini . . ." while couples put quarters in slots to watch peep shows of George Stathakis dying in his barrel, holding his pet turtle, or have their photos taken in barrel-jumping poses.

The original Niagara Falls Museum is now just north of the Rainbow Bridge, away from the monsters of Clifton Hill. Thomas Barnett founded it at Table Rock in 1827; and it was moved across to the American side, then back again. It has a notable collection of Egyptian artifacts, a large display of fossils, and a floor of early American, Aztec, and Eskimo exhibits, but is best known for its Daredevil

In Fifi's Footsteps

Hall of Fame, commemorating the rope walkers, gorge runners, and barrel jumpers, and containing some of the original barrels.

There is another daredevil display, with more boats and barrels at the Whirlpool Rapids—part of a viewing platform at the river's edge, beside the haystack waves that swallowed Channel-swimmer Captain Matthew Webb and knocked the funnel off Captain Joel Robinson's old *Maid of the Mist* as she lurched downstream on her last Niagara voyage. It is reached by yet another elevator and a 240-foot tunnel through the wall of the gorge. On the opposite shore, the river is removing the last traces of the Great Gorge Railway. Across from the platform is the spot where a train was derailed in 1917, throwing 14 tourists to their deaths in the rapids. It was Niagara's worst accident—although a similar derailment on the Canadian side two years earlier killed 13, most of them children on a Sunday school outing from Toronto.

The Great Gorge Route was a truly international railway. After 1902, for $1 a trip, the tourist could be trundled along both sides of the river and over two bridges, at Queenston/Lewiston and across the Upper Steel Arch Bridge, just below the falls. It was an electric trolley line, with grass growing between the tracks and overhead lamps lighting it by night. The cars had open sides, and there was no nicer way of enjoying Niagara—but for the fact that the gorge crumbled, as ever, rocks fell, and disaster was never far away. In July 1913 a garbage-disposal unit on the American side broke at the wrong moment, showering its contents on a passing train. The line was abandoned because of persistent rockfalls. In 1935, some 5,000 tons of gorge wall fell on the tracks near the Whirlpool Rapids on the American side and the company, too, caved in.

All Niagara's man-made circuses are about to be overshadowed by the expansion of Marineland and Game Farm, a mile above the falls on the Canadian side, into a theme park of Disneyland proportions. The present park, which opened in the early '60s, is the biggest commercial attraction in the area. It has a 4,000-seat aqua-show theater with performing dolphins, three killer whales, circus acts, and an aquarium. Three hundred small deer, a herd of buffalo, llamas, elk, wolves, and scores of other animals wander in the 75-acre farm outside. Another 1,000 acres are being developed at a cost of $75 million and will contain 4 miles of canal for boat rides, 10 miles of railway with steam trains imported from Yugoslavia, a monorail running through a jungle populated by lions and tigers, and a new 15,000-seat stadium for the viewing of bigger and better whales. The centerpiece, to be ready in the mid-1980s, is a 300-foot-high artificial mountain with a castle on top and a European village below.

The river of stunts and accidents flows between Goat Island and the Whirlpool, but the river of battle goes all the way from Lake Erie to Lake Ontario, its banks dotted with forts, graveyards, and markers recalling two centuries of struggle between French and Indians, British and French, and Americans and Canadians for mastery of the frontier. The tide of history flowed against the current, from north to south, so a historical tour should begin at the river's mouth—Old Fort Niagara on the American side.

Three flags fly over it: the lilies of Bourbon France, the British flag minus the cross of St. Patrick, and the fifteen-star American flag that inspired Francis Scott Key to write "The Star-Spangled Banner"—a reminder that the fort had several tenants. It has been restored to show several periods

In Fifi's Footsteps

at once: the Gate of the Five Nations, with its great door and drawbridge, designed by the French to lure the Iroquois in to trade while curbing their warlike instincts; two British blockhouses, and, most impressive, de Léry's stone chateau, the House of Peace, built in 1726. The original four-foot walls are intact and the gentle-looking upper dormer windows conceal heavy iron cannon. The American heroine Fanny Doyle is remembered here. When her soldier husband was captured by the British during the War of 1812 she took his place, carrying hot shot to the guns. According to her commander, under fire, she showed the courage of the Maid of Orleans.

On the ground floor lies the well, once bricked up by the British and still supposedly haunted by the headless ghost of the French officer decapitated in a duel. The guardroom beside it contains one long wooden bunk, big enough for thirty or forty soldiers to sleep side by side.

There are dungeons at the rear, their walls scratched by the names of French prisoners, which once held a torture apparatus on which wretches could be strangled, partly or completely. By contrast, the downstairs dining room and council chamber is pleasant and spacious. There the Joncaires held court and there Captain Pouchot surrendered the fort to Sir William Johnson. Later Johnson would use the room to entertain Indian chiefs and sign treaties with them that gave King George control over half of North America.

The old fort sits placidly by a broad expanse of shining river and sparkling lake, its grassy earthworks neatly trimmed and its parade ground smooth as a golf fairway. When La Salle and Hennepin landed there and built the first bark cabin, it was a tangle of bush. In its trading days, it was surrounded by a fairground of tents, and under siege it became a swarming refugee camp of starving whites and Indians, with wolves howling outside. Now the sentries who guard the walls on summer days—students in period dress—look out on a marina crowded with pretty white pleasure boats.

Across the river mouth sits Niagara-on-the-Lake, seat of Governor Simcoe and the first Parliament of Upper Canada. The original village, burned to the ground by the Americans on a winter night in 1813, has been rebuilt, then restored as a charming little Victorian town. The main street is as wholesome as an old-fashioned sticky bun, and even the government liquor store has the facade of an olde curiosity shoppe. In 1962 Niagara-on-the-Lake discovered George Bernard Shaw and held a festival of his plays in its century-old courthouse, which was still in use, with prisoners in the cells. The festival grew, an 830-seat Shaw Theatre was built and the town now ranks second to Stratford, Ontario, as a center of summer theater in Canada.

Navy Hall, which was too damp and depressing for the Simcoes to live in, survives, encased in new stone walls, beside the restored log buildings of Fort George. So does part of Butler's barracks, where the colonel and his raiders settled after their depredations across the border. The fort, built by Simcoe in 1796–99 was destroyed and rebuilt during the War of 1812, so only the stone powder magazine is original. But today's stark, squarish log buildings probably give a better idea of the rough life of the ordinary redcoat or bluecoat soldier than the French castle opposite. When it was being restored in the 1930s, the skeleton of a horse was dug up. Its lower legs had been cut off, as if to fit a coffin, so it may have been Alfred, General Brock's beloved charger, to whom he said good-bye before leading his last attack on foot. Brock was originally buried at Fort George,

In Fifi's Footsteps

and Alfred was paraded at his funeral. The horse may have been given a funeral of his own when he died.

Heading south and upstream, the historic route follows along the rich flatlands that were once the bottom of ancient Lake Iroquois to the looming face of the escarpment where the first break occurred, the river spilled down 250 feet, and the falls were born. On the left is Lewiston, where Louis Joncaire built his first trading post, the *Magazin Royal*, at the foot of the Crawl-on-All-Fours section of the portage; where Captain Montresor erected his tramway to haul goods up the cliff face, and Mrs. Hustler invented her cocktail.

Queenston, on the right bank, remembers Mackenzie, its most violent resident, and Laura Secord, the heroine who walked her cow past the American troops to warn the British in 1813. It was 1860, and she was eighty-six years old, before her deed was rewarded. The Prince of Wales heard of her while he was at Niagara, watching Blondin, and sent her 100 gold sovereigns. Her house, too, waited a long time for proper recognition as a historic site. It was privately owned until 1969, when the Laura Secord Candy Company bought it, rebuilt it, since it was crumbling from rot, and refurnished it with pine chairs and period kitchen utensils. Energetic tourists can walk Laura's nineteen-mile route. Maps are provided, but not cows.

Both Lewiston and Queenston are pretty little places, unspoiled in this century (although devastated by war in the last) for the heavy onslaughts of industry or commerce passed them by.

The Brock Monument on Queenston Heights marks the American position General Sir Isaac Brock tried to reach in his gallant uphill charge on October 13, 1812. The spot where he was shot down by an Ohio sharpshooter is near the foot of the escarpment, marked by a small stone cenotaph. The monument, 210 feet high and bristling with stone lions and classical symbols of war, has a violent history of its own. When the original column was 48 feet high, Lieutenant-Governor Sir Peregrine Maitland, who had laid the cornerstone, learned that under that stone Mackenzie's rebels had inserted a whiskey bottle and a copy of his *Colonial Advocate*. Sir Peregrine ripped down the column, removed the offending artifacts, and rebuilt it. It was completed in 1825, a Tuscan column 135 feet tall. The bodies of Brock and Lieutenant-Colonel John Macdonell, who had led the second fatal charge, were taken from their graves at Fort George and laid in a vault beneath it. But on Good Friday, 1840, Benjamin Lett, an Irish-Canadian, who had been one of Mackenzie's followers, crossed the river from his refuge in the United States, planted a charge of gunpowder at the base of the column and blew it up, destroying most of it. The bodies of Brock and Macdonell were moved once more, to a graveyard at Queenston. They were reinterred in a vault below the present monument when it was finished in 1856.

All went well until April 5, 1929, when an electrical storm tore off the outstretched arm of the huge statue of Brock on top. Workmen discovered that the head and shoulders were loose, so large parts of the statue were replaced. Brock now holds a lightning rod in his hand and has another sticking out of his hat. Visitors can climb a spiral stairway inside the shaft and share the statue's superb view of the battlefield below and the orchards and river mouth beyond. Or they can follow, through well-preserved parkland, the course of the battle. Slightly to the west of the Brock Monument you can see the remains of two British redoubts built in 1814—Fort Drummond and Fort

In Fifi's Footsteps

Riall. The site of the Redan Battery, which held back Brock and Macdonell, is marked by a bronze tablet.

Just upriver from the Queenston killing ground is the Devil's Hole, scene of a still more gruesome massacre. The Robert Moses Parkway now streaks along the portage trail where, on September 14, 1763, John Stedman's wagon train was cut to pieces and thrown into the gorge by Seneca raiders. Ninety men, including soldiers who came to the rescue, were either scalped on the path or thrown, alive, over the brink. Visitors can go down to the hole from Whirlpool State Park, enter the cave, and listen for the watery voices that warned La Salle of his impending doom.

But it's hard to brood for long on ancient warnings or horrors of long ago when the scene is dominated by today's wonders—the giant Canadian powerhouses, Sir Adam Beck 1 and 2, and the even larger Robert Moses Plant on the American side. Power Vista, a viewing gallery above the Moses turbines, contains a theater and museum explaining how the immense hydroelectric scheme works. A 40-foot model of the area provides an overview of the power canals, conduits, and reservoirs on both sides of the river which bleed off the strength of Niagara and put it to good use. It's a reminder that these man-made rivers and lakes, when seen from the air, dwarf both the falls and the gorge. They spread out, unruffled, saving their energy for the moment their waters plummet down their 24-foot-diameter pipes and hit the colossal turbine blades. White foam eddies from the outlets 375 feet below Power Vista, but there is no thunder and pillar of spray. The force is spent.

Ontario Hydro used to tell its story in the Hall of Memory Museum, attached to Adam Beck 1 power station, but this was closed in 1976 to save money. The floral clock, beside it, was built by Ontario Hydro in 1950 and planted by the Niagara Parks Commission. It is modeled on one in Princes' Gardens, Edinburgh, but much larger—40 feet in diameter with hour and minute hands weighing 500 pounds apiece and a face picked out by 24,000 plants. Three rooms underneath the clock house the mechanism and electrical equipment.

The plants come from the Parks Commission's School of Horticulture (formerly its Training School for Apprentice Gardeners) just upstream from the clock. Its 100 acres, open to visitors, display a brilliant variety of blooms raised by its students, ranging from spring flowering bulbs (April 15–30), flowering Japanese cherries (May 10–20), lilacs, rhododendrons, and irises (May and June) followed by peonies, roses, hardy chrysanthemums, perennial borders, and rock garden plants lasting until fall or the first frost. It is North America's only resident school for gardeners. A dozen graduate each year—all of whom are much in demand by parks throughout the continent. The school grounds contain every kind of garden from formal layouts to natural gardens and vegetable gardens, ponds, fountains; even a wedding chapel (usually booked solid for months in advance).

Between the school gardens and the Whirlpool nestles Niagara Glen, a wild natural beauty spot of lichen-covered rocks, fern grottoes, and leafy dells, different from any other scenery along the Niagara frontier. It looks primeval and is probably the oldest, untouched part of the gorge. Here, at some point in prehistory, the river paused in its steady erosion of a bed for itself to broaden out and form two streams around an island perched on the brink of its falls, as Goat Island perches today. The eastern stream was the stronger, and it gradually demolished the island, smashing it into great chunks of dolomite rock and heaps of loose shale, which it elbowed over to the west side. Wintergreen Point, a promontory on the western gorge wall, is part of the ancestral river bank and stood in relationship to the ancient falls as Table Rock does to the present Horseshoe. The glen below is ancient, abandoned riverbed. The Parks Commission has provided stairways, paths, and a restaurant above, but otherwise left it to its primordial peace. The glen is Niagara's natural chapel; a place to ponder and worship.

Back to more recent history. The trail of battle leads to Lundy's Lane, now a major highway westward out of Niagara Falls, Ontario, and the battlefield's most prominent marker is the city water tower. It replaces the viewing towers of the early 1800s, when the site, still littered with the debris of war, drew tourists from all over. Now memories of this bloodiest battle of the War of 1812—a battle neither side won—are confined to the slopes of Drummond Hill Churchyard. The grass which long refused to grow there, after nearly 300 bodies, British, Canadian, and American, were burned on a pyre of fence rails, is now tough and springy. Markers commemorate "Two Unknown U.S. Soldiers" here, nine more there, with more elaborate stones put up by the families of officer victims and a plinth, erected 1885, "In Honour of the Victory Gained by the British and Canadian Forces On This Field, Fighting for the Unity of the Empire." Nearby there is a small Lundy's Lane museum containing military relics and part of one of the coffins used for Brock, Canada's most-buried general.

The Niagara River Parkway south from Niagara Falls to Fort Erie passes a monument commemorating the battle of Chippawa, where General Winfield Scott's Americans, wearing the gray, undyed uniforms later adopted at West

Point, routed the nearsighted General Phineas Riall, who thought they were raw militiamen.

Beyond Chippawa comes a further trace of William Lyon Mackenzie—the marked site of the riverside property owned by Captain Samuel McAfee where he kept the boat used by Mackenzie to escape to Grand Island. McAfee distracted a detachment of British troopers out for Mackenzie's blood while the rebel got away.

Old Fort Erie is actually new Fort Erie, since it is a rebuilt version of the third fort on the strategic site guarding the inlet of the Niagara River from Lake Erie. The first and second British forts, which took the place of an old French trading post, were destroyed by storm-driven ice floes. The third was still unfinished in May 1813, when the then-victorious Americans advanced upon it. The British blew up the powder magazine and left. The Americans evacuated it and burned it two months later. It changed hands twice after that, was besieged by the British for six weeks in 1814, and finally abandoned and blown up by the Americans near the end of the war. More than 2,000 men died in these battles. A 30-foot monument covers the mass grave of 153 of them whose remains were found during the restoration of the fort. Next to Old Fort Niagara, it is the most impressive of Niagara's military restorations, and its museum holds a fascinating collection of old weapons and medals. A rarity is the Canadian General Service Medal, 1866–70, with a bar on its red-white-and-red ribbon engraved *The Fenian Raid, 1866*. The site of the Fenian landing and the principal fight with the raiders is about a mile north of the old fort.

The last official American invaders of Canada sailed home across the river from Fort Erie. Appropriately the old fort now sits in the shadow of the Peace Bridge to Buffalo, opened in 1927 to celebrate a century of relative calm on the frontier.

A new battle began on the frontier in the mid-twentieth century—not nation against nation or man against man, or even man against the elements; but man against the devastation he himself had caused. The fight to preserve or restore the natural beauty of the area had been more or less won through public control and the parks concept. Through international agreement, the falls had been allowed to continue spilling enough water to remain a spectacle, while the power authorities milked off enough for their needs, mostly by night. But the strategic position of *Onguiaahra*, the throatway, which gave it commercial advantage as the gateway to the Upper Lakes and its power as the main exit of their water system, also made it their sewage pipe. The industrial muck of Cleveland and Detroit and anything Chicago did not flush down the Mississippi system arrived at the falls, to be augmented by 75 million gallons a day of raw sewage and industrial waste from Niagara Falls, New York.

In the early '60s Lake Erie was declared ecologically dead—an expanse of dirty water, inhabited only by the foulest of creatures, which would eventually stagnate. Well, that hasn't happened. Pollution controls have removed much of the nastiness. Niagara Falls, New York, has a new control system, which began in 1978, and if it works according to plan, the salmon in the lower Niagara will be edible once more.

The river is not jumping with fish as it was in Mrs. Simcoe's day. (Lest we become too nostalgic for those days, let it be said that the river banks are no longer crawling with rattlesnakes or patrolled by marauding bears and wolves.)

But you can catch twenty-pound cohoe and forty-pound chinook salmon both in the upper and lower rivers, plus rainbow and brown trout. These West Coast salmon, introduced in Lake Ontario, swim up to the base of the falls. Up above, there are Atlantic salmon stocked from Michigan. Apart from its violent rapids, where only a fish would venture, most of the Niagara is fishable by boat. The river is so deep in places that you need a boat equipped with depth-finders and temperature gauge, and "down-rigger" gear with 10-pound weights to attract salmon cruising perhaps 73 feet down. Life is returning to the waters.

But up beside the original Cayuga Creek at the southern end of Niagara Falls, New York, that once-woody inlet sheltered by Cayuga Island where La Salle built his ship, the *Griffon*, a new horror struck in 1978. An old stream called the Love Canal, after real estate promoter William Love who dug it in the 1890s, had been used for twenty-three years as a dump for chemical waste. When the dumping ended in the 1950s, it was filled in and deeded to the local school board for $1; the board built a school on it and sold the land around for development as a subdivision.

The chemicals worked their way to the surface, burning the feet of children and dogs playing on the site. There were 82 different substances, 11 believed to cause cancer. An unusually large number of birth defects and miscarriages occurred among residents. A thirty-four-year-old man, found to be suffering from lymph cancer, remembered swimming in the canal as a boy and developing boils the size of silver dollars. The New York State health commissioner declared Love Canal a "great and imminent peril," and nearly a hundred families were evacuated. It was a reminder that beauty and danger go hand in hand at Niagara, although this danger could have been avoided if environmentalists had been as active in the 1930s and 1940s as they are now.

If La Salle had built his *Griffon* on the same spot 300 years later, chemicals would have rotted the keel before it was launched.

A visit to Niagara must end with the spectacle of the falls by night, lit by 8 million candlepower of multicolored beams. Here man and nature work in harmony for once; the power of Niagara is used to glorify Niagara, glowing on the sparkling brink, scintillating in the gushing drop, whipped-cream foam, and soaring spray. The changing colors reflect the rainbow that forms in the mist by sunlight but without the garishness of noon; their radiance is gentle. One moment the American falls are painted a pastel green while the spume below shines blue-white like the ice bridge, the little Luna cascades bridally pure, and the Horseshoe is a dusky-red volcano. Then pale blue spreads from Terrapin Point to Table Rock and the American cataract is suffused by pink. The voluble Victorians who expended their Niagaras of ink on the daytime view should be with us to describe it. Father Hennepin would achieve sainthood.

It is early September, and the couples watching are mostly in their forties and fifties. They stroll quietly along the promenade of Victoria Park and pause, mutely staring from the iron rail. Then a camera clicks. A young girl relaxes her pose and tells her boyfriend, "It's all show biz, isn't it?" It is, and has been for thousands of years, since the wild river first burst its banks. Niagara is an eternal show but ever-changing, ever-new.

Bibliography

Alexander, Sir James Edward. *Transatlantic sketches, comprising the most interesting scenes in North and South America and the West Indies.* London: Richard Bentley, 1833. 2 vols.

Babcock, Louis L. *The War of 1812 on the Niagara Frontier.* Buffalo: Buffalo Historical Society, 1969.

Bird, Isabella Lucy. *An Englishwoman in America.* London: John Murray, 1856.

Braider, Donald. *The Niagara* in *The Rivers of America Series.* New York: Holt Rinehart and Winston, 1972.

Burke, Andrew. *Burke's Descriptive Guide, or the Visitor's Guide to Niagara Falls by an Old Resident.* Buffalo, 1852.

Campbell, Marjorie Freeman. *Niagara, Hinge of the Golden Arc.* Toronto: Ryerson Press, 1958.

Campbell, Patrick. *Travels in North America.* Toronto: The Champlain Society, 1937.

Costain, Thomas B. *The White and the Gold: The French Regime in Canada.* Toronto: Doubleday Canada, 1954.

Creighton, Donald. *A History of Canada.* Toronto: Macmillan, 1964.

Denison, Merrill. *The People's Power*. Toronto: McClelland and Stewart, 1960.
De Veaux, Samuel. *The Falls of Niagara: A Tourist Guide to This Wonder of Nature*. Buffalo: William B. Hayden, 1839.
Dow, Charles Mason. *Anthology and Bibliography of Niagara Falls*. Albany: State of New York, 1921. 2 vols.
Dunlop, William. *Tiger Dunlop's Upper Canada*. Toronto: McClelland and Stewart, 1967.
Edgar, Lady. *General Brock* (Makers of Canada series). New York: Oxford University Press, 1926.
Flexner, James T. *Mohawk Baronet*. New York: Harper, 1959.
Flick, Alexander. *History of the State of New York*. New York: Columbia University Press, 1933.
Forrester, G. C. *The Falls of Niagara*. New York: Van Nostrand, 1928.
Graham, Lloyd. *The Niagara Country*. New York: Sloan and Pearce, 1949.
Greenhill, Ralph, and Mahoney, Thomas D. *Niagara*. Toronto: University of Toronto Press, 1969.
Guillet, Edwin C. *Early Life in Upper Canada*. Toronto: Ontario Publishing Co., 1933.
Hennepin, Louis. *A new discovery of a vast land in North America, extending above four thousand miles between New France and New Mexico*. London, 1698.
Howard, Robert West. *Thundergate: The Forts of Niagara*. Englewood Cliffs, N.J.: Prentice-Hall, 1968.
Howells, William Dean. "Niagara First and Last," *The Niagara Book*. Buffalo: Underhill and Nichols, 1893.
Hubert, Archer Butler. *The Niagara River*. New York: G. P. Putnam's Sons, 1908.
Hutchison, Bruce. *The Struggle for the Border*. Toronto: Longmans, 1955.
Jeffrys, C. W. *The Picture Gallery of Canadian History*. Toronto: Ryerson Press, 1945.
Kilbourn, William. *The Firebrand. William Lyon Mackenzie and the Rebellion in Upper Canada*. Toronto: Clarke Irwin, 1956.
Kiwanis Club of Stamford, Ontario, Inc. *Niagara Falls, Canada. A History of the City and the World Famous Beauty Spot*. Niagara Falls, Ont.: Kiwanis Club, 1967.

Bibliography

Lahontan, Baron de. *Voyages to North America.* Chicago: A. C. McClurg, 1905. 2 vols.

Loker, Donald E. *Guide to Niagara Falls.* Buffalo: Henry Stewart Inc. and M. Spitalny and Son, 1969.

MacLean, Harrison John. *The Fate of the* Griffon. Toronto: Griffin House, 1974.

McIlwraith, H. N. *Sir Frederick Haldimand* (Makers of Canada series). New York: Oxford University Press, 1926.

Morden, James C. *Historic Niagara Falls.* Lundy's Lane Historical Society, 1932.

Morison, Samuel Eliot. *The Oxford History of the American People.* New York: Oxford University Press, 1965.

O'Brien, Andy. *Daredevils of Niagara.* Toronto: Ryerson Press, 1964.

Parkman, Francis. *La Salle and the Discovery of the Great West.* New York: New American Library, 1963. (reprint)

———. *The Jesuits in North America.* Boston: Little Brown, 1885.

Porter, Peter A. *A Brief History of Old Fort Niagara.* Buffalo: Mathews-Northrup, 1896.

———. *Official Guide, Niagara Falls.* Buffalo: Mathews-Northrup, 1901.

Pound, Arthur. *Johnson of the Mohawks.* New York: Macmillan, 1930.

Robertson, John Ross. *Landmarks of Toronto.* Toronto: William Briggs, 1894.

Robinson, Percy J. *Toronto During the French Regime.* Toronto: University of Toronto Press, 1965.

Rogers, Major Robert. *Journals.* 1765.

Rowe, Percy. *Niagara Falls and Falls.* Toronto: Simon and Schuster, 1976.

Rutledge, Joseph Lister. *Century of Conflict.* Toronto: Doubleday, 1956.

Samuel, Sigmund. *The Seven Years' War in Canada.* Toronto: Ryerson Press, 1934.

Scott, Duncan C. *John Graves Simcoe* (Makers of Canada series). New York: Oxford University Press, 1926.

Severance, Frank. *Studies of the Niagara Frontier.* Buffalo: Buffalo Historical Society, 1911.

Tovell, Walter M. *Niagara Falls: Story of a River*. Toronto: University of Toronto, 1966.

Trollope, Anthony. *North America*. Philadelphia: J. B. Lippincott, 1862. 2 vols.

Vinal, Theodora. *Niagara Portage, from Past to Present*. Buffalo: Henry Stewart, 1948.

Way, Ronald L. *Ontario's Niagara Parks, A History*. Niagara Falls, Ont.: Niagara Parks Commission, 1960.

Woods, Nicholas A. *The Prince of Wales in Canada and the United States*. London: Bradbury and Evans, 1861.

Yates, Raymond F. *The Old Lockport and Niagara Falls Strap Railroad*. Niagara Falls, N.Y.: Niagara County Historical Society, 1950.

——. *The Niagara Story*. East Aurora, N.Y.: Henry Stewart, 1959.

Index

Abbott, Francis, 125–26, 237
Adams, Dean, 213
Albany, New York, 36, 38, 42, 45, 100, 142
Alexander, James Edward, 125
Allen, Sadie, 188
Amherst, Jeffrey, 59, 62
Amherstburg, 103–4, 107
Armstrong, John, 108, 112
Arnold, Benedict, 93
Audubon, John J., 231
Avery, Samuel, 237

Barclay, Robert, 155, 246
Barnett, Thomas, 155, 246
Barnum, Phineas T., 162, 231, 240
Batavia, New York, 107, 109
Beachy, Lincoln, 195, 196
Beall, John Yates, 176
Beck, Adam, 219, 220–21, 223–26
Bellini, Henry, 170–71
Berlin (Kitchener), Ontario, 218–21
Bernhardt, Sarah, 233
Bigot, François, 47–49, 52, 56

Black Rock, 91, 102, 119, 137, 178
Blondin (Jean François Gravelet), 163–69, 182, 199, 246
Bonaparte, Jerome "Fifi," 228
Bonaparte, Jerome Napoleon, 228
Bonnefons, Jean Carmine, 154
Bonnycastle, Richard, 153
Boughton Hill, 21, 32, 34, 39
Bourbon, Louis de, Prince de Condé, 20–21
Boya, Nathan, 199
Braddock, Edward, 49, 50
Brant, Joseph, 66, 68, 78, 79
Brant, Molly, 66, 67
Brébeuf, Jean de, 9, 13, 16
Brock, Isaac, 87, 94, 96–99, 100, 251–53, 255
Brown, Jacob, 109, 112–14
Brown, John, 118
Brûlé, Étienne, 11–16, 34
Brush, Charles, 211
Buck, Leiffert L., 147–48
Buffalo, New York, 107, 135,

138, 142, 156, 188, 197, 202, 209–11, 232, 236, 256
Burgoyne, John, 66
Burke, Andrew, 9–11
Burnet, William, 38, 39
Butler, John, 66–68, 73
Butterfield, George, 201

Calverley, Clifford, 172
Campbell, Walter G., 189
Cavelier, René-Robert, Sieur de la Salle. *See* La Salle, Sieur de
Champlain, Samuel de, 11–13, 15
Charlevoix, Pierre de, 20
Chauncey, Isaac, 101–2, 111–13
Chippawa, 74, 109–10, 113, 129, 134, 222, 223, 241, 256
Church, Frederick, 159, 239
Claus, Daniel, 66
Clay, Clement Claiborne, 242–43
Clay, Henry, 93
Cleveland, Grover, 160
Clinton, De Witt, 88, 93
Clinton, George, 45–46
Coke, E. T., 123
Colcord, Harry, 164–66
Colie, Alice, 236–37
Cooper, James Fenimore, 88
Cotten, Joseph, 202
Crawl-on-All-Fours (Niagara portage), 8, 21, 37, 48, 59, 63, 251
Curtis, George William, 152

Davies, Thomas, 82–83
Davis, Annie, 176
Davis, Saul, 155

De Creux (historian), 15–16
De Forest, Anna, 236
De Leon, "Professor," 172
Denonville, Marquis de, 32, 35–36, 39
Detroit, 38, 61, 96–97, 100, 103
Devil's Hole, 25, 59, 181, 253
Dickens, Charles, 156–57, 160, 231
Dieskau, Ludwig August von, 50–51
Dixon, Sam "Daring," 172
Dongan, Thomas, 36
Dorsheimer, William, 238
Doyle, Arthur Conan, 245
Doyle, Fanny, 249
Drew, Allen, 136
Drummond, Gordon, 114–15
Dufferin, Lord, 159, 239
Dunninger, Joseph, 245

Edison, Thomas, 213
Edward, Prince, of England, 75
Edward, Prince of Wales (later Edward VII), 156, 166–67, 182, 211, 251
Ellett, Charles, 143–45
Erie, Pennsylvania (Presque Ile), 102
Erie Canal, 142, 210
Eustis, William, 93
Evershed, Thomas, 212

Falls View Bridge, 148–50
Farini, Guillermo Antonio (William Hunt), 167–70
Fitzgibbon, James, 102
Flack, Robert, 189

Index

Forsyth, William, 81, 117–18, 121, 123, 129, 154
Fort Condé, 20, 24, 28, 35, 39
Fort Crèvecoeur, 28, 29
Fort Erie, 65, 92, 101, 109, 112, 178–79, 230, 241, 256
Fort Frontenac, 22, 32, 54
Fort George, 82, 87, 98, 100, 109, 113, 250
Fort Little Niagara, 48, 55
Fort Niagara (Old), 21, 30–31, 61, 67–68, 72, 77, 98, 107, 248–50
Fort Schlosser, 74, 82, 102

Gironkouthie, Chief, 29
Goat Island, 85, 120–21, 127, 136, 201, 235–41, 254
Graham, Carlisle D., 187–88
Grand Island, 93, 129, 133, 137–38
Grass Island, 191
Gravelet, Jean François. *See* Blondin
Greeley, Horace, 174–75, 243
Griffon (ship), 21–28, 207, 258–59

Haldimand, Frederick, 67, 73
Hall, Basil, 154
Harris, James, 202–3
Harrison, William Henry, 96, 106, 108–9
Hartling, Murray, 207
Hawthorne, Nathaniel, 126–28
Hayes, John R., 205–6
Hazlett, George, 188
Heacock, Burrel, 234–35

Head, Francis Bond, 129–30, 132
Hennepin, Louis, 2, 13, 17–25, 82, 128, 230, 249, 259
Hennepin Point, 230–31
Henson, Josiah, 126, 173
Hill, William (Red), Sr., 194–97, 234
Hill, William (Red), Jr., 197–98
Hillaret, Moyse, 22, 29
Hinu legend, 9, 10, 29
Honeycutt, James, 204–5, 207
Honeymoon Bridge (Upper Steel Arch), 149–52, 247
Hooker, S., 152–53
Hopkins, Jack, 207
Houdini, Harry, 244–45
House of Peace, The, 31, 39–41, 45, 47–49, 52–53, 56–57, 98, 108, 209, 249
Howe, William, 66, 68
Howison, John, 121
Huellet, Thomas, 143–44
Hull, William, 95–97
Hunt, William. *See* Farini, Guillermo Antonio
Hurlbutt, W. H., 159
Hustler, Mrs. Thomas, 88, 259

Jameson, Anna, 123
Jenkins, I. F., 170
Johnson, Guy, 65–66
Johnson, John, 65, 68
Johnson, Peter Brant, 65
Johnson, William, 32, 41–46, 48, 50–51, 54–57, 60–63, 67, 249
Joncaire, Daniel, 37, 47, 51, 53, 56, 211, 249

Joncaire, Louis Thomas, Sieur de Chabert, 30, 32–37, 39, 42–44, 249
Joncaire, Magdelene le Guay, 36–37
Joncaire, Philippe, 37, 45, 52, 57, 249
Jones, James H., 182–83

Kalm, Peter, 20
Keech, Clifford, 206–7
Kelvin, Lord (William Thomson), 213
Kemble, Fanny, 231
Kendall, William, 187
Key, Francis Scott, 248
King, William Lyon Mackenzie, 139, 243
Kingston, Ontario, 71, 112–13
Kipling, Rudyard, 142
Kirke, David, and brothers, 14–15

Lafayette, Marquis de, 231, 239
La Fleur, Sergeant, 29
Lahontan, Baron de, 19, 32–33
La Motte-Cadillac, Mme. de, 37
La Motte de Lussière, 17
Landreth, Alex, 233
La Salle, Sieur de, 16–29, 34, 249
Lasker, Seymour, 203
Latrobe, Charles Joseph, 123
Leach, Bobby, 193–96
Léry, Gaspard Chaussegros de, 40, 57, 65
Lett, Benjamin, 252
Lewiston, New York, 7, 8, 37, 88, 108, 127, 136, 187, 189, 225, 247

Lincoln, Abraham, 156, 177
Lockport, New York, 142
Loftberg, Gustav, 202–3
Longueuil, Baron de, 37, 39
Lount, Samuel, 133, 243
Love, William, 258
Luc (pilot of *Griffon*), 21, 25–28
Lundy's Lane, 113, 115, 255
Lussier, Jean, 196–97
Lyell, Charles, 4

McCauslin, Robert, 3–4
McCloy, Jack, 185
McClure, Joseph, 107–9
Macdonell, John, 99, 100, 252
McIntyre, James, 183
Mackenzie, William Lyon, 120–22, 129–39, 243–44, 251, 256
MacLean, John, 27–28
McLeod, Dick, 230
McMullen, Rowland, 169
MacNab, Allan, 135–37
Maid of the Mist legend, 9–11
Maitland, Peregrine, 252
Marryat, Frederick, 126
Mason, James Murray, 174–75
Matheson, James, 124
Mathews, Peter, 133, 243
Maude, John, 86
Merritt, William Hamilton, 142–43
Moir, Jim, 229
Monroe, Marilyn, 202
Montcalm, Marquis de, 49, 53
Montgomery, John, 132–33, 138
Montgomery, Richard, 93
Montreal, 22, 34–36, 39, 51, 54, 107
Montresor, John, 63, 65–66

Index

Moore, Tom, 86–87, 231
Moraviantown, 106
Morison, Samuel Eliot, 8, 94
Mouton, Romain, 166–67
Mowat, Oliver, 159, 216
Murphy, Rowley, 27

Navy Hall, 71, 72, 74, 250
Navy Island, 119, 133–34, 136–37, 139
Niagara Falls, New York (Manchester), 88, 117, 124, 135, 142, 193, 196, 211–12, 229–30, 258
Niagara Falls, Ontario (Stamford), 83, 110, 117, 199, 217, 229, 241, 255
Niagara-on-the-Lake (Newark), 71, 73, 80, 82, 108, 250
Nissen, Peter, 190

Oakes, Harry, 243
Olmsted, Frederick Law, 238–39
O'Mahoney, John, 177–78, 180
O'Neill, John, 178–80
Onguiaahra, 16, 257
Oswego, New York, 39, 45, 51, 55, 113

Papineau, Louis Joseph, 131
Parkman, Francis, 19, 159
Patch, Sam, 122
Patterson, Elizabeth, 228
Péan, Angélique, 47–48
Péan, Jean, 47–48
Peere, Stephen, 171–72
Percy, Charles Alexander, 189
Perry, Oliver Hazard, 102–5, 108, 175

Plewman, W. R., 224
Pontiac, Chief, 60–62
Porter, Augustus, 92, 209–10, 235–36, 241
Porter, Peter Buell, 92–93, 110, 209, 235–36
Potts, William, 188
Pouchot, François, 53, 55–57, 249
Prideaux, John, 54–56, 69
Procter, Henry A., 104, 106–8
Prospect Point, 160, 231, 237

Quattrochi, John, 206
Queenston, Ontario, 94, 98–102, 108–9, 112, 135, 142, 222–23, 247

Railway Suspension Bridge, 145–49
Rainbow Bridge, 246
Rechatin, Henri, 200–1
Rede, Andrew, 124
Riall, Phineas, 110, 113–14, 256
Richardson, Henry Hobson, 238
Ripley, Robert, 246
Robinson, Joel, 182–83, 247
Rochefoucauld, Duc de la, 77–78, 242
Rochester, New York, 21, 122, 133–34, 138–39
Roebling, John, 143–47
Roth, Ignatius, 234
Rough, James, 119–20
Russell, William Howard, 157–58

Sackets Harbor, New York, 111–13

Sagard, Gabriel, 14
St. Laurent, Mme., 75
Sandusky, Ohio, 105, 175–76
Schoellkopf, Joseph, 210–11, 215
Schultz, Christian, 87
Scott, James, 187
Scott, Winfield, 100, 109–14, 137–38, 255
Secord, Laura, 101–2, 114
Seed, Frank O., 151
Sellers, Coleman, 213
Shaw, George Bernard, 250
Siemens, Wilhelm, 211
Simcoe, Elizabeth Posthuma, 71–77, 84, 257
Simcoe, John Graves, 71–72, 75, 77, 80–81, 88, 250
Sims, George, 238
Slidell, John, 175
Smyth, Alexander, 91–94, 98
Snider, C. H. J., 27
Spanish Aero Car, 200
Spelterini, Maria, 172–73
Stanton, Eldridge, Mr. and Mrs., 234–35
Stathakis, George, 197
Stedman, John, 59, 61–62, 89, 235, 253
Stephens, Charles, 195–96
Stowe, Harriet Beecher, 126, 173–74, 231
Stuart-Wortley, Lady Emmeline, 152
Sullivan, John, 68
Syracuse, New York, 189

Table Rock, 118, 121–22, 124, 128–29, 153–56, 193, 217, 232, 242, 259
Taylor, Anna Edson, 190–94
Tecumseh, Chief, 78, 94, 96–98, 106–7
Terrapin Point, 125, 205, 241, 259
Tesla, Nicola, 213–14
Tiyonaga, "King Hendrick," 43, 51–52, 78
Tonti, Alphonse de, 37
Tonti, Enrico de, 17, 21–22, 26, 29, 34
Tonti, Lorenzo, 17
Toronto, 14, 82, 101, 130–31, 247
Torres-Quevedo, Leonardo, 200
Trollope, Anthony, 157

Ussher, James, 3

Vail, Orrie, 26–27
Van Buren, Martin, 137–38, 141
Vanderlyn, John, 83
Van Rensselaer, Stephen, 98, 100

Wadsworth, William, 100
Wagenfuhrer, Martha, 188
Walsh, Homan, 143, 148
Warburton, George, 153
Warren, Peter, 41–42, 44
Washington, George, 49, 66, 68, 134
Waterton, Charles, 154
Way, Ronald L., 239
Webb, Matthew, 184–87, 247
Weisenberg, Catherine, 43, 65–66

Index

Welch, Thomas V., 239
Weld, Isaac, 83–86
Welland Canal, 142, 179
White, Berry Hill, 238
Whitman, Walt, 157–58
Whitney, James, 219–21
Whitney, Parkhurst, 118, 236
Wilde, Oscar, 231

Willard, Maude, 188–89, 191
Wolfe, James, 46, 95, 99
Woodward, Deanne, 204–7
Woodward, Roger, 204–7

Yeo, James, 112–13, 116
Youngstown, New York, 108, 231

NIAGARA FALLS, ONTARIO

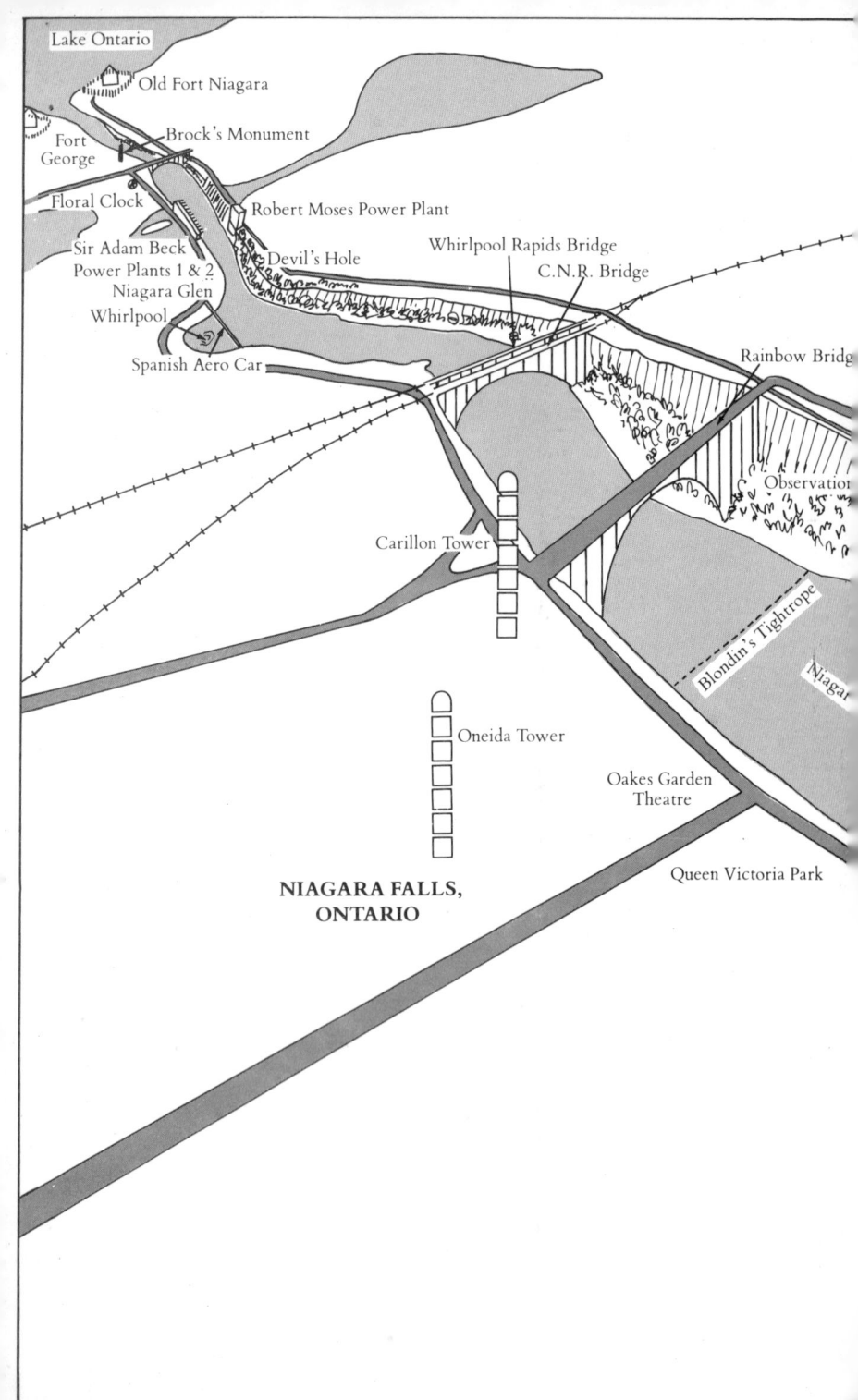

- Lake Ontario
- Old Fort Niagara
- Brock's Monument
- Fort George
- Floral Clock
- Robert Moses Power Plant
- Sir Adam Beck Power Plants 1 & 2
- Devil's Hole
- Whirlpool Rapids Bridge
- C.N.R. Bridge
- Niagara Glen
- Whirlpool
- Spanish Aero Car
- Rainbow Bridge
- Observation
- Carillon Tower
- Blondin's Tightrope
- Niagara
- Oneida Tower
- Oakes Garden Theatre
- Queen Victoria Park